COSMOPOLITAN
Survival
Guide

COSMOPOLITAN
Survival
Guide

ANGELA PHILLIPS

DORLING KINDERSLEY
London • New York • Stuttgart • Moscow

A Dorling Kindersley Book

Project Editor Charyn Jones
Editor Nasim Mawji
Senior Art Editor Ann Burnham
Art Editor John Dinsdale
Managing Editor Susannah Marriott
Managing Art Editor Toni Kay
Photography Andy Crawford
D.T.P. Designer Karen Ruane
Production Controllers
Manjit Sihra Antony Heller
Production Manager Maryann Rogers

•

*Dedicated to the young women in
my life: Rachel, Jacquie, Caroline and
Joanna. May their lives turn out to be
everything they wanted.*

First published in Great Britain in 1996 by
Dorling Kindersley Limited,
9 Henrietta Street, London WC2E 8PS

Visit us on the World Wide Web at
http://www.dk.com

A CIP catalogue record for this book is available
from the British Library.

ISBN 0 7513 0319 4

Reproduced by Colourscan, Singapore
Printed and bound in Italy by
New Interlitho, Milan

CONTENTS

VALUING YOURSELF

HEALTHY LIVING

FOREWORD
by the Editor of Cosmopolitan

Whenever I talk to other young women, I sense a wonderful optimism in the air. It's there not only because women today are stronger, braver, more exceptional than ever, but also because, despite the ever more competitive and stressful society in which we live, the opportunities are there, should we wish to grab them. And what's more, many more women than ever before are taking control of their destiny. The result is that today's women are taking time to work out what they want from life, through travel, education, spirituality and general interests. And most important of all, they refuse to be categorized.

Women today are far more likely to follow their hearts and do what they really want. They won't be forced into roles simply to make other people happy. If you want a full-time career, great. If you want to work flexi-time and pursue other interests, wonderful. If you want to stay at home and bring up children, that's great too. And if you want to have a career *and* children, it's up to you. What's important is that you are doing what *you* want to do.

As I see it, it is this freedom from rigid stereotypes that is the key to women's progress. Women are more independent than ever, free from other people's control, financially savvy, self-motivated, and self-reliant. They are not dependent on the support of men or others. The key to self-sufficiency and liberty is confidence – the confidence to follow your instincts, to know who you are and to develop your talents to the full. If you feel confident, you feel safe. If you feel safe, you also feel brave. You feel brave and courageous; you can survive anything.

The *Cosmopolitan Survival Guide* is designed to empower women in every aspect of life, practical and emotional, and to build confidence. It provides you with the tools to enjoy life fully, to be free-spirited and, most of all, to be inspired to take on any challenge, on your terms. They say the future is female and there is no doubt that it is a brilliant time to be a young woman with your whole life ahead of you. Enjoy the book and enjoy yourself.

INTRODUCTION

Today's women are mould breakers. We cannot follow the old rules. One of the most important things we have learned is that real change only starts to happen when we ask the unaskable: Why shouldn't women be financially independent? Why aren't we enjoying sex as much as we could? What is wrong with mothers going out to work? Why can't men programme washing machines or pick up their socks? That is why this guide is different. It recognizes that we must ask the questions that make sense in our own lives before we can find answers. So, rather than providing "pat" answers, this book helps *you* to do the asking.

The opening chapters are all about you. They invite you to look at yourself, both inside and out. They start from the premise that your happiness is important and that you are most likely to get the best out of life if you know what you really want. The section on colour and body shape will help you to work out what enhances you rather than what designers want to sell this season. Discussions on health detail exactly what you can do to make sure you feel the best you can both physically and mentally. This section also explores the factors that prevent you from being as healthy as you could be and suggests ways to change them.

Relationships form the core of all our lives. How are we formed as human beings? How do the patterns of childhood reach out into our adult lives? This section helps you learn about yourself and, through learning, to improve relationships with the people you care about. There is also your working life to consider. How can you decide what work to do and organize yourself to get the most you can from it? Finally, there is a practical section where instructions really are important because when your car tyre punctures or your house catches fire, you haven't got time to think, you just have to act. At the back of the book is space for recording personal details and planning for the future.

I hope this guide will be a useful companion as you pick your own route through the, as yet, uncharted waters of your own future. Good luck!

Angela Phillips

STAGES OF LIFE

L IFE, FOR ALL OF US, is a gradual transition from total dependence, through a period of learning, to independence. For some of us, real independence is only a brief period between the time when we were mothered and the time when we become mothers ourselves. For others, that gap has widened: motherhood is postponed, or avoided, and careers take precedence. But our independence is never absolute. As our knowledge and understanding grow, it is our turn to pass them on and, through doing so, to renew the cycle.

FINDING YOUR WAY IN LIFE

Mother-daughter relationship 96–98

Terrible teens 113

Knowing what you want 14–17

Body image 18–23

FRIENDSHIP

Making new friends 99

Old and new friendships 112

Taming jealousy 118–19

Valuing friends 127

Building a community 154

GETTING A JOB

Focusing your ambition 130–31

The right job for you 132–35

Writing your CV 137, 185

Asserting yourself 16

Selling yourself 136

STARTING A RELATIONSHIP

Exploring sensuality 104–106

Commitment 100–101

Negotiating safer sex 76, 101

Choosing contraception 58–62

Sexual health 76–81

STAYING HEALTHY

Healthy eating 34–37

Psychology of food 38–39

Assessing your fitness 42–44

Choosing exercise 46–51

Regular health checks 66–75

CHOOSING TO BE A PARENT

The decision to be child-free 111

Pregnancy 64–65, 80

Becoming a mother 108–115

Maternity rights 186

Parent-child relationships 96

RUNNING A HOME

OUT AND ABOUT

RELAXATION

SURVIVING A CRISIS

ACHIEVING JOB SATISFACTION

RESOLVING ARGUMENTS

JUGGLING MOTHERHOOD AND WORK

THE LATER YEARS

Interpreting body language

Choosing colours that suit you

Defending yourself

VALUING YOURSELF

We all have a capacity for joy. It comes not from the esteem of others (though that is important), not from material things (though it helps to have enough of them), but from ourselves. It is our pleasure in our own bodies that makes us stretch and smile at the touch of the sun, or climb a mountain to see how the world looks from the top. If you value yourself, you will take every opportunity that presents itself to climb a little higher knowing that the effort will have been worth it even if the rewards turn out to be few. It is the valuation you put on yourself that will, in the end, be reflected back to you by the people in your life. Use the following pages to assess your strengths and priorities, and learn to value yourself.

THE REAL YOU

For some people, self-belief comes easily. They have grown up taking centre stage in their own lives and basking in the esteem of people who care for them. Others grow up feeling like a bit player with a walk-on part in someone else's drama. To discover the real you might involve rewriting the script, with you in the main role, playing the life you want for yourself. This exercise is designed to help you look at the person you are and consider whether you feel happy with yourself and with the control you have over your life.

QUESTIONNAIRE

IF YOU WERE AN ANIMAL, WHICH WOULD YOU BE?

- ☐ A cat, curled up purring by the fire.
- ☐ A hedgehog, sticking pins into allcomers.
- ☐ A budgie, cheeping peevishly to get a word in.
- ☐ A wolf, stalking alone and howling in the night.
- ☐ A lioness, proud and powerful.
- ☐ A tiger, restlessly prowling her cage.
- ☐ A bee, forever busy, never still.
- ☐ An elephant, lumbering and a little ludicrous.
- ☐ A cow, sitting quietly while she is milked.

- ☐ A bird, freewheeling in the sky.
- ☐ A sad dog, alone and abandoned.
- ☐ A Labrador, jumping up and knocking things over.
- ☐ A mad dog with sharp fangs, biting and snarling.
- ☐ A cheetah, sleek and predatory.
- ☐ A mouse, poised to run away.
- ☐ A tortoise, hidden in its shell.
- ☐ A beast of burden.
- ☐ A lowly worm.

Considering yourself

Perhaps you are different animals at different times, with different people, or in different circumstances. You may feel like a cat at home and a hedgehog at work. You may feel like a mad dog for a few days of each month, but like a cheetah for the rest of the time. Do you sense that the different parts balance out, or is one side of you preventing the whole you from functioning well? Do you like your animal or despise it? If you do not like it, what does this tell you about yourself? Choose an animal you would prefer to be. Imagining yourself in a more positive role may help you to become more positive about yourself.

ANIMAL ANALYSIS

A budgie cheeping, a wolf howling, a tiger pacing.

All these animals suggest frustration. As babies we cry with frustration if milk is delayed. As adults we expect to be able to solve our own problems. If you are not getting what you want, is it because you are not putting your point clearly enough (see page 116), or could it be that your needs cannot be met without disadvantaging someone else? When needs clash you cannot assume that yours are the most important, but nor should anyone else assume that yours are less important. Perhaps you feel frustrated with a process that is going too slowly for you. Frustration can be the motor of progress if you focus it rather than howling at the moon.

The mad dog or the sad dog.

You may feel like both of these. Anger is often the flip side of misery: you lash out because you feel uncared for. The mad dog visits most of us occasionally and so does the sad dog. A burst of anger can sometimes have the same effect as a crack of thunder: the rain comes, the sky clears and you feel better again. But if you feel permanently angry or permanently sad, you need to start looking for reasons. These feelings have a habit of eating you up; they corrode not only the person they invade, but also the people close by. Anger and unhappiness can be passed on from one generation to another like a gene – but it is in your power to stop the cycle (see page 96).

The cat, the lioness, the bird and the cheetah.

If you chose these, you probably have a positive image of who you are, or at least who you want to be: quiet and content, calm and strong, happy-go-lucky or totally directed. If you are attracted to one of these images but feel stuck in some other persona, you need to consider whether your present life is leading you in the right direction or whether you need to reassess it. You may feel that all these images are unattainable dreams available only to the privileged few. Certainly financial circumstances, ill health, discrimination, and the need to care for others create enormous obstacles to finding and expressing yourself, but very often it is the change in your perception of yourself that will precede a change in material circumstances rather than the other way around (see page 14).

A beast of burden, a cow, a bee.

All these images imply a lack of control. You feel that someone else is pulling your strings. You may find that the "someone else" is hidden inside you. Perhaps you were brought up believing that to be loved you must be good, and that being good means catering to the demands of others, not yourself. The desire to care for others is a valuable one that is often underrated in our work-orientated world, but care itself is devalued if it is given grudgingly. If you feel this way about yourself, perhaps you need to step back a little, look at your own needs and do something to change the situation (see page 16).

A hedgehog, a tortoise or a mouse.

These animals suggest that you are defined by your defences. The walls you have built certainly have their place: they protect you from experiences that are too powerful or frightening. You may have grown your shell as a response to something way back in your childhood that you could not handle. This protective layer may have helped you to avoid further harm, but are you sure you still need it? Now that you are an adult you may be able to risk dropping your guard and allowing people a little closer. After all, you are now big enough to say no and mean it (see page 16).

An elephant, a lowly worm, a Labrador dog.

If you chose these, you are not taking yourself seriously and you probably do not expect anyone else to either. If you expect to get stepped on, you almost certainly will be. You may believe that the worm's role in irrigating the soil will eventually be recognized for the important job it really is, but do not bet on it – you need to get out from under those feet.

The elephant is the fool at the feast. By waving her own inadequacies like a flag, she makes others feel strong and protective. You are a good person to be around, but beware of using your ability to clown as a cover-up for your own fears of being not quite up to scratch. You may fear that if you start to take yourself seriously, you may lose your status in the group, but if you do not, you may get left behind.

The good thing about the Labrador is her eagerness to try something new. Time and experience will steady you and, if you take yourself more seriously, your enthusiasm will take you far (see page 14).

THINKING ABOUT WHAT YOU WANT

• GETTING WHAT YOU WANT

W E ARE ALL SO USED TO PLAYING OUT THE PARTS others have given us that we have learned to think of ourselves in categories. We are labelled first by our relationship to our family: daughter, mother, wife, aunt; and second by our relationship to work: doctor, shop assistant, child-carer. From very early in life we learn to hide, or to curb, those desires or skills that do not seem to fit in with what is expected of us. If, at age four, your father laughed at your attempts to dance, you may not only feel too inhibited to dance as an adult, but find yourself hiding your body in case it is deemed ugly or awkward. If you had a slow start at school, your sense of failure may have coloured your whole educational life. If the only time you spent alone with your father was when he helped with your science homework, you may have found yourself, years later, slogging through a science degree without stopping to ask if the subject really interested you.

CHALLENGING EXPECTATIONS

Social expectation is a powerful force. It can trap us in roles that feel constricting, but when a wind of change blows through society, expectations also change and profoundly affect what we anticipate from life. In the years before the feminist movement of the 1970s, girls did so much worse than boys in maths that it was assumed that mathematical ability was genetically programmed on the Y chromosome. As expectations changed, and female educators started to encourage girls, the results began to improve. In Britain, in just 10 years, the number of girls attaining higher grades in maths increased by 35 per cent; now they are level with boys. In both Britain and the United States, a high level of male unemployment, accompanied by an increase in lone parenthood, has changed expectations in the black community in a couple of generations. Black women, recognizing the need for self-reliance, are now twice as likely as their male peers to graduate from college.

POSITIVE EXPECTATIONS These can help us channel our energies toward getting better at the things we do best. But they can also make it impossible for us to think about what we ourselves want because we are so busy trying to do what other people expect. Operating against social expectations can be an uphill struggle.

NEGATIVE EXPECTATIONS These can trap us forever inside a distorted vision of our capabilities. This negative vision probably has a more important influence than either intellectual capacity or even social class in shaping a child's future.

66 My parents expected me to meet a nice boy at college, get a job, settle down and have babies. It wasn't easy to tell them that the boy was a girl and that I had dropped out of college to join a band. 99

Children whose parents are unsuccessful, and who live among people who feel marginal and powerless, can grow up without ever having a glimpse of a world in which they themselves could be powerful and influential. It takes both imagination and determination to see a way out of such a world and to find the persistence to make that vision a reality. The important thing is to believe in your own power to change; if you can imagine yourself in a different place, you are already on your way there.

NAME: **Kathryn Page** OCCUPATION: **Teacher** AGE: **34**	*"I was abused by my stepfather, and I had a baby when I was 15; she was adopted. I dropped out of school and then spent 10 years hanging out with men who treated me badly. By that time I had two young children to care for. I saw an advertisement for educational opportunities for young mothers. I studied for seven years; it gave me such a feeling of control. Even though I had to cope with poverty and racial abuse, I knew it was the only way to change my life. Everything will be better for my kids now."*

CREATING YOUR OWN EXPECTATIONS

Like most girls you may have spent your childhood years with dolls, practising to be an adult woman who would one day be expected to look after a house and children, as well as working to earn a living. You may have developed a strong sense of the responsibility that goes with being a woman, possibly to the exclusion of any pleasures not directly associated with caring. If loving others becomes the only pleasure, it leaves you dangerously dependent on others to provide happiness. Creating your own expectations means having the courage to think about what makes you happy.

You may feel that achieving will make you happy – getting a degree, landing the right job, being promoted. These goals may well satisfy most of your needs, but if you are struggling to fulfil responsibilities at work, and then rushing to meet the care requirements of the people you love, you may not have stopped to ask yourself whether the balance of your life is right. Are you looking after your own need for physical and emotional fulfilment? Do you even remember what it felt like just to be able to play?

Think back to a time in your early childhood, before examinations or grades interfered, before you needed to worry about jobs or lovers or babies. What made you happy? Maybe it was baking cakes, squidging your hands in dough, or playing with a hose in the back garden. Perhaps you remember being carried on a broad back to watch a carnival procession, or singing in the school choir. Maybe you climbed a tree in the garden and got right to the top, or helped your friend to build a den. What was the pleasure about? Was it the sense of accomplishment, the physicality of the experience, the excitement? Think of a way of bringing that sense back again, perhaps through singing, dancing, riding, walking, painting or modelling with clay, and plan to do something about it.

SOME EXCUSES FOR NEVER DOING WHAT YOU WANT

How many of these apply to you and how many more can you add?
- I am too tired.
- I am too busy.
- I have to drink with colleagues after work to get on.
- My mother needs me, my children need me, my partner needs me.
- I do not know what I want.
- I enjoy being a martyr.
- If I do not do well, my parents will be disappointed.
- If I do too well, my friends won't want to know me.

GETTING WHAT YOU WANT

ASSERTING YOURSELF

Assertiveness is about respecting yourself, but it is also about respecting others' rights. It stems from self-confidence, it cannot replace it.

■ A person who is genuinely confident will not be afraid of listening to another point of view and considering what someone else has to say. She will change her own position if she is proved wrong, but if not, she will quietly, confidently and clearly press her own case.

■ Nobody can be absolutely confident all the time – nor should they be. Total certainty implies a rigidity and resistance to learning and changing that is more indicative of weakness and lack of imagination than of strength and flexibility.

■ Assertiveness is as much about knowing when to admit you are wrong and feeling able to say you are not sure, as it is about being heard when you know you are right.

Knowing what you want is 90 per cent of getting what you want, but it is the other 10 per cent that may make all the difference to your life. Learning to act confidently will not only help you to be heard, it will also build your confidence because it creates the kind of positive expectations from other people that will in turn feed into your positive estimation of yourself. Sometimes we block this positive feedback by failing to project the things we feel sure about, confusing ourselves as well as the people we are trying to convince. For women, the problem may be increased when men are present because male conversational styles tend to marginalize us. The style men use is not better at getting things done, in fact it is often less effective, but in mixed groups its very directness dominates. Understanding the following differences in conversational style may help you to get heard.

FOUR AVOIDABLE COMMUNICATION PROBLEMS

APOLOGIZING *"I'm sorry about this, but I have got three questions to ask. I hope you don't mind, they are probably pretty trivial, but ..."*

This speaker was a woman. Her first question was answered, the next two were then lost in the discussion. She did not try to press her points and seemed surprised when one of the co-ordinators (a woman) insisted on returning to her questions. The meeting was dominated by three men who all spoke directly, often interrupting and cutting in to make a point; none apologized. One said something that was contradicted by another member of the group. He did not respond but later came forward with a suggestion that indicated that he had completely changed his mind. His suggestion was welcomed. No one commented on the change of direction.

Women are more likely than men to use a placatory style or to admit weakness as a conversational strategy to get attention or information, or to encourage participation from other members of a group. Men, on the other hand, tend to avoid asking questions rather than risk being seen as weak.

In mixed groups you may need to adapt your style in order to be heard: make your point simply, without the placatory preamble; if you are being ignored, repeat your remark; avoid making any reference to things that you cannot do or things you feel doubtful about, stick with what you can do and what you feel certain about. If you are in a position to do so, try to create space in which other women can be heard by quietly returning to the points they have made and passing the conversation "ball" back to them.

INDIRECT QUESTIONS *"When I say to my son, 'Would you like to help me with the washing up?' he says, 'No, thank you,' and sits down in front of the television. He interprets my request as a question and answers accordingly. He wouldn't like to wash up but, if I tell him to, he will comply with my request. I have now learned to say, 'Please do the washing up'. It seems rude to me, but it works better."*

Indirect speech patterns work very well among those who understand them. Some people prefer taking instructions from those who give them indirectly because they appear to be enabling rather than directive and so allow the person in the subordinate position to make a decision. Others find this manipulative and prefer to be given straightforward directions that allow them to say yes or no.

The important thing is to spot which kind of group, or person, you are talking to. If indirectness is seen as a sign of weakness, your attempts to intervene in this way will be ignored. You can either adapt your style or, if this is an on-going relationship, try to talk about the difference in your way of communicating so that you each learn to respect the other's approach.

MAKING EXCUSES *"I know that I should have handed in a better paper, but I was very busy on another project and my flatmate used my computer and the printer ran out of ink and then the bus was late and then I got very tired and I had a hangover and I didn't have time."*

An excuse is usually provided in a wheedling voice, always with the implication that some other thing or person is at fault. An excuse leaves the impression that you are not in control; it is different from a reason.

A reason is a simple explanation given as a matter of courtesy. A reason, supplied only when it is necessary, shows that you have a grasp of the situation and are prepared to take responsibility for your part in it.

SQUEAKING NOT SPEAKING One common strand that links apologizing, indirect questions, excuses (and anger) is voice level: all such interventions tend to end with a rise in tone. In contrast, clear instructions, direct speech and decisive interventions mostly end with a level or downward inflection. If you want to be heard, talk in a level tone.

THE POWER OF CLOTHING

"I dreamt that I had arrived at this important conference wearing a bikini. The feeling of humiliation was still with me when I woke up."

Men can hide in the uniformity of a grey suit and simply make themselves invisible. Everything a woman wears makes a statement about how she feels about herself and the world. Since your clothes are an extension of you, it makes sense to use them positively.

■ Clothes that shout, "Look at me!" are fine if you have a voice and style loud enough to match. If not, your presence as a person will be overshadowed.

■ Unless you are very confident about clothes, do not buy something new for a big event. Go in comfortable clothing that you won't have to think about. Avoid ill-fitting clothes: skirts you have to tug at, straps that fall off, anything that makes you feel self-conscious.

BRIEF ENCOUNTERS

Body language can also say a lot about your confidence and affect how other people respond to you.

RELAXED CONFIDENCE
These two women are confident and relaxed with one another. No one person is trying to dominate and neither of them appears submissive.

SUBTLE CONTROL
By standing at an angle and showing less of her body, the woman on the left is holding something back. She can assess the person she is meeting while subtly controlling the encounter.

NERVOUS DEFENCE
Crossed arms are protective. The woman on the left is nervous and defending herself from unwanted attention, even aggression, from a woman who clearly feels in control.

GOOD RAPPORT
These women are good friends, their gestures leave their bodies open to one another. They are not defensive.

The External You

• Body Language • Feeling Happy with Your Body • Understanding Colour

For women, clothes, make-up, hair and jewellery are like paint palettes. Where men have been allowed to be creative in the public arena, as painters, sculptors and craftsmen, women have, traditionally, been confined to the private arena where they have turned their creativity to making quilts, pots, hangings and clothes. Self-adornment is as old as our knowledge of human history and yet it is rarely seen for what it is: a unique act of self-expression that is pleasurable and accessible to all.

Body Language

The way we choose to present our bodies is as much a part of how we interact with the world as the words we speak. When Madonna dresses in a black lace corset set off by bright red lips, she is shouting, "Look at me, I am a woman, I am powerful, I can have you on my own terms". And when the actress Demi Moore posed naked and pregnant on the cover of *Vanity Fair* magazine, she was saying, "Share with me the pleasure of my unique human creation".

Your clothes, too, reveal a great deal about the way you feel about yourself. You may think that you can wear a skin-tight wisp of a dress, but if you hate being looked at, you will not look bold, just uncomfortable. You will hunch your shoulders, hide behind your hair, avoid making eye contact and signal awkwardness and discomfort with your body language. Far better to wear something that you feel comfortable in and that won't undermine your confidence.

When teenage girls choose to clothe themselves in shapeless black, for example, they may be signalling some of the following ideas:
- Ambivalence about the power of their bodies, preferring to keep them hidden and "under wraps".
- Independence, in choosing a colour long associated with age rather than youth.
- Identification with a particular peer group, by dressing in a similar style to friends, even if it is outside the fashion statements decreed by the adult world.

The great advantage of shapeless dark clothing is that it acts like a chrysalis, giving you time to establish your place in the world on your own terms. It allows you to choose who will look at your body rather than obliging you to put yourself on display for allcomers. You can find other outlets for your creativity – or go in for magnificent nail varnish. As you learn to be more confident, you may choose to wear garments that emphasize your sexuality rather than concealing it, or you may always prefer a style that allows you to blend in with the crowd. What's important is not what you wear but how you feel about wearing it.

FEELING HAPPY WITH YOUR BODY

Most women grow up feeling critical of their bodies. We are brought up with an ideal image of how we should be and spend the rest of our lives fixated by the bits of our bodies that do not measure up: a fat bum, stick legs or small breasts. It makes more sense to take a step back, look at our whole bodies, not isolated elements, and get a feel for the shape. Wearing clothes to fit the shape you really are, rather than the shape advertisements hold out as perfection, not only feels more comfortable, it also looks better.

YOUR BUILD

Your proportions will not change – they are determined by your bone structure, height and weight – but the right clothes can flatter your size. If you are tiny, it is usually unwise to wear huge patterns or a great deal of clutter. Stick with small patterns (or none at all) and neat jewellery. If you are big and broad, you can use boldly designed fabric patterns to go with your size, and experiment with dangly jewellery and even huge hats.

SHOULDERS NARROWER THAN HIPS Wear tops that accentuate your shape. If you have a narrow waist, choose clothes that nip in at the waist. If you have a broad waist, choose a dropped-waist style or clothes that gently flare out toward the bottom. Look for hairstyles that create a balance with your hips, such as a short bob, which gives width.

NARROW SHOULDERS, NARROW HIPS You have a straight up and down, vertical line and, particularly if you are tall, will gain advantage from introducing some horizontals. Contrasting tops and bottoms, belts, and jackets that are double breasted or have wide lapels or collars will all suit you. Try wearing baggy tops over narrow bottoms or narrow tops with wide bottoms, and be as daring as you like with short skirts. Wear your hair short or in a bob, but if you have long hair, experiment with styles that lift it away from your shoulders and break up the sense of a long vertical line.

BROAD SHOULDERS, BROAD HIPS Look for clothes that show off your shoulders and emphasize your waist. Avoid the temptation to disappear into a tent if you feel you are bigger than the norm. Be bold, and try clothes that follow your shape. You can wear your hair in an exuberant style to match an exuberant body. Go for loose curls or a medium bob, perhaps with a fringe if your hair is straight.

BROAD SHOULDERS, NARROWER HIPS You are able to wear softly cut tops or dresses that would flop on someone with narrow shoulders. Belt tops at the waist or wear them long over trousers or narrow skirts to create a triangular feel – wide at the top and narrow at the bottom. Unless you are quite tall, longer skirts or trousers will suit you better than short skirts, which may make you look too top-heavy. If you are tall, try to wear your hair in a long bob, crop it short, or sweep it up close to your head.

BODY SHAPE
Avoid the temptation to disappear into baggy, tent-like clothing. Follow the line of your body.

UNDERSTANDING COLOUR

The right colours for you are the ones that enhance your own colouring. Taupe may be all the rage this year, but if it does not suit you, no amount of money will make you look good in it. The international mass marketing of fashion clothing may be good for manufacturers and for keeping prices down, but designers seem to make few concessions to the fact that people come in a vast range of skin tones and hair colourings.

To understand more about your own colouring you need to take a long, hard look at yourself. It might help to do this with a couple of friends so that you can see how different you all are. Sit down in front of a mirror with a white sheet around your shoulders and then ask a friend to hold different colours against your face. Forget what your mother has told you or the colours you prefer, just look in the mirror. Does the colour make your eyes light up? Does it make your skin look bright or dull? Does it enhance your colouring or drain it away?

WARM COLOURS
Traditional Rajasthani dress, with its rich jewel colours and glittering threads, reflects light into the face and eyes.

CHECK THE REFLECTION

Colour reflects in your skin as well as contrasting with it. If you are very pale, wearing radiant pink puts colour in your face, whereas red makes you look paler, and white looks deathly. If you have muddy, combination skin, olive greens and yellows will push your skin colour toward yellow, whereas warm blues or cool reds will tilt it the other way, making you look brighter. Golden brown skin will look dull with khakis and bright with clear, warm colours. Look in the mirror and see for yourself.

CONSIDER THE CONTRAST

If you try to reflect in your clothes the colour contrasts in your face, you will enhance your colouring rather than swamp it. If, for example, you have very dark hair and pale skin, or very dark skin and bright eyes, you have high contrast. Echo it by wearing bold patterns in contrasting colours. If, on the other hand, you have pale blonde hair and pale skin, or olive skin and sun-bleached hair, you have very low contrast and will look better in closely toning, plain colours. If you have olive or light brown skin and dark hair, or mid-brown hair with a rosy complexion, go for medium contrasts of tone and pattern. Don't worry; you are not absolutely confined to a particular level of contrast. If you are an ash blonde with a love of the dramatic, alter the contrast by wearing bright lipstick or dramatic eye make-up, or by dyeing your hair.

THE COLOUR OF CULTURE

The colours and fabrics worn across the world show just how much colour, tone and contrast vary according to culture, colouring and climate.

HIGH CONTRAST Nigerian and Ghanaian fabrics often come in the high-contrast colours that work well with dark skin: blue and white, green and white, yellow and black. Spanish fashions too team bright primaries with black or white.
MEDIUM CONTRAST Indian saris are often made in jewel colours with glittery threads. In Thailand and China, bright colours may be teamed with black, but plain or small-patterned fabrics are often shiny to reflect light into eyes, hair and skin.
LOW CONTRAST Northern European designers go for low-contrast mixtures of beige and white, soft pink and apricot, heather and grey, with pearls rather than diamonds; all mixtures that enhance a soft, pink complexion and kill most others.

BOLD CONTRASTS
In Ghana, warm dark skin looks good with bright, often high-contrast patterns that would swamp a duller complexion.

YOUR COLOUR GUIDE

The colours you wear can make your face look duller or brighter, just as they can enhance your colouring or swamp it.

There are three different elements to play with when choosing colour: the basic fabric colour, the contrast between colours, and the pattern. The combination that suits you best is the one that echoes your own blend of colouring and contrast. Colour contrast, the contrast between your skin colour and your hair and eyes, is your starting point.

High contrast If you have dark hair and light skin, you are high contrast. The whites of the eyes and teeth offer a high level of contrast against darker skin (which is why there is no medium contrast for dark colouring).

Medium contrast If you have skin, hair and eyes that are all in the same basic colour range, but with highlights in your hair or rosy cheeks, for example, you are medium contrast.

Low contrast If the degree of difference in colour tone between your hair, skin and eyes is more subdued and subtle, you are low contrast.

Patterns Big designs look best with high-contrast colouring. Low-contrast hair and skin team better with plain colours or small patterns.

The five case studies shown in this chart represent different skin tone and hair colour contrasts. See which type you resemble most closely – you may even be a combination of categories. You can then use this information to experiment with different colour mixes, and perhaps to try colours that you wouldn't normally have considered.

DELICATE COLOURING

Very light pink with no olive tones.
• **Be cautious with black.**

High contrast
You can wear most colours, but go for cool rather than warm tones. Your basics are blue and green with touches of the dramatic, such as hot pink or purple. You can cope with high-contrast patterns. If you wear black, team it with white.

Medium contrast
Go for a basic tone that reflects your hair or eye colour and look for combinations that work with it. Don't opt for big contrasts or bright patterns.

Low contrast (see below)
Subdued colours such as light yellow, cream, light blue and pink will suit you best. Choose subtle colour combinations.

Zoe's *pale skin and dark blonde hair make her low contrast.*

She looks best in plain, clear blues and dark camel or creamy colours with gold to create sparkle.

ZOE'S KEY COLOURS

HIGH COLOURING

Rosy cheeks, a tendency to blush.
• **Avoid reds and bright pinks.**

High contrast
Cool blues and greens look good; so too do beige and black. You can wear contrasting patterns of stripes or dots.

Medium contrast (see below)
Bold patterns will swamp you, so experiment with more low-key designs and colour mixes. Try gold and warm browns to pick up the highlights in your hair. Wear black sparingly; it will take the sparkle out of your colouring.

Low contrast
Stick with cool blues and greens and small patterns. If you have blue eyes, outfits in beige or cream will create a look of cool elegance. Blondes can look stunning in black, but don't team it with white and avoid jewellery that sparkles.

Kirsty's *high colouring and dark red hair make her medium contrast.*

She looks good in burnt golds and browns highlighted with touches of warm blue or purple.

KIRSTY'S KEY COLOURS

COMBINATION COLOURING

Brown skin with a yellow tone; pink skin with olive tones.
• **Look for clear colours; avoid beige, olive, yellow and ochre.**

High contrast (see below)
Opt for black, navy and dark grey, with bright colour near your face or with contrasting patterns in clear colours.

Medium contrast
Dark, clear, basic colours like navy, dark brown and white look good, but avoid contrasting patterns. You will probably look good in cool reds, green, pink and warmer blues. Avoid colours that tip toward yellow or orange.

Low contrast
Stick to clear colours, avoiding black. Try understated combinations and vary the colours, but choose clear pinks, blues and greens.

Shoko's *skin has yellow tones and, with her dark hair, she is high contrast.*

Dark basics suit her, but with something more colourful near her face, like deep red from the cool end of the spectrum.

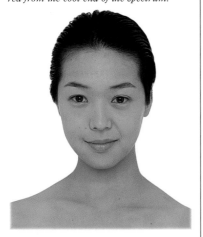

OLIVE OR MEDIUM COLOURING

Warm brown colouring.
• **Be wary of black.**

High contrast (see below)
Truly dramatic colours like hot orange, red and purple, and big, contrasting patterns will look marvellous. Wear black with gold to increase contrast, but away from the face. Avoid muddy colours.

Medium contrast
Try colours that bring out the gold in your skin – greens, yellows, oranges – mixed with warm purples or blues. Avoid brightly contrasting colours: they will swamp you.

Low contrast
Close colour combinations are best. Avoid anything too near to your skin colour: it will have a dulling effect. Creamy colours can look stunning, mixed with gold to create sparkle.

Marije's *dark hair and sparkling eyes make her high contrast.*

She can wear strong colours such as green and red mixed with warm purples or blues, with black as a basic.

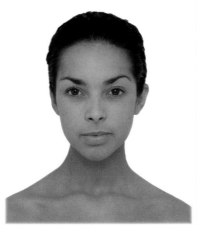

BROWN OR BLACK COLOURING

Dark skin with warm or blue tones.
• **Be bold with colour.**

High contrast
Wear bright colours in high-contrast patterns. If you have a warm tone to your skin, go for oranges and warm reds. Cooler colours will suit skin with blue tones. Avoid muted browns and khakis which will make you look drab. If you wear black, use contrasting colours too, or add gold for sparkle near your face.

Low contrast (see below)
Wear strong colours, warm or cool according to your skin tone. Keep to subtle colour contrasts, such as blue and green, pink and red. Rich, dark browns and creams suit you, but not khaki or grey. When wearing black, choose a stronger colour near your face.

Carine's *dark skin and dark hair make her low contrast.*

She looks wonderful in bright, warm colour combinations, with dark brown or dark green as a basic.

SHOKO'S KEY COLOURS

MARIJE'S KEY COLOURS

CARINE'S KEY COLOURS

FEELING SAFE

• PRACTICAL SELF-DEFENCE • IF THE WORST HAPPENS • YOUR NATURAL WEAPONS

JOHN JAMESON WAS TRAVELLING HOME from work late one evening. It was a cold, dark, winter night and he was heading for the bus stop. A group of young men came toward him. One of them stabbed him, and said later that he was drunk and did not remember doing it.

Stories like this do not make the headlines because attacks of this kind are commonplace. A young man is at least twice as likely to be attacked in public as a young woman of the same age and background. Young men, according to all surveys of risk, are the group most likely to experience violent victimization. Yet, according to criminologist Elizabeth Stanko, "women report fear at levels which are three times that of men". Feminist geographer Rachel Pain describes women's fear as "more a pervading sense of alertness than a momentary terror".

Fear is rarely rational, it is usually a shadowy reflection of a past trauma that may have been experienced personally or passed on through our shared culture. Women feel afraid because we carry with us a deeply held cultural belief that we are at risk of sexual interference from dangerous strangers. In reality, rape by a stranger is not a common occurrence, and in fact statistics show that most rapists are known by their victims. In Britain, rape accounts for less than 2 per cent of recorded violent crime (although it is recognized that rape is under-reported). But it only takes one rape, well-advertised through the media, to imprison an entire community of women. Though we fear the dangerous stranger, clearly women are more at risk from putting misplaced trust in the men they know than in putting their trust where it belongs – in themselves.

Fear creates its own cycle. The more frightened we are, the less powerful we feel and the easier it is for men to remind us of our weakness. The first step in defending ourselves must be to confront our fear and redirect it so that we learn to identify and avoid real, rather than imagined, danger.

PROTECTING YOUR PERSONAL SPACE

Unwarranted sexual intrusion is a way in which some men try to bolster their own feelings of inadequacy. By putting us down, they feel "up". They are not trying to "be nice", and in repelling them we are not "uptight". We have a right to defend ourselves against all invasions of our personal space, from sexual harassment, touching and name calling to unwanted sexual advances.

Making it clear to those who make unwanted advances that you will not give in to them (see opposite) offers a good chance of stopping the behaviour. It also increases your self-confidence, rather than allowing your harasser to undermine it, and self-confidence will enable you to deal with potentially dangerous situations.

VIOLENCE: THE FACTS

■ In a 1988 British crime survey, one woman in three said she was afraid of going out after dark. Young men, the most vulnerable group, are the least likely to admit to being afraid.

■ 90 per cent of violent assaults on women are carried out by someone they know.

■ 85 per cent of female murder victims are killed by someone they know.

■ In Britain, 60 women a year are killed by their partners.

■ 68 per cent of rapists are known to their victims.

SAFETY AWARENESS TRY TO IMAGINE WHICH WOULD BE YOUR MOST LIKELY RESPONSE TO THESE SITUATIONS.

Some young men on the bus start making sexual suggestions in a loud voice. Do you:

1. Bury your head in your book.
2. Go bright red and/or cry.
3. Move to sit nearer the driver.
4. Verbally abuse them with equally lewd suggestions.
5. Pick on the weakest member, look at him and say that you don't play with children, and move away.

A man at work keeps trying to corner you and touch you up. Do you:

1. Creep around the office trying to avoid him and hoping that he will stop.
2. Put on a brave face, keep smiling and try to ignore it.
3. Tell him very firmly that you want him to stop immediately.
4. Report your harasser to either his superior or yours and ask for help.

You accept a lift home from a party. The driver asks to come in for coffee but you feel wary. Do you:

1. Say yes and hope he won't stay long.
2. Say no and get out of the car.
3. Get your keys out before the car stops and then open the door before saying no.
4. Say your brother/partner/father is staying and you can't invite him in.

A new client asks you to meet him alone to discuss a big sale. Do you:

1. Gleefully rush out, thinking about the commission.
2. Ask for the phone number and address and say your assistant will ring back and confirm.
3. Ask him to meet you at your office.
4. Leave the address and phone number and arrange to call the office as soon as you arrive.

ANALYSIS

1 This might work if you can really ignore them, but it might also make them step up their insults to try to get a rise out of you.

2 You will have confirmed their power and that will make you feel even more powerless.

3 A dignified withdrawal will leave them without a target, without making them think they have won. Sitting closer to the driver may give you the confidence to ignore them.

4 By engaging them, you are inviting them to keep it up and to start again next time they see you.

5 If you can pull it off, you will come away feeling empowered rather than weakened by the encounter, but judge carefully whether you can easily get away.

1 You are telling him you are frightened of him. He will go on doing it.

2 You are telling him that you might even agree to being fondled. He will go on doing it.

3 You are making your position clear and letting him know that he is an irritation, not a threat. He might stop.

4 You are safeguarding your position and the position of other women. It would be better still to combine this with **3** above so that he knows exactly where he stands. If he is your boss, confide in another woman, preferably one with a similar level of responsibility to his, or inform your trades union or personnel department (see page 143).

1 You are putting yourself at risk. He may be a wonderful person, but if your instinct is telling you to be wary, listen to it. If he is a nice guy, he can get your number and ring you some other time.

2 He may take no for an answer, but you are alone with him in his car. Perhaps you should have thought ahead.

3 Well planned; you can do this without appearing to be rude. This will make it clear that you are in control and that you are not going to have second thoughts. You are one step ahead of him.

4 This may be a good strategy if he has not already checked whether you live alone. If you are really anxious, it would be best to combine it with **3** above.

1 You are putting yourself at risk. You know nothing about him and nobody knows where you are going. He could very easily take advantage of this situation.

2 You are telling him that at least one other person knows his name, address and telephone number. If his intentions are not straightforward, he will probably try some other target.

3 This is a good strategy because he will then be seen by others, but it may not be practical.

4 You should always make sure that someone knows where you are going and, by phoning back to base, he will know that you are in contact. If his intentions are not good, he may try another target.

PRACTICAL SELF-DEFENCE

Use your fear, do not try to ignore it. Courage, built on an understanding of risk, will keep you far safer than bravado built by ignoring danger.

DO NOT BE A STRANGER We all feel safer in familiar surroundings, among people who know us and care about our safety. Even a big city is made up of small communities, so get to know yours. Chat to elderly neighbours; notice the appearance of a new baby on the block; take the time to discuss the news when you buy your paper; sympathize when the woman at the checkout is looking tired; be aware of who is driving the bus you take to work every day. Be visible, be known.

AVOID DANGER Attacks do not often happen on a crowded street in the rush hour. Avoid underpasses, alleyways and parks, even if it means taking the longer route. When travelling on public transport, sit close to a door and change carriages if you find yourself alone or in the company of a lone man. If you take a taxi, use a licensed cab and take its registration number. If you call for a cab, ask for the number when you call and make a note of it. If you enjoy isolated country walks, look for places where you can see anyone coming and take steps to avoid meeting them. If you walk along a dark, quiet street, use the outside edge of the pavement or even the road if there is little traffic.

RUN AWAY If you feel afraid, move away from the situation. Do not give the other person the benefit of the doubt. If you think you are being followed, cross the road, run to a place where there are lots of people, or into a shop or a café. Perhaps he really was just asking the time, but a man who cares about women's safety should not approach a lone woman in a secluded area. He should understand her fear.

USE YOUR VOICE While a scream is better than no sound at all, it is better still to learn how to shout. A loud, firm "No" may actually throw an attacker off. He expects fear, not challenge. It will also help you to feel strong and angry rather than weak and frightened, and anger releases energy whereas fear can paralyse. Loud shouting will attract attention, so it may bring you help as well. If you think you wouldn't be able to shout, you may feel more confident carrying a rape alarm.

DO NOT BE MOVED If someone tries to make you go with them, stand your ground. If he is trying to move you, he clearly thinks he would be safer elsewhere. That means you are safer where you are. If you are in a car, look for a chance to get out; if you are being pulled, do not co-operate, a dead weight is harder to move than someone who is walking.

FIGHT There is a simple rule to fighting: do not do it unless you have no other option, but if you find yourself alone with a person who clearly means you harm, it does help to know how to fight. Women are often so afraid of being hurt that they become passive in the face of threat. Fighting back means turning fear into anger and accepting that you might be hurt (see pages 28–29).

IF THE WORST HAPPENS

If you are attacked or raped, understand that whatever action you took (or did not take) you are not responsible for what has happened. Try to avoid self-recrimination and "if only". Responsibility for violence lies 100 per cent in the hands of the aggressor.

IMMEDIATE ACTION

• Although you do not have to report the assault to the police, consider that your attacker may have assaulted other women and he may strike again. If it is someone you know, you may be reluctant to report it, but remember that a recent survey showed that 68 per cent of rapists are known to their victims.

• Either go straight to a police station, phone the police, or, failing that, tell someone you trust what has happened straight away and ask them to phone the police. They will be able to provide corroborating evidence of your state of mind and appearance if the case goes to court.

• Call a friend or family member for support. The next few hours may be hard.

• Do not wash, shower or change your clothes: you may lose vital evidence.

• The police will refer you to a doctor who will collect forensic evidence (you can ask to see a female doctor), but you should also make an urgent appointment to see your own doctor, who can prescribe morning-after contraception, arrange for tests and provide any necessary treatment. Your doctor may also be called as a witness when the case comes to court.

• Write down everything you can remember about the event. It may help you to deal with it as well as providing a vital record for a case that could take up to two years to come to court.

LONG-TERM ACTION

Any attack on our personal space, be it through looking, touching, name calling or physical harm, makes us more vulnerable. We need to rebuild our sense of bodily security in just the same way that a householder needs to mend the door and reinforce the locks after a burglary.

PRACTICAL ACTION You may want to take practical measures. Use taxis, improve the lighting outside your home, cut back a hedge that screens a window or door. Police crime prevention officers can offer practical advice.

EMOTIONAL ACTION It may be enough to talk about the attack with friends until the fear is out of your system. If you would like professional emotional support, rape crisis centres provide counsellors who will help you to express the whole range of your feelings – from fear and grief at the loss of your old self-confidence, all the way through to rage against the person who has caused you this pain. Most importantly, they can guide you in the task of rebuilding your confidence in the world. If there are no rape crisis centres where you live, talk to your doctor about counselling. You may also find that self-defence lessons help you to rebuild a sense of yourself as a strong and independent person.

RAPE TRIALS

Although the attack has been against you, court action will be taken by the state. You will be a witness at the trial. Some police forces have set up special rape teams with female officers trained to provide sensitive support. If your assailant is caught, and if the prosecution goes ahead (many do not for lack of supporting evidence), you will have to retell your story in court and cope with cross-questioning from your attacker's defence lawyers. In Britain and Australia, you cannot be identified in news reports.

SEE ALSO
•PAGE 61 Emergency Contraception
•PAGE 77 Vaginal Infections
•PAGES 187–88 Useful Addresses

YOUR NATURAL WEAPONS

According to American Justice Department figures, women who defended themselves against rape were twice as likely to escape as those who did not. But fighting back can be worse than doing nothing if you do not know how to use your body, and self-defence classes are a must if you seriously want to be able to defend yourself. Even if the last thing you can ever imagine is being able to fight back, it is still worth taking some lessons. Many gyms run "boxercise" sessions where you can practise raining blows on to a leather bag. Failing that, pair up with a friend and take it in turns to hold a pillow for your partner to punch. Shout out which part of the body you are punching as you do so. You may never have to make use of your knowledge, but it will certainly make you feel stronger and less vulnerable. If you feel more confident, you are less likely to be a target.

Fighting back is not what an assailant expects. He may let go to protect himself. Strike quickly and effectively using the following ideas and seize the moment of shock to run away.

- Door keys, held in your hand, give a hard edge should you need to hit out.
- An umbrella can be used to keep an assailant beyond arm's length for long enough for you to turn and run.
- Shoes (harder soled ones are best) form effective weapons, particularly if you kick with the side or the heel rather than the toe.
- Your fist is harder than your fingers and more difficult to grasp. Keep your thumb outside your fist, otherwise you might break your fingers when you punch. Punch with force, aiming with the flat front of your fist.
- Your knee may be useful, but if you are close enough to use it, you are unlikely to have room to do so. Do not wait for the opportunity, use something else first.
- The top of your head is a blunt instrument but a powerful one.
- Your teeth are your sharpest natural weapon – try not to be squeamish about sinking them into an assailant if you get the opportunity.

WHERE TO HURT

Your instinct may be to scratch his face or kick out, but your biggest weapon is the element of surprise and you can only use that once. Unless you know how to make the first strike effective, you may be making yourself more vulnerable. An assailant is likely to be bigger and stronger than you are, so it is important to go for the places where you can inflict the most pain or damage. It is safer to use your heel or the side of your shoe and aim at a low target like his shin or foot, rather than kick up at his groin. He may just grab your foot and pull you over. If your hands are free, make a fist and hit him hard on the nose or Adam's apple. It will do more damage than scratching, and a fist is not as easy to grab as extended fingers. Learn a couple of simple, quick yet powerful moves. The illustrations opposite show where to make yourself felt. Start by standing as steadily as you can. Plant both feet on the ground, legs a little apart, knees slightly bent, keeping your weight low. If you root yourself to the spot, you are harder to drag away or to knock over. You can strike lower and you can also lend more weight to your force.

PHYSICAL SELF-DEFENCE

PUNCH THE NOSE OR THROAT
*Clench your fingers in a fist, keeping
your thumb out and wrapped around
the outside. Put the force of your body
weight behind the punch, but not so
that you unbalance yourself. Punch
with the flat front of your fist.*

TWO-FINGERED POKE TO EYES
*This will temporarily distort his vision,
giving you a chance to run. Make sure
that his hands are not close enough to
grab your fingers. Act quickly and catch
him by surprise.*

**HEEL OF
PALM TO CHIN**
*Bend your hand
back and thrust
forward, aiming
with the flat heel of
the hand. Catch him
under the chin or
nose. This is one of
the most powerful
and effective moves.*

**SCRATCH
THE FACE**
*The sight of his
own blood might
be enough to make
him back off. He may
get worried about not
being able to account
for obvious scratches.*

**GRIP AND TWIST
TO GROIN**
*This can only produce results
if the positioning is correct.
Reach up and under,
grip securely and twist
forcefully. Keep out of the range
of his arms in case he tries to
grab or punch you.*

KNEE KICK TO GROIN
*This is an obvious vulnerable
area. Some argue that hitting
an assailant here will only
make him more angry, but
if you strike forcefully, it
is guaranteed to disable
him, at least momentarily,
and it will give you a
chance to run.*

HEEL KICK TO SHIN
*This is a useful move to free
yourself if you are being held
from behind. It is especially
effective if you are wearing
heels. Stamp your heel down
on his foot or kick
backward like a
donkey, aiming
for his shin or groin.*

SHOUTING
*A loud shout of anger will have more impact
than a scream of terror. It can unfreeze you
and empower you. An attacker will react as
any other human being and feel scared.*

Eating healthily

Exercising

Knowing your body

Diffusing anger

HEALTHY LIVING

Do you remember being five years old, when you jumped out of bed in the morning and every day was an adventure? That is what good health should feel like – not just the absence of disease but a positive feeling of wellbeing. Worries, work and overindulgence have a way of taking the edge off that zest, but it is possible to recapture or to hang on to some of that limitless energy and optimism. The pages that follow examine health-related issues from diet to exercise and will help you to target any areas that need attention.

How Healthy are You?

STAYING HEALTHY IS NOT ABOUT ABSTINENCE and self-denial, it is about embracing a lifestyle that allows you to feel your best. The feeling of positive health will be different for each one of us. For some, a life without chocolate would be unbearable, for others, an alcohol-free existence would be purgatory. Since health is above all about happiness, we must create our own balance, a balance that will change from time to time as our lives change.

You can use this questionnaire to evaluate how healthy you are. It covers most aspects of daily life, and aims to give an indication of your current state of health. Be honest with your answers and use the scores to highlight areas for improvement and to enable you to spot changes you might want to make. If, for example, you have a sedentary job and you use a car and lift whenever possible, you might want to try being more active during the day.

QUESTIONNAIRE

FRESH FRUIT AND VEGETABLES
Do you eat them:

☐ Rarely. *(Score 5)*

☐ Most days. *(Score 2)*

☐ At every meal. *(Score 1)*

SWEETS, CHOCOLATES AND CAKES
Do you:

☐ Binge, especially when you feel low. *(Score 5)*

☐ Enjoy them occasionally. *(Score 2)*

☐ Avoid them like the plague. *(Score 1)*

FRIED FOODS
Do you eat them:

☐ Most days. *(Score 5)*

☐ Once a week or less. *(Score 2)*

☐ Never. *(Score 1)*

ALCOHOL
Do you drink:

☐ Heavily – more than 3 units a day. *(Score 5)*

☐ Moderately – less than 3 units a day. *(Score 2)*

☐ Never. *(Score 1)*

(A unit is a glass of wine, a measure of spirits or half a pint of beer.)

LIQUIDS
Do you drink water, caffeine-free drinks or pure fruit juices:

☐ Never. *(Score 5)*

☐ Occasionally. *(Score 2)*

☐ Several times a day. *(Score 1)*

SLEEPING PATTERNS
Do you wake early or during the night and worry:

☐ Often. *(Score 5)*

☐ Rarely. *(Score 2)*

☐ Never. *(Score 1)*

WAKING UP
First thing in the morning do you:

- [ ] Feel terrible, cough and/or feel stiff. (*Score 5*)
- [ ] Feel ready to go after a cup of something. (*Score 2*)
- [ ] Bounce up and start rushing around. (*Score 1*)

EXERCISE
Do you take vigorous exercise, such as cycling, running or squash for 20 minutes or more:

- [ ] Never. (*Score 5*)
- [ ] Two or three times a week most weeks. (*Score 2*)
- [ ] More than three times a week every week. (*Score 1*)

RECOVERY RATE
When you climb stairs do you:

- [ ] Pant and slow down after about 20 stairs. (*Score 5*)
- [ ] Pant and slow down after 40 stairs. (*Score 2*)
- [ ] Walk up 60 stairs and recover quickly. (*Score 1*)

DAILY ACTIVITY
In your daily life do you:

- [ ] Drive to work and remain mostly sedentary during the day. (*Score 5*)
- [ ] Walk or cycle at least 30 minutes a day and use stairs rather than lifts. (*Score 2*)
- [ ] Have a physically demanding job or occupation. (*Score 1*)

ANSWERS AND ANALYSIS

If you smoke regularly, add 30 points to your score.
If you regularly drink more than 3 units a day, more than twice a week, add 30 to your score.
If you regularly use class A (hard) drugs, add 50 to your score.
If you starve yourself, binge-eat, or vomit after eating, add 50 to your score.

If you scored between 10 and 12
You are almost certainly very fit indeed, but are you sure you are not over-controlling yourself? A rigid programme of diet and exercise with no late nights and not even an occasional treat may be a sign of obsession. Are you afraid that if you give a little you will fall apart? It is possible that you are overdoing it.

If you scored between 13 and 26
You have a healthy lifestyle, but make sure that it is not the exercise you are skimping on. If you are under 20, you are a credit to your generation. Just the occasional self-indulgence will not hurt; you have plenty of time to make up for it. If you are over 40, then keep going as you are and you should keep aches, pains and the other less pleasant signs of ageing at bay for a while.

If you scored between 27 and 37
If you are under 30, you are probably not yet noticing the effects of your lifestyle because you bounce back so easily, but it is time to take a look at yourself and try to incorporate some healthier habits into your daily life. If you are pregnant, or considering pregnancy, you need to shape up quickly because this lifestyle is not doing you, or your baby, any good.

If you scored between 38 and 60
A little self-indulgence is a wonderful thing, but too much can lead you along the road to self-destruction. If you are truthful with yourself, you probably aren't feeling very healthy. Start by changing the easy things. You may find, for example, that by adding better food to your diet you will begin to tip the balance toward health, and feel more able to cut down on smoking or drinking and take more exercise. If you are over 35 (or considering pregnancy), you need to take immediate action. If you are under 25, you have a little longer in which to turn your life around, though bad habits are difficult to break. You may find this hard to believe, but you really will feel happier if you allow yourself to be healthier.

If you scored over 60
You have some habits that will soon affect your health seriously. You may need professional help to find out what is pushing you down this destructive road (see pages 40–41).

FOOD AND YOU

• GOOD FOOD • THE RULES OF HEALTHY EATING

FROM OUR EARLIEST MOMENTS, thoughts of love, security and comfort (as well as defiance, denial and control) have been tied up with food. Sharing food is recognized as a symbol of friendship and in many cultures food rituals and taboos are also a symbol of belonging. There is also the matter of pleasure. Good food appeals to our senses, and the creation of special dishes appeals to our creative instincts. Little wonder then that our feelings about food are so complicated.

GOOD FOOD

Human beings evolved on a diet of fresh, locally grown food, softened through grinding and heating, and combined to improve its flavour. Food was not genetically manipulated to grow faster, nor grown with chemical fertilizers to make it bigger. It was not dusted with pesticides to keep insects and disease at bay, nor was it cut unripe and then stored. It was not refined to remove part of its nutrient qualities, nor mixed with chemicals to preserve it and change its colour. Nor was it combined, as today, with animal fat, salt and sugar to alter the flavour and consistency.

Food was not all perfect either. It rotted, became infested and did not always last through the winter months. People used to die of food poisoning and suffer deficiency diseases. However, we have swapped those problems for new ones: heart disease, diabetes, behavioural problems and cancers have all been linked to the way we eat; so it makes sense to eat fresh and well-prepared food. We should be able to acquire all the nutrients we need through a balanced, healthy diet; but at certain times in life we may need extra supplements.

FRESH FOODS
A healthy diet includes plenty of fresh, unrefined food.

SPECIAL FOODS FOR WOMEN

SPECIAL NUTRIENT	WHEN YOU NEED IT	WHERE TO FIND IT
Folate (B vitamin) 	You need folate before puberty and throughout your childbearing years. It protects against spina bifida, a malformation of the central nervous system, in babies; so it is important to eat enough in the months *before*, as well as during, pregnancy.	Beans, peas, parsley, walnuts, wholemeal bread, bananas and green leafy vegetables such as broccoli. Supplements (in synthetic form as folic acid) should not be necessary if you eat green vegetables every day.
Calcium 	You particularly need calcium in childhood, during pregnancy and in the approach to menopause and after. Calcium builds strong bones and teeth and guards against osteoporosis (brittle bones) in later life.	Green vegetables, milk products, nuts, sunflower seeds, beans, dried fruit and tiny fish eaten with the bones. In Western countries milk products are the major source of calcium. If you cannot tolerate milk, make sure you compensate with other calcium-rich foods.
Vitamin D 	Vitamin D is essential in childhood and then approaching and after the menopause. It helps the body to absorb calcium to make strong bones.	Manufactured in the body from sunshine, vitamin D is also found in eggs and fish oils and is added to margarine and some milk. Darker-skinned people who live in a cold climate may need supplements.
Iron 	All menstruating women need to be sure that they are getting enough iron since it is lost in blood. In pregnancy your iron levels should be checked and, if necessary, boosted with supplements. Lack of iron in the blood leads to anaemia (see page 73).	Green leafy vegetables, egg yolks, fish, liver, red meat, dried fruit, cereal, nuts, bread and haricot beans. Iron is best absorbed if it is eaten at the same time as vitamin C. Iron supplements should only be necessary if you are anaemic. Cooking in iron pots increases the iron content of food.
Vitamin B6 	There is some evidence that women who suffer from premenstrual syndrome (see page 56) can benefit from supplements of vitamin B6.	Wheatgerm, brewer's yeast, peanuts, bananas, soft fruit, mushrooms, fresh fish, poultry and pork. If you take supplements it may be better to take the whole range of B vitamins as they interact with each other in ways that are not yet fully understood.
Evening primrose oil	Evening primrose oil contains gammalinolenic acid, which is claimed to ease premenstrual syndrome (see page 56) and to improve various skin conditions.	In capsule form from pharmacists and health food shops.

THE RULES OF HEALTHY EATING

It is easy to eat well. You do not need to count calories or understand much about nutrition. You do need to understand that in Western industrialized countries we eat too much refined sugar, too much animal fat and far too little dietary fibre and vitamins. Much of the reason for this overconsumption is our growing reliance on prepacked, convenience foods that contain large quantities of hidden fats and sugars and are often stripped of fibre and vitamins. If you prepare your own food to the following basic rules, your diet will look after itself.

FRESH FRUIT AND VEGETABLES   Make sure that you include green vegetables at most meals; they provide a range of B vitamins (in particular folate). Yellow vegetables are a good source of vitamin A, and citrus fruit, sweet peppers and potatoes contain vitamin C, which guards against infection. Eat vegetables fresh if you can, frozen if you have to, and tinned if there is no alternative. Vitamins are lost in the cooking process, particularly if you throw away the cooking water. The healthiest (and tastiest) way to prepare vegetables is to steam them.

COMPLEX CARBOHYDRATES   These should be the foundation of every meal. They provide a range of vitamins and minerals, as well as energy and fibre, which is vital to your internal health. Complex carbohydrates are found in bread (wholewheat and soda bread, naan and pitta bread), pasta, porridge, rice, potatoes and couscous. Sugared breakfast cereals, cakes and biscuits, and other foods

SNACKS, TREATS AND JUNK FOOD

If you cut refined sugar and animal fat out of your diet, and keep even vegetable oils to a minimum, you are unlikely to become overweight and will certainly feel more energetic and fit. If you cannot imagine life without treats, however, stick to the following rules:

■ Never eat a chocolate bar or any other type of junk food *instead* of a good meal.

■ Always treat your body to the good healthy food it deserves *before* abusing it with the bad food that you crave.

FRESH FRUIT
Eating fresh fruit provides the best source of vitamin C.

APPETIZING MEALS
Savour every mouthful at mealtimes. Choose fresh, flavourful dishes, such as this vegetable couscous and tropical fruit salad. Food should bring pleasure, not guilt.

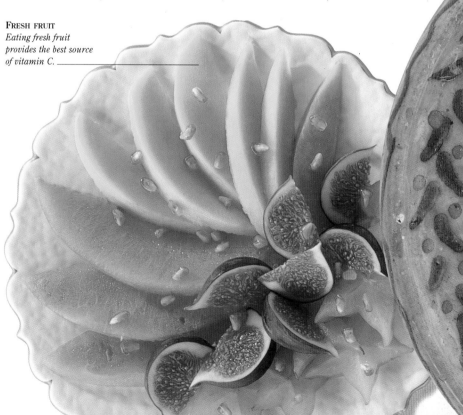

containing sugar and fats, also provide energy. However, they provide no other nutrients so they tend to be used up fast to give you a burst of energy. The rest is stored as fat in the body, leaving you lethargic and ready for another meal.

PROTEINS These are necessary for the growth and repair of body tissue, and protein-rich foods also contain B vitamins and some minerals. Eating protein foods slows down the digestion of other foods and stops you becoming hungry again immediately, so it is useful to eat some at every main meal. Fish, meat, poultry, dairy products, beans and pulses, eggs and nuts are all high in protein.

In most Western countries, animal proteins (including dairy products) are consumed to excess; a healthier source is combinations of grains and beans, for example, beans and wholewheat bread or dhal with rice. These proteins are also high in fibre and do not contain harmful animal fats, which are associated with high levels of heart disease.

LIQUID IN YOUR DIET

■ About 60 per cent of the body consists of water and you need to drink plenty to keep your kidneys working well.
■ Always drink as much water as your thirst dictates, but avoid sweet, sugary drinks.

CHICKPEAS
These are a good source of protein, especially for vegetarians.

COURGETTES
An excellent choice for folate.

CARROTS
A rich source of vitamin A and fibre.

COUSCOUS
Contains protein from semolina grains.

> **" I felt a sense of pride in my ability to control myself. My mother was constantly dieting and failing. This was something I could do better than her. "**

WHEN FOOD MAKES YOU ILL

• BODY BATTLES • KICKING THOSE HABITS

SOME PEOPLE CANNOT TOLERATE PARTICULAR FOODS because they lack the enzymes to break them down properly. As a result, they may have chronic stomach or digestive problems or suffer from low energy levels. Other people may be allergic to specific proteins in foods and may react with something as mild as a rash or as serious as a severe asthma attack. Food additives, pesticides and preservatives have also been connected with a range of health problems varying from hyperactivity to cancer. But perhaps the most common food problem for women lies in our minds.

BODY BATTLES

Do you see food as a potential enemy, a potent force with the power to invade and overwhelm you? If this feels true to you, then you are not alone. For many women, and some men, the attempt to control their relationship with food is a life-long struggle. All eating disorders stem, in some way, from our image of ourselves and our place in the world. Often they conceal deeper fears about whether we are loveable; whether we are in control; whether we can cope with big changes ahead of us. This is why eating disorders often occur (or recur) in times of crisis. The problem can start at various stages in life:

• In childhood. Starvation is often used to resist adult control, as Sheila McLeod explains in *The Art of Starvation*, it can be used "to triumph over the wills of others and over the chaos ensuing from their conflicting demands".

• In puberty. For some girls, controlling food intake (which includes over-eating), is a way of avoiding becoming a woman.

• As a young woman. It may be a response to the overwhelming onslaught of images that tells young women they ought to be thin, making the battle to control food intake a battle to become desirable.

OVEREATING

It is fine to go out and eat a banana split on your birthday just because you like it. It is not fine to eat one and then order another one straight away. Nor is it fun to hide food in your bedroom and eat it silently, guiltily, when you think no one is looking, and to feel a sense of fear if you are far away from food for an hour or two. Real overeating is not evidence of a zest for life, or even pleasure in food, it stems from feelings of worthlessness. It is a way of dropping out of a world in which you are judged by the way you look, and where it may seem easier to hide within your body. You may tell yourself that you enjoy this self-enforced feeding, but in fact every mouthful is tainted with self-loathing. The hole inside that you are desperate to fill is not hunger, it is some other kind of emptiness and food cannot fill it.

You may have tried dieting and found that you feel miserable and defeated; in fact, dieting is remarkably ineffective for most people. Studies show that 98 per cent of dieters regain the lost weight within five years, and most end up weighing more than before. You need to find out why it is that you seek comfort this way. Choosing a healthier way of eating will enable you to find your ideal weight and to start enjoying the food that you eat now without even tasting it.

ANOREXIA NERVOSA

Self-starvation is a problem of growing severity in industrialized societies. It usually starts between puberty and adulthood. Some young women manage to starve themselves to death. This psychological disease, which is not easy to treat, is clearly connected with the Western obsession with slimness. Girls are expected to conform to an increasingly androgynous, idealized version of womanhood at earlier and earlier ages. Girls as young as six have been treated for anorexia because they have become so afraid of getting fat that they refuse to eat.

When a child gains weight in the years before puberty – a perfectly normal development – she may already have internalized a fear of being fat and, as a result, may start to refuse food. For an anorexic, the realization that she can assume control over a body that has seemed out of control may lead to an even greater effort of will. She no longer sees what she looks like; she is now engaged in a battle with her own flesh.

BULIMIA

Bulimics overeat compulsively, but then vomit to rid themselves of the food they have guiltily consumed. In a sense, a bulimic has the desire of a compulsive eater without the iron will of an anorexic, so vomiting becomes the way to cope with the conflicting desires of the body and the mind – to eat and yet never to get fat. The bingeing will seem totally uncontrollable and then the urge to rid the body of the "polluting" food is equally irresistible.

While it may be possible to control weight gain in this way, the effects are seriously damaging to health. Bulimics can injure the stomach lining and intestines by constantly regurgitating acids as they vomit. They are also likely to become seriously malnourished.

CREATING CHANGE

A mild eating disorder may resolve when a period of crisis is over and normal behaviour returns. A young woman who has been overeating, or starving, may find that a change of environment allows her to "start again", to slip out of old patterns and find a healthy relationship with her body. This might be a holiday, or leaving home to go to college. Some find that the problem is intractable without help (see page 40). Many self-help books deal with eating problems, and self-help groups with members who have had similar experiences can be invaluable (see pages 187–88).

ALLERGIES

Eczema, asthma, migraine, irritable bowel syndrome and a number of other chronic conditions can be caused by the body's overreaction to eating a particular food. The chemical histamine is created and released into the bloodstream, initially as a protection against the ingestion of a "foreign" protein. The reaction may cause anything from a mild skin irritation or rash to a life-threatening asthmatic attack.

■ The most common food allergies are to milk products (other than human milk), wheat, nuts, eggs, chocolate, citrus fruit and some food colourings.

■ If you suffer from a chronic condition, which could be allergic in origin, talk to your doctor about an elimination diet or to a homeopath about allergy tests; both may help to pinpoint your particular sensitivity so you can avoid that food in future.

■ You may be advised to keep a supply of antihistamine tablets in case of future attacks.

KICKING THOSE HABITS

Why do we smoke, drink to excess, starve ourselves, find a hand in the biscuit box without even knowing how it got there, when we know these things are bad for us? The answer is nearly always "because I enjoy it". A pleasure becomes a habit when we no longer do it just because we like it, but because we cannot manage without it.

HOOKED ON CHEMICALS

Caffeine, alcohol, nicotine and sugar are some of the chemicals implicated in addiction. All these substances have a mood-altering effect. Some people feel the buzz and then allow it to die away until the next time. Others take some more so they can get that buzz back as soon as possible. Gradually the body will adjust to the chemical so that more is needed just to stay ahead of the body's defences and to feel the rush as the chemical hits the spot. Once the metabolism has adjusted to a steady level of chemical, any drop in that level will be interpreted as a threat by the body. If you feel cravings, become bad tempered, or worse, you have reached the level of dependency and you need the chemical just to feel normal.

PSYCHOLOGICAL DEPENDENCY

Some people are locked into a cycle of self-destructive behaviour which, at least at the start, provides a comforting barrier between themselves and the world. The habit may be purely behavioural – starving, overworking, overeating, playing computer games – or it may provide the psychological underpinning of a chemical addiction. This psychological attachment is the reason why some people find it hard to stay off cigarettes or alcohol even when they have managed to get the chemical out of their system; it is also the reason why the apparently simple use of willpower rarely works. If you are psychologically addicted, you will find yourself drawn back to the behaviour or the habit. You need to deal with the emotional element of your habit if you are ever to loosen its grip on your life.

MAKING AN ACTION PLAN

You may be denying the fact that you have a habit at all. If this is the case, it is time to stop making excuses for yourself. You will feel much better when you are the one in control of your life.

FACING UP You cannot give up a habit until you know you have got it, so the first

❝ I wanted to get pregnant, and knew that I would have to stop smoking first. I couldn't have lived with myself if I had harmed my baby. **❞**

NAME: **Pam Johns**

OCCUPATION: **Computer programmer**

AGE: **33**

"If I went into a bar I would stay there until I was so drunk I had to be helped home. I told myself it wasn't addiction because I didn't drink at home. I insisted that I knew how to have a good time. The truth dawned on me when I realized that I was avoiding going out on a Friday night because I knew that I would end up dead drunk and in a stranger's bed. I had to face the fact that I couldn't control my drinking."

step may simply be owning up to yourself that you are hooked. This apparently simple step can be surprisingly difficult to take.

FEELING SURE You have to know why you want to give a habit up. Perhaps it is because you know you are drinking away money that should be shared with your family, or because you caught sight of your reflection in a window and hated the way you looked. One strategy that might help is to write down what you think the reason might be for giving up and leave it somewhere where you will see it often.

FORGIVING YOURSELF If you are psychologically hooked, feeling bad about yourself may be the root of your habit. Learning to feel good about yourself could be another stage on the road to recovery. Perhaps you are turning to chemicals or chronic overwork because:
• You feel unable to open up to another person and ask for help or for love.
• You are punishing yourself.
• You feel that nobody loves you so there is no reason to care about yourself.
• The chemical numbs your mind and stops you feeling anything.
• You are afraid of feeling pleasure.
• Eating, drinking or smoking are the only ways you know to comfort yourself.
• You are afraid that if you let go, you will fall apart.
You may also find that other people's attitudes toward your habit add to your feelings of self-loathing: you feel despised so you despise yourself even more. By pinpointing your problem you can begin to work on it yourself, but you may need professional help to deal with deep-seated feelings (see page 93).

GETTING SUPPORT Tell your friends about your decision and ask them not to tempt you. If you suspect that "coming off" will throw you completely off balance emotionally, you may need more formal help. Self-help groups are particularly useful because other members provide reassurance and support while preventing you from making excuses to yourself (see page 93).

BREAKING THE PATTERN Addictive behaviour is often ritualized. Perhaps you always smoke when you are talking on the telephone or after a meal. Do you find that you stuff yourself with sweets while watching television, or that you drink while preparing supper? Learn to recognize and cut these links. Hold the telephone in the hand in which you usually hold your cigarette; go for a walk as soon as the meal is over; give up watching television or teach yourself to knit; try to get someone else to prepare supper.

REWARDING YOURSELF Most people associate "giving up" with discomfort and pain. Reverse this by rewarding yourself for your efforts – though try not to turn the reward into a substitute habit. If your habit costs you money, save it for a special purpose: a trip, a new dress, a facial or a massage.

If your habit does not involve cost, plan to do things you do not usually allow yourself time or money for. Since habits are so often rooted in low self-esteem, it will probably do you good to take your own needs seriously.

HARD DRUGS
■ If you are addicted to hard drugs or tranquillizers, you may need medical help to see you through the period of physical withdrawal (see pages 187–88).

■ Once the chemical addiction has been overcome, you will have to tackle the psychological and emotional issues or you will simply slide back into addiction.

■ You may want to consider individual or group psychotherapy, or join a specialist group for people with similar problems (see pages 187–88).

EXERCISE AND YOU

- FITNESS TESTS • FITTING EXERCISE INTO YOUR LIFE
- SELF-HELP EXERCISE PLANS • HOME WORKOUT
- EXERCISING WITH OTHERS

OUR BODIES WERE MADE FOR MOVING and carrying, but today, more and more, we use cars, escalators and lifts and are rarely called upon to pick up anything much heavier than a spoon. The energy we should expend in movement is stored up as fat, or released in bursts of aggression. Very often the first real sign that our bodies are untested comes with having a baby. Babies need carrying and they get heavier by the day. An aching back may be a sign of trouble to come. However, it is in middle age that we really start to feel the creaking joints that tire easily when walking up stairs, lungs unaccustomed to being used, a heart that pounds with effort and, as we get older, bones that break too easily.

WHY EXERCISE?

Exercise is the lubricant that keeps our bodies and minds in working order, but it is not always easy to fit in to busy routines, especially for those of us who hate sports and have little reason to exercise during our day-to-day life.

If you enjoy sports, you are probably out there exercising already. If you have been temporarily grounded by a disability, ask for advice from your doctor and then an exercise professional before starting; there is certainly some form of sport you can still enjoy. If you dread the thought of any exercise, you probably have a psychological, rather than a physical, barrier to jump. Start with the quiz opposite and discover whether you are just making excuses for not exercising, then set yourself a low, achievable goal. Twenty minutes exercise twice a week will not turn you into a wrestler, but it is 40 minutes better than nothing at all.

WHICH EXERCISE?

Swimming is the easiest form of exercise if you are overweight, have a disability, or have simply not moved for a long time, because your joints are supported by the water and you will not get hot and sweaty. If there are no special sessions at a local pool to suit you, try to swim at the quietest time of the day. Many swimming pools now organize water aerobics or step classes for those who want something more interesting and sociable than just swimming up and down.

Women-only gyms can be a comfort for women who feel self-conscious about their bodies. Some arrange classes for women with disabilities, and beginners' classes are usually slow enough for even the creakiest joints and most nervous newcomers. There may be a special session for older people too at your sports centre and, if there is not, take a group along and start your own.

TEN COMMON EXCUSES FOR NOT MOVING WHY ARE YOU RESISTING EXERCISE?

Tick off all the excuses that you make for not doing any exercise:

1. I do not have time.

2. I have a bad back, knee, ankle, etc.

3. I am too old.

4. There is nowhere to do it.

5. I hate getting sweaty and jiggling up and down.

6. I am happy with my body the way it is.

7. I am hopelessly unco-ordinated and feel foolish.

8. I prefer to spend my free time sitting down.

9. I am too fat. I am too embarrassed to wear a leotard.

10. I do not enjoy it.

ANALYSIS

Deep-down resistance

If you have ticked numbers **2**, **3**, **7** or **9**, your major concern may be self-consciousness. It can be hard to join a gym, for example, if you feel that everyone else is slim, beautiful and more adept than you.

Remember, however little you do, and however slow you are, it is better to have started, and do not think that buying an exercise video will do the trick. If you have a very high level of resistance, you are unlikely to exercise alone so the video will never be played. You probably need some form of external discipline to get you going. Look out for special classes or team up with a friend for moral support. She can stop you from backsliding in the early days.

Once you have got started you will almost certainly find you feel so much better that you will want to keep going.

If you have a physical disability, get clearance from your doctor and consult an exercise professional first.

Low resistance

If you have ticked **5**, **6**, **8** or **10**, face the fact that you are not taking exercise seriously. Maybe you are too young to care and hope to make up for your sloth in later years.

Why not learn a sport, or take up dancing? You can choose from many different types of dance, such as salsa or rock and roll, which are popular. You may be able to find classes where you can go regularly, have fun, meet people and get some exercise at the same time.

If you played a sport at school, consider a revival. You may be able to join a local netball or hockey team, or perhaps a tennis club.

If you spend your life in front of a television or computer screen, try to increase your energy levels by walking briskly for an hour a day.

Practical difficulties

If you have ticked **1** or **4**, you need to put some creative thought into this.

If it is work that is keeping you stationary, consider whether you are overworking and may be less productive than you could be if you paid more attention to your health. Why not make the following changes to your daily routine: cycle to work (or to the nearest station); work out in your lunch hour at a gym; organize or join a sports club at work; or make yourself leave earlier twice a week to take care of your own needs.

If you care for children, your free time will be squeezed. Try to carve out 20 minutes, two or three times a week, by getting someone else to care for them; if the children are old enough, they can join in too.

If the problem is lack of facilities, see pages 48–49 for exercises you can do at home.

SWIMMING
A good general exercise that supports the limbs and works the heart and lungs.

FITNESS TESTS

Fitness can be defined in many ways – physical fitness, mental fitness, emotional fitness – but it is often confused with looking healthy. A slim, rosy-cheeked woman may be regarded as fit by her friends just because of her slimness, but looking physically fit does not necessarily entail good mental or medical health. Physical fitness can be loosely defined as using your heart, lungs and muscles to their optimum efficiency (see page 74). Here are some easy tests that you can do at home to establish your current level of stamina, muscular endurance and strength. Whatever level you are, plan to increase your fitness gradually, using the ideas on pages 46–51. Do not attempt any exercise without first warming up (see page 48), and although you don't have to wear special clothing, well-fitting sports shoes will protect your joints – they come in different styles for different sports.

MONITORING YOUR HEART RATE

Take your pulse at regular intervals after exercise to assess your fitness level.

Use two fingers to feel your pulse

1 Find your resting pulse rate, either on your wrist or at the side of your neck, using two fingers. Count the number of beats in 15 seconds and multiply by 4 to show your rate for one minute. This is your personal base line. Fill it in on the chart. If your rate is over 100 beats per minute, check with your doctor before you attempt any energetic activity.

2 Do one minute's worth of vigorous exercise, such as jumping jacks (right), running on the spot or back and forth between two points. Take your pulse again. It will be higher because your heart has been working hard. Record it on your chart.

Bend your knees and land on your heels when doing jumping jacks

3 Continue taking your pulse at 15-second intervals and record it on your chart until it returns to normal. If you repeat the test every week, you may see that you return to normal after a shorter time and this is an indicator that your exercise plan is working and you are fitter than before.

YOUR PULSE RATE (BEATS PER MINUTE)

Time	Pulse rate
At rest	
After 1 minute's exercise	
15 seconds later	
30 seconds later	
45 seconds later	
1 minute later	

TARGET PULSE RATE (BEATS PER MINUTE)

Age	At rest	After exercise
18–29	70–77	86–90
30–39	72–79	88–95
40–49	74–81	90–97
50+	76–83	92–99

MUSCULAR ENDURANCE TEST: CURL-UP

Count how many you can do in one minute and compare
with the chart. Note your weekly improvement.

TARGET FOR ONE MINUTE

Under 35 yrs	Over 36 yrs	Score
39	39	Excellent
34	29	Good
25	18	Average
16	10	Fair
10	4	Poor

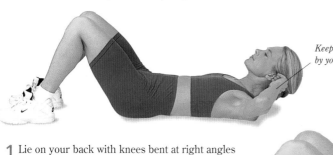

*Keep your hands
by your ears*

3 Pause in this top position and breathe in. As you
breathe out, slowly curl back down again, but
without putting your head back on the floor.
Repeat the exercise, counting the
number of curl-ups completed
in one minute.

1 Lie on your back with knees bent at right angles
and your lower back pressed into the ground.
Keep your feet flat on the floor, hip-width apart.
Place your fingers by your ears so that they
gently support your head. Breathe in.

2 As you breathe out, curl your shoulders
up and off the floor in a slow and
controlled movement. Keep your
tummy muscles tight and be careful
not to strain your back or neck.

MUSCULAR STRENGTH TEST: PRESS-UP

Repeat this exercise over one minute and compare with the chart.

TARGET FOR ONE MINUTE

Under 35 yrs	Over 36 yrs	Score
40	35	Excellent
33	30	Good
25	19	Average
14	10	Fair
5	3	Poor

1 Place your hands flat on the ground, facing forward,
shoulder-width apart and level with your ears.
Bend your knees and cross your ankles.
Breathe in before you
exert yourself.

2 Breathe out,
lowering
your body weight
by bending your
arms and taking your chin
nearer the floor. Keep your
back in a straight line;
do not let it sway.

3 Slowly straighten
your arms,
lifting your body
weight, but do
not lock them.
Repeat for one
minute, counting the number
of completed press-ups.

*Bend your arms to
lower your body*

*Do not let your
lower back dip*

FITTING EXERCISE INTO YOUR LIFE

Sometimes it can be particularly difficult to get out and take exercise. You may be kept at home by children or sick family members. You may find that the combined pressure of home and work simply leaves no time for you. Or perhaps you are afraid to run in the streets and cannot afford to use specialized sports facilities. In the long term you need to find a better solution to your physical confinement, but in the short term there are always ways of doing some exercise to help make you that bit fitter. Always begin any exercise with a few minutes of warming up and stretching (see page 48) and then start slowly, before stretching again and cooling down. This prevents cramps and stiffness, which can make you feel so uncomfortable that you might stop exercising.

WALKING AND CYCLING

Most of us have to go out during the day, so on some of these trips you could forsake the car or public transport and try some of the following ideas:
- If you always drive, try parking your car further away each day so that you are forced to walk to your destination, remembering to allow yourself the necessary extra ten minutes' travelling time.
- If you take a bus, try walking one bus stop further than you need to, or get off one stop early.
- Use stairs instead of lifts or get out one or two floors early. On an escalator, walk up rather than stand.
- Use a bicycle for all short trips. Consider cycling to work if you live near enough, but take adequate safety measures and always wear protective gear.
- On a bicycle, fit a baby seat if necessary, but make sure you provide maximum protection – use a baby helmet, too.

EXERCISING WITH A BABY

If you are at home with a baby, include her (or him) in your exercise routine once she is at least three months old and able to hold her head up. By this point your stomach muscles should be ready to work again too. Choose a time when your baby is awake and alert and try the following exercises to work different parts of your body:

ABDOMINAL MUSCLES Lie on the floor with your knees up and your back well supported. Lift your baby up on your shins where she can watch your face. Lift your head and shoulders gradually off the ground and stretch out toward her, then lower yourself. Do this ten times at first, gradually increasing the number.

UPPER BODY Lie on the floor with your baby on your stomach. Holding her firmly under her arms with both hands, straighten your arms slowly so that she is at arms' length and gently lower her again. Do this as often as you can manage and she enjoys.

PLANNING FOR EXERCISE

- Write out an hour-by-hour analysis of what you do in a typical day, starting with the time you get up and ending with your bedtime.
- Try to fit at least an hour's exercise into your daily routine, such as half an hour of stretching in the morning and a walk in the evening.

PELVIC SQUEEZES

Toning up your pelvic floor (the muscles that surround your vagina) helps prevent incontinence (involuntary urination) and can improve your experience of sex. It is particularly important during and after pregnancy.
- Find the muscles by stopping and starting your urine flow – the pelvic floor muscles control this.
- Now that you have found the muscles, use them; squeeze in and out while you wash up, while you wait at bus stops – anytime you are standing still.

SELF-HELP EXERCISE PLANS

Exercising alone requires a level of discipline. There is no one to chivvy you along and no one to compete with, but some people prefer to be in sole control of their time this way. If you feel constrained by the discipline of classes, hate to be "herded around", or simply find it hard to fit into a schedule because your life is too complicated, you will be more likely to stick to an exercise programme of your own making. You can easily integrate exercise into your daily routine by walking or cycling, as suggested opposite, or you could try one of the following ideas.

SWIMMING

Pools often mark off a few lanes in the early morning, at midday and in the evening for people who want to swim lengths. Build up to 20 minutes' swimming, gradually increasing the distance as you get fitter.

ADVANTAGES Swimming exercises the whole body, including the heart and lungs, and increases flexibility; it is ideal for good all-round fitness. It is excellent for those with back problems (it's best to swim on your back as flat in the water as possible) or joint problems.

DISADVANTAGES Swimming endless lengths can be monotonous. High chlorine levels can be unpleasant: ozone-treated pools have lower levels of chlorine.

USING A GYM

All gyms induct new users: a trained instructor should show you how to use the equipment and the correct way to do exercises to prevent injury. Always start with a 10-minute period of aerobic exercise on a cycle, treadmill, step or rowing machine to warm up, followed by stretches (see page 48). If you lift weights, begin with 10 or 12 repetitions of light weights, increasing them as you get stronger. You can intersperse periods of weight training with aerobic exercise to keep up the aerobic effect. Always cool down and stretch at the end of a session.

ADVANTAGES You can exercise your whole body in safe and private surroundings. For those with knee and back problems there is a high degree of control and no need to do any high-impact jumping, which can damage joints.

DISADVANTAGES Some gyms are expensive and they can be crowded with rippling muscles and lycra, which you may find daunting. You also miss out on the benefits of fresh air and sunshine.

JOGGING

Many cities have marked out, supervised running or cycling tracks in parks. If yours does not, work out your own circuit. Try to keep going for 20 minutes to start with, slowing down when you get tired and then speeding up again. Invest in good trainers to absorb some of the impact of running on hard surfaces.

ADVANTAGES Aerobic exercise is good for the heart and circulation, lungs and legs. It costs nothing and can be done at your convenience.

DISADVANTAGES Jogging or cycling in city areas is not much fun if car-borne pollution is high and the parks are unpleasant. You may also feel vulnerable jogging on your own so try to enlist a friend.

HOME WORKOUT

WARMING UP

■ Jog on the spot or run up and down stairs for five minutes to start blood circulating through your muscles.
■ Do the stretches on page 50, then slowly start your exercises.

If you can't get out to exercise or if you haven't got time, follow a personal workout routine at home. This 30-minute programme, with the addition of curl-ups and press-ups from page 45, works the main muscles in the body. You don't need weights or lycra: bags of rice and a pair of pyjamas will do.

CHEST AND ARM CONDITIONING

Try to do this exercise for at least 30 seconds, then run on the spot for 3 minutes.

Keep your arms straight, but do not lock your elbows

Press the weights upward

1 Stand with your feet about shoulder-width apart, knees slightly bent. Hold 1kg (2lb) weights (or a 1kg (2lb) bag of rice) in each hand, in front of your thighs.

2 Raise your arms slowly to the sides, up to your shoulders, and then lower them to your thighs. Keep the movement slow and controlled.

3 Raise the weights to shoulder level. Your palms should be facing forward.

4 Press the weights up in a strong and controlled movement, then lower slowly and return to the starting position. Repeat the exercise.

THIGH TONER

Strengthen your legs with this exercise and follow with 3 minutes of jogging.

1 Stand up straight with your feet hip-width apart and your arms out in front of you.

2 Bend your knees, push your bottom out behind as if sitting on an imaginary chair, and extend your arms forward as if to grab an imaginary bar. Do this as slowly as you can, controlling the movement with your thigh muscles and keeping your back straight.

3 Use your legs to push yourself up and bring your arms to your sides. You should be able to feel your thigh muscles working. Start with 10 repetitions, building up as your body gets used to the exercise.

CALF STRENGTHENING

Tone your calf muscles on the stairs for 30 seconds.
■ Stand at the bottom with one foot on the step above and, allowing your top leg to take all the weight, step up slowly.
■ Step down on to the other foot and repeat. Keep it slow, making sure your whole foot is on the step and that you can feel your muscles working. Repeat, this time starting with the other foot.
■ Speed up, but do not use the bottom step as a springboard or you will reduce the effort.

BUTTOCK TIGHTENER

Use this exercise to firm and tone, then jog on the spot for 3 minutes.

1 Kneel forward with your weight supported on your forearms and your back straight.

2 Lift one leg and straighten it behind you. Lift it slowly up and down, keeping your back straight, your head in line with your body. The movement should be controlled: do not jerk your leg up.

Keep your hips aligned

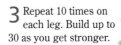

3 Repeat 10 times on each leg. Build up to 30 as you get stronger.

COOLING DOWN

■ Walk around or jog slowly for a few minutes to keep the blood circulating through your muscles.
■ Slowly lower your body into a squat, then rise to standing again without using your hands to help you. This cools down the leg muscles and those in your back.
■ Repeat the stretches you did to warm up as part of your cooling down.

BASIC COMPONENTS

Any exercise programme should combine different kinds of exercise in order to improve your heart and lung capacity, your endurance, strength and flexibility as well as co-ordination and balance.

■ **Aerobic exercise** This strengthens the heart and lungs and improves bone density. It includes any brisk movement that you keep up continuously for at least 20 minutes, such as stepping or jogging.

■ **Stretching** This improves flexibility and co-ordination, increases blood flow through the body and reduces muscle soreness.

■ **Weight training and strength work** Good for improving muscle tone, endurance and stamina.

STRETCHING

Before you do any exercise it is very important to do some slow stretches to protect your muscles, ligaments and tendons from tearing during your exercise programme. These are not exercises that you bounce into; they should be done slowly and thoroughly, whether you are going out for a jog or simply doing a few sit-ups. Concentrate on the leg and arm muscles and those in the back and hold each stretch for a few seconds.

LEGS Gentle lunges will stretch out your calves; for your hamstrings, stretch one leg in front of you, bend the other and, pressing your bottom back, bring your chest toward the outstretched thigh. For your front thighs, bring your foot to your buttocks, keeping your knees together, and hold.

ARMS Clasp your hands together and stretch your arms out in front of you, then stretch them backward and gently upward. Stretch up one arm, then bend it and, placing your hand on your upper back, gently press back your upper arm.

WHOLE BODY Using the muscles in your calves and thighs, stretch up on to your toes as slowly as you can and stretch your linked hands high above your head.

EXERCISING WITH OTHERS

Classes or clubs provide opportunities not only for getting fit but also for making friends. If you lack the necessary motivation to run around a park on your own, the company and thought of a get-together afterward might stiffen your resolve.

AEROBICS, DANCERCISE AND BODY-CONDITIONING CLASSES

Exercise classes should be run by a trained fitness instructor who can advise you on suitable classes for your fitness level and ensure that you are doing the exercises correctly. A good class will include a warm-up and cool-down period, which is essential to prevent injury and stiffness. If you have leg, back or knee injuries, tell the instructor and avoid high-impact exercises, or anything that involves toe touching and may cause strain.

ADVANTAGES Good music, encouragement and planning mean that classes provide an ideal way to work your whole body in a concentrated one-hour session. They are usually indoors so you are protected in bad weather. The level of commitment is low (the class will still go on without you).

DISADVANTAGES It can be hard to keep up if you have poor co-ordination, but take heart, your co-ordination will improve with your fitness level.

TEAM SPORTS

Your local leisure centre or sports facility may be able to put you in touch with teams or clubs; some advertise for new members. Watch the team first to get a sense of the skill level.

ADVANTAGES This is a good way to get aerobic exercise, increase muscle tone and improve your social life.

DISADVANTAGES You have to like other people who like sports, accept a pretty high level of commitment and not be too fussy about getting soaking wet, boiling hot or freezing cold according to the weather.

SOCIAL SPORTS

Many social sports are also club sports and membership can be pricey, but you may find subsidized facilities if you look around. Sports such as tennis, squash, golf and riding will improve your general fitness level if you participate regularly.

ADVANTAGES Social sports can require less commitment than team sports. Tennis, golf and riding are suitable even for seasoned couch potatoes, but do not attempt squash unless you are already exercising.

DISADVANTAGES Some social sports are expensive to start. You will need some lessons and appropriate equipment and, probably, membership of a club.

DANCING

Any form of dancing in which you move vigorously for at least 20 minutes at a stretch is aerobic. The controlled forms, such as ballroom, rock and roll, and Latin, will also improve muscle tone, balance, co-ordination and reaction time.

ADVANTAGES This is probably the most enjoyable exercise of all and an excellent way of meeting people; even more fun if you enjoy the music.

DISDVANTAGES If you feel self-conscious about your body or ability, you might feel overexposed at a dance class but, if you fancy it, you should still have a go; there will be others in the same position.

DANCE CLASSES
The better you get, the more fun you will have.

THE FEMALE BODY

- ## YOUR MONTHLY CYCLE
- ## SYMPTOMS AND STRATEGIES

U NIQUE AMONG MAMMALS, women have periods that neither signal a fertile time nor give any indication of desires. Our blood is a symbol of our difference and of the power to give life. It is a secret signal, a clock within clocks, counting out the years and the days. A woman will experience monthly periods for about half of her life. The four or five days of bleeding are only the end point of a cycle that affects almost every part of our bodies. The better we know the many different things that are happening throughout the month, the easier it is to live with our fluctuating moods, changing body shape, and the peaks and troughs of energy and desire.

HOW HORMONES WORK

The endocrine system is the system of glands which produces the hormones that control all our body processes, from feeling happy to growing, from milk production to our response to stress. When, for example, the level of oestrogen released by the ovaries drops, FSH (follicle-stimulating hormone) is released and the ovary will start ripening a new egg. The ripening egg follicle produces higher levels of oestrogen, which triggers the release of LH (luteinizing hormone). The developing egg then switches to progesterone production, which thickens the lining of the uterus and acts on the breasts, preparing for pregnancy. If the progesterone levels drop, menstruation starts.

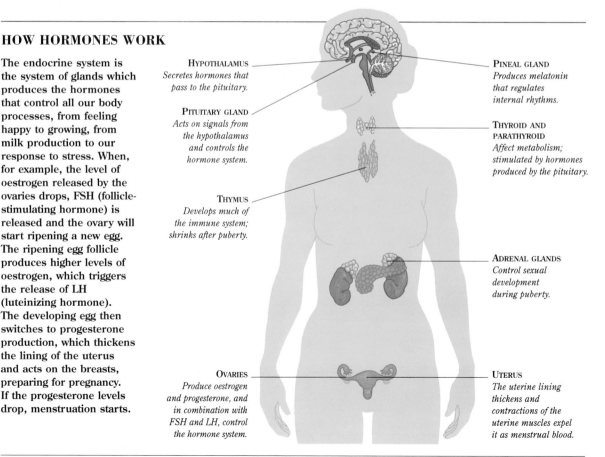

HYPOTHALAMUS
Secretes hormones that pass to the pituitary.

PITUITARY GLAND
Acts on signals from the hypothalamus and controls the hormone system.

THYMUS
Develops much of the immune system; shrinks after puberty.

OVARIES
Produce oestrogen and progesterone, and in combination with FSH and LH, control the hormone system.

PINEAL GLAND
Produces melatonin that regulates internal rhythms.

THYROID AND PARATHYROID
Affect metabolism; stimulated by hormones produced by the pituitary.

ADRENAL GLANDS
Control sexual development during puberty.

UTERUS
The uterine lining thickens and contractions of the uterine muscles expel it as menstrual blood.

PUBERTY

Periods usually begin between the ages of 11 and 14, sometimes earlier, sometimes later. This is a sign that hormones have stimulated the ovaries to start to release eggs (see opposite). However, ovulation (the production of eggs) does not usually get underway immediately, so the first few cycles may be irregular, and bleeding is often scanty and brownish in colour. Mood swings may be particularly pronounced, partly because they coincide with a new awareness of sexual feelings and all the other worries of growing up, and partly because the swings of mood are themselves new and unexpected.

THE FERTILE YEARS

When your cycles settle down into a pattern, there may not necessarily be 28 days between periods, but however long or short the whole cycle, the period between ovulation and menstruation will be around 14 days.

Look at the diagram on page 55 and use it to track your cycle. If you are having regular cycles with fertile mucus, you are almost certainly fertile. If your mucus does not change, this may be evidence that you are not ovulating and therefore not fertile. It is possible to have occasional cycles when no egg is produced, even if you are normally fertile. These are called anovular cycles and they may feel different from your normal ones. You may find that symptoms such as water retention are also less pronounced. If you are using some form of hormonal contraceptive (see page 60), you will not be having fertile cycles and the changes will even out across the month.

MID-LIFE FERTILITY

Fertility does not end suddenly. In your forties, your cycles may start to change in length. You may experience mood swings when you have had none before, or find that your mood has mellowed. Some women experience new symptoms such as much heavier periods – these may be caused by fibroids (see page 79) – or menstrual cramps. Some women experience hot flushes (see page 57).

Sudden changes should always be checked by a doctor, but the changes are probably just a sign that your body is moving into a new phase. You are less fertile. You may skip periods for several months only to find that they have started again. It is hard to be sure exactly when ovulation stops, but the general rule is that you should keep using birth control, if necessary, for two years after your periods have stopped if you are under 50, and for one year if you are over 50.

MENOPAUSE

Ovulation finally stops completely around the age of 50, though it is possible to reach menopause much earlier. The often uncomfortable symptoms (see page 57) and mood swings of this time of change will also stop. Oestrogen levels drop to a lower level, some coming from the ovaries and the rest from the adrenal glands. This may mean that the walls of the vagina become drier. Menopause often coincides with other changes and many women find themselves, for the first time in years, able to concentrate on their own needs. This new-found independence can be frightening, but it can also be exhilarating.

WEIGHT GAIN AT PUBERTY

The weight gain that often accompanies puberty may be a cause of particular anxiety, but eating normally and keeping up a reasonable level of exercise will enable it to stabilize.

---

66 I finally realize that I like my cycle. If I snap or feel exhausted I can forgive myself because I know I will feel different tomorrow. Since I learned to accept that this is part of me I have stopped fighting myself. 99

SEE ALSO

•PAGES 58–63 Contraception
•PAGE 57 Hormone Replacement Therapy
•PAGES 56–57 Symptoms and Strategies

YOUR MONTHLY CYCLE

We are born with ovaries containing some 400,000 follicles. During the fertile years, roughly once a month, one of these follicles starts to ripen and an egg begins to develop. At the same time, the sex hormone oestrogen is produced. When the follicle is ripe, it ruptures and releases an egg. The ruptured follicle continues to produce oestrogen and then progesterone too. If the egg is not fertilized, the follicle breaks down after about 14 days, and menstruation occurs.

HORMONES

Oestrogen acts on the lining of the womb, making it thicken in readiness for pregnancy. It peaks at about mid-cycle when the egg is released and then rises again just before the end of the cycle. If the egg is fertilized, the oestrogen level continues to climb, otherwise it will drop to pre-ovulation levels.

Progesterone rises only if you have ovulated. It will continue to rise if you are pregnant but will drop sharply, just before menstruation, if you are not.

VAGINAL DISCHARGE

Cervical mucus varies throughout the month: at certain times you will be unaware of the vaginal discharge; at other times it is obvious. Toward ovulation it becomes wet and slippery, like egg white, to help the sperm on its way. After ovulation it becomes tacky and drier again. Observing this change in mucus is the most reliable way of pinpointing ovulation. Sperm can survive for several days if fertile mucus is present; without it, the sperm will die. This is the time to make love if you want to get pregnant or, if not, to be extra-careful or avoid sex.

There are other changes during your cycle: your body temperature, for example, rises just before ovulation. The change is only a fraction of a degree, but it can be detected with a basal body thermometer (see chart opposite).

PHYSICAL CHANGES

Your weight may fluctuate, rising in the second half of your cycle and falling during menstruation. This is due to water retention. Some women feel bloated in the days before a period (see page 56). You may find that you need to urinate frequently before your period as the water level adjusts. The increased level of progesterone may also soften your muscles (you may be more prone to sporting injuries before a period). Progesterone can also cause temporary constipation.

MOOD CHANGES

You may feel energetic and sexy in the early part of the cycle and downcast in the second half. If you can look forward to the upswings rather than dreading the down ones, you can change your whole attitude to your cycle. You may need more sleep at the end of your cycle, or you may sleep badly and feel tired. You may also crave sugary things in the days before your period is due because of temporarily low blood sugar, and some women get a sudden surge in sexual interest. It may help to chart these changes in a personal menstrual diary (see pages 180–81). It is often better to expect them than to fight against them.

THE MIND-BODY LINK

No one has been able to unravel the subtle connections between mind and body that may allow us, at some unconscious level, to alter our cycles. We have all experienced the effect that stress can have in shortening or lengthening cycles: periods that arrive 10 days late when we are consumed with worry about unprotected sex, or arrive early when we are due to take an exam. Anthropologist Chris Knight speculates that this subconscious link lies behind the secret of menstrual synchrony – the mysterious force that causes cycles to coincide among women who live collectively. He suggests that it was the means by which women through history have forged co-operative links and thereby created communities.

CHARTING YOUR MONTHLY CYCLE

Length of cycle	21	22	23	24	25	26	27	28	29	30	31	32	33	34	35	36
First fertile day	3	4	5	6	7	8	9	10	11	12	13	14	15	16	17	18
Last fertile day	10	11	12	13	14	15	16	17	18	19	20	21	22	23	24	25

Keep a daily record of your menstrual cycle. Day 1 is the first day of bleeding. The chart below is for 28 days, but your own cycle may be shorter or longer, as shown above. Ovulation should occur 14 days before your next period is due; so whatever the length of your cycle, be aware that the extra days come before ovulation, that is, day 14 of a regular 28-day cycle or day 16 of a 30-day cycle. Sperm can live for up to five days in the fallopian tubes.

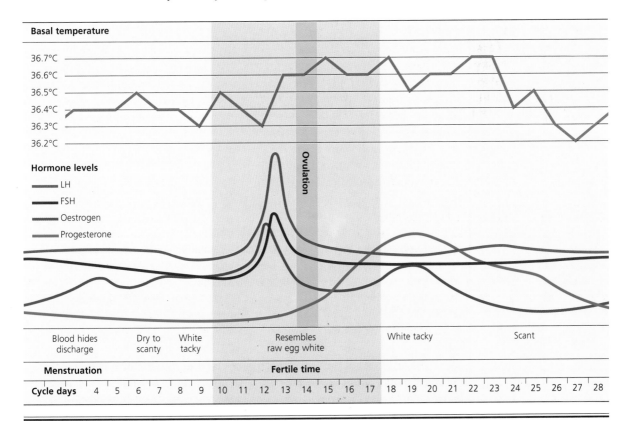

SYMPTOMS AND STRATEGIES

For many of us, the menstrual ebb and flow barely ruffles the surface of our existence. For others, mood swings, cramps and bloating can cause anything from mild irritation to serious disruption. Here are some strategies for coping.

PREMENSTRUAL SYNDROME

Premenstrual syndrome, or PMS, describes all the negative changes that occur in the second half of the menstrual cycle. Some women have PMS all their fertile life; others find it appears for the first time in their forties. The symptoms are thought to be triggered by hormonal changes and may include depression, aggression, headaches, tiredness, bloating, clumsiness and, often, exacerbation of chronic problems like eczema. It helps to make a chart of symptoms (see pages 180–81) for at least three months to get a clear picture of any cyclical changes. There is no cure for PMS because it is not a disease, just a variation in what feels normal.

TREATING YOURSELF There are ways of handling the severity of PMS by yourself:
• Tolerance for caffeine and alcohol is likely to be reduced premenstrually, so it helps to cut down.
• Your blood sugar level may be low the day before a period, so remember to eat little and often and avoid junk food to keep your energy levels high.
• Deal with aggressive feelings by exercising. It may help to run up and down the stairs or punch a pillow to avoid yelling at someone.
Some women find additional relief in alternative therapies such as acupuncture. Each therapy works according to very different principles. Do make sure that the person you consult is trained and certified by the relevant professional body.

MEDICAL TREATMENT Your doctor may suggest a hormone treatment based on progesterone. Trials have not shown this to be very effective, but individual women swear by it, and if you are very troubled by mood swings, it might help. If your major problem is breast tenderness and bloating, your doctor may prescribe evening primrose oil or vitamin B6 (see page 35). Do not take more than 100mg a day of vitamin B6 without medical approval.

PERIOD PAINS

Painful periods are caused by the action of prostaglandin, which makes the womb contract to expel the lining. Some women feel no pain at all, some experience mild cramping at the start of bleeding and a minority are virtually incapacitated for up to 48 hours. If the pattern is regular, then this pain is clearly normal – for you. If the pain is becoming more severe and lasting longer than before, you should see your doctor. You may have a more serious medical condition (see page 81).

TREATING YOURSELF Increasing the flow of blood to your pelvic organs helps to relieve painful cramps. Stand with your feet apart and your hands on your hips. Move your hips in a full circle, rather like a belly dancer, first one way and then the other. Repeat about 10 times.

DYSMENORRHOEA

Very painful periods, with intense, lower abdominal cramps and backache, are known as dysmenorrhoea. The pain may be so severe that you vomit. The condition becomes less severe if you use the contraceptive pill and as you grow older.
■ Pain-killers can help relieve abdominal pains.
■ A hot-water bottle may be comforting.
■ If the pains are particularly severe, you should go to a doctor, who may prescribe an anti-prostaglandin drug.
■ Exercises, such as hip circles, or yoga, may help to relieve the discomfort.

MEDICAL TREATMENT Most women cope with period pains by taking over-the-counter pain-killers. If pain is interfering with your ability to carry out normal activities, ask your doctor for advice. The most likely treatment will be with mefenamic acid, an anti-prostaglandin. This drug should be taken at the first indication of cramps. Take the tablets with food as they can cause stomach upsets.

BLEEDING PROBLEMS

Spotting between periods may be due to hormonal changes in mid-life or to pregnancy, but it should always be investigated by a doctor. Heavy bleeding is most common in the teenage years and before the menopause. It is also sensible to see a doctor if previously light periods suddenly become heavy. The cause is almost certainly hormonal, but there may be some other problem. If heavy periods continue, you should have a blood test (see page 73) to check for anaemia.

MEDICAL TREATMENT For heavy bleeding, the contraceptive pill, or some other progesterone-based hormone, may be prescribed for women under 35. If heavy bleeding is accompanied by pain, mefenamic acid, prescribed for pain relief, will usually also reduce the flow. For those over 35, heavy bleeding may be caused by fibroids; since the most effective treatment is hysterectomy, you may prefer to live with it until the menopause puts a natural end to the problem.

HOT FLUSHES AND VAGINAL DRYNESS

Hot flushes and vaginal dryness are the only symptoms that can be attributed solely to the menopause and lowered oestrogen levels. Flushes (or flashes) are described as a sensation of heat that sweeps over the upper body, sometimes followed by heavy sweating and then chills. For some women they present little or no problem; others find them very disturbing, particularly at night. Some women feel upset by flushes because they signal the end of fertility. Others welcome them as a sign of approaching freedom. Vaginal dryness is unlikely to occur for several years after periods cease.

TREATING YOURSELF People are most unlikely to spot the change even if you feel that you must be glowing like a beacon! As your system settles down, the flushes will stop without any treatment. If you have no other symptoms of the menopause, vaginal dryness can be alleviated by using water-soluble lubricants and taking time over sexual intercourse.

MEDICAL TREATMENT If flushes are interfering with your life, you might consider hormone replacement therapy (HRT) to replace the dwindling level of oestrogen and alleviate sometimes uncomfortable symptoms. It can be administered as pills, patches, creams or implants under the skin and will do the following:
- Stop hot flushes and vaginal dryness.
- Prevent bone loss, which accelerates after the menopause (see page 75).
- Reduce the risk of heart attack and stroke.
- Replace lost oestrogen, which helps the skin retain moisture, thus slowing down the formation of lines and wrinkles.

IS HORMONE REPLACEMENT THERAPY RIGHT FOR YOU?

If you decide to try HRT, see your doctor for regular checks. HRT is not advised if you have:
- A family history of breast cancer.
- A personal history of oestrogen-dependent tumours.
- Uncontrolled high blood pressure.
- Recent heart disease.
- Oestrogen-dependent conditions such as endometriosis or fibroids.

66 The type
of contraceptive
I use fits in with
my needs and
lifestyle. 99

CONTRACEPTION

• BARRIER METHODS • HORMONAL METHODS
• OTHER METHODS • ABORTION

THE ABILITY TO DECIDE WHEN, WITH WHOM and whether or not we will have babies has been one of the most important changes in the lives of twentieth-century women. The ability to control our fertility has allowed us to enter the workplace on the same terms as men and to make critical decisions about how we organize our lives. Some contraception will also provide protection against sexually transmitted infections.

WHICH CONTRACEPTIVE?

Tick the boxes that apply to you, then read along the row to assess the method you use.

	Condom		Diaphragm		IUD		Combined pill		Progestogen method		Sterilization	
Yours is a long-term, steady relationship.	M	L	M	L	M	L	H	L	H	L	H	L
You suspect your partner is unfaithful but assume he uses a condom.	M	L	M	M	M	L	H	M	H	M	H	M
You have had 2 or more partners this year.	M	L	M	M	M	VH	H	H	H	H	H	H
You are not in a relationship but if the opportunity for sex arises, you will probably take it.	M	L	M	M	M	VH	H	H	H	H	H	H
You are sexually confident.	●		●		–		–		–		–	
You are not very sexually confident.	●		–		●		●		●		●	
You are under 20.	●		●		▲		●		●		▲	
You are between 20 and 35.	●		●		●		●		●		●	
You are between 35 and 45.	●		●		●		●		●		●	
You are over 45.	●		●		▲		▲		▲		●	
You smoke.	●		●		●		▲		●		●	
You are overweight.	●		●		●		▲		●		●	
You have a family history of heart disease or high blood pressure.	●		●		●		▲		●		●	
You have liver problems.	●		●		●		▲		▲		●	
You suffer from urinary tract infections.	●		▲		●		●		●		●	
Pregnancy would be a disaster.	–		–		●		●		●		●	
Pregnancy would not be unwelcome, or you are prepared to consider abortion.	●		●		–		–		–		–	

INTERPRETING THE CHART

The blue columns show effectiveness and the green columns the risk of infection for each type of contraception on the following scale:

L=Low   H=High
M=Medium VH=Very high

The method that shows the highest effectiveness and the lowest risk is probably best for you.

KEY

● This method is suitable

● Check this method with your doctor and/or return for regular screening

▲ This method is not suitable

– There is no contraindication but the method is not specifically recommended

NOTE: IUD, Combined pill, Progestogen method
The chart assumes these methods are used alone. Infection risk falls when they are used with a barrier method.

BARRIER METHODS

Barrier methods of contraception include the condom – different types for men and women – and the diaphragm or cap. They all act by preventing the sperm from reaching the egg. The choice of barrier method depends on your preference (see opposite). The diaphragm is placed in the vagina to cover the cervix, and is held in position by a springy ring. The cap is thimble-shaped and smaller than the diaphragm and is held in place by suction; both should be used with spermicide. **ADVANTAGES** These are the only contraceptives that guard against infection. Condoms protect against transmission of the HIV virus as well as other sexually transmitted infections. The diaphragm and cap, used with a spermicide, provide some protection against other, less dangerous but more widespread infections. **DISADVANTAGES** Male condoms may be difficult to use if your partner has problems getting or maintaining an erection. Condoms not put on properly may come off during intercourse. Diaphragms may not be advised if you have recurrent cystitis.

> **WARNING**
> If you or your partner has sex outside your relationship, you should use a condom even if it is not your main method of contraception.

❝ Carrying condoms is a statement of sexual maturity. It says I take responsibility for my sexual desires. ❞

USING BARRIER METHODS

THE CONDOM

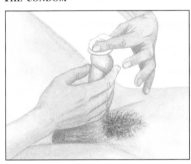

1 Squeeze the end of the condom to let out air and to create space for sperm. Place it over the top of the erect penis.

2 Unroll the condom down over the penis. A fingernail or ring can be enough to tear a condom, so take care.

THE DIAPHRAGM OR CAP

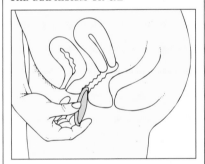

1 Apply spermicide to both sides of a diaphragm, but to only the inside of a cap, avoiding the rim. Squeeze the rim.

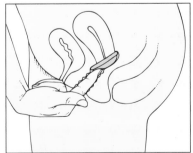

2 Insert into the vagina. Use your finger to ensure it is held over the cervix by the rim.

THE FEMALE CONDOM

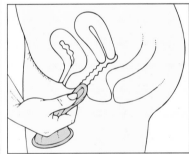

1 Squeeze the ring at the closed end of the condom into an oval and insert into the vagina.

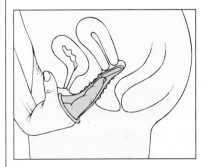

2 Manoeuvre the ring up past the pubic bone to the cervix. The end hangs 5cm (2in) outside the vagina.

HORMONAL METHODS

Hormonal methods of birth control use synthetic versions of the hormones that control menstruation, ovulation and pregnancy. They subtly alter the body's hormone balance in order to interfere with the process of conception. Hormone-based contraception is available on prescription as pills, implants and injections.

COMBINED ORAL CONTRACEPTIVE PILLS

These pills contain low doses of both oestrogen and progestogen in different combinations. They prevent ovulation and control a woman's cycle over a 28-day period. One pill is taken every day at approximately the same time.

ADVANTAGES They are reliable, easy to use and can reduce heavy bleeding and period pain. They also provide some protection against pelvic inflammatory disease (see page 79).

DISADVANTAGES The combined pill, particularly if it contains the progestogens gestodene or desogestrel, is not suitable for women with a history of circulatory disease, or for those over the age of 35 who smoke, because it is associated with an increased incidence of blood clotting. The combined pill is not recommended for women with diseases of the liver (such as hepatitis) or with severe depression. It is not recommended for breastfeeding women. There has also been evidence of an association with breast cancer among those starting the pill in their teens and taking it for a long period of time. It provides no protection against HIV infection or other sexually transmitted diseases (STDs).

Blood clots (thrombosis) are a rare but potentially very serious side effect of combined contraceptives. Clots in the vein (deep vein thrombosis) can travel through the bloodstream to the lungs, causing injury and, very occasionally, death. The estimated risk of blood clots in the veins are:
- 5 per 100,000 women for healthy non-pill users.
- 15 per 100,000 women for most combined pill users.
- 30 per 100,000 women for those using combined pills containing gestodene or desogestrel.
- 60 per 100,000 women for pregnant women.

PROGESTOGEN CONTRACEPTIVES

Progestogen, the synthetic form of the hormone progesterone, causes the cervix to produce a thick mucus that prevents sperm from entering the uterus, thus preventing fertilization. The progestogen-only pill must be taken at the same time every day without a break; it is a little more effective than condoms in preventing pregnancy.

Implants consist of tiny plastic tubes of progestogen inserted under the skin – usually in the upper arm – under a local anaesthetic. They release progestogen straight into the bloodstream and can be effective for up to five years.

Injections of progestogen, usually into the buttocks, last up to three months. They are not approved in all countries.

Some IUDs also contain progestogen (see page 61).

FORGETTING TO TAKE THE PILL

You must act immediately:
- If the combined pill is over 12 hours late, use another method of contraception for 7 days.
- If you use the progestogen-only pill, and you are more than three hours late taking it, use another contraceptive method for the remainder of the cycle.

ADVANTAGES These contraceptives are not associated with circulatory problems. Implants and injections last for a long period of time and no effort is required by the user. Implants and injections are highly effective, pills only slightly less so. They can be used by breastfeeding women.

DISADVANTAGES Progestogen contraceptives may cause erratic and breakthrough bleeding. Because they work by thickening the cervical mucus, they are effective against uterine pregnancy, although ectopic pregnancies (where the egg is implanted in the lining of the fallopian tube) are still a possibility. Injections are also associated with weight gain, decreased libido, acne, headaches, a delay in the return of fertility when the method is stopped, and, in some studies, with bone loss (which may lead to brittle bones in later life). These more serious side effects are not associated with other progestogen methods. If the pill is not taken at the same time every day, there is only a three-hour margin of error, which may be a problem for women who lead disorganized lives or who travel frequently to different time zones. These contraceptives may be less effective for women weighing over 70kg (11 stones), and provide no protection against STDs.

INTRAUTERINE DEVICE (IUD)

The IUD is a device that is inserted into the uterus and works by preventing sperm reaching the egg or by preventing the egg from being implanted in the uterus. It is placed in the uterus by a doctor and must be removed by a doctor. The two threads attached to the base of the IUD can be left to protrude a short way into the vagina; this can be a way of checking that it is still in place. It is essential to ensure that there is no infection present when the IUD is fitted.

ADVANTAGES Once an IUD is in place, you can forget about it, knowing that it is highly effective as a contraceptive. An IUD does not intrude into lovemaking.

DISADVANTAGES The IUD is associated with a higher incidence of pelvic infection than other forms of contraception. It may also increase bleeding and menstrual pain. The IUD is not advised for women under 25 or for those who are not in steady relationships.

EMERGENCY CONTRACEPTION

■ If an IUD is inserted up to five days after unprotected intercourse, it will usually be effective in preventing pregnancy.

■ The morning-after pill, which contains both oestrogen and progestogen, can be taken within 72 hours of unprotected intercourse to prevent unwanted pregnancy. Check with your doctor or clinic.

HOW THE IUD WORKS

A pregnancy rarely develops when there is a foreign body in the uterus, such as an IUD. In modern IUDs, copper wire, or a slow-release hormone, is added to the tiny plastic device to improve its effectiveness.

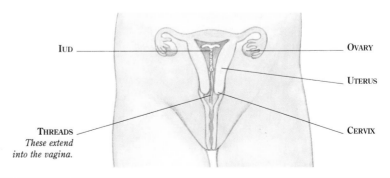

IUD

OVARY

UTERUS

THREADS
*These extend
into the vagina.*

CERVIX

OTHER METHODS

There may be times in your life when you really do not want to have to use either chemical or barrier methods of contraception. You may have religious objections, you may prefer something that seems more in tune with your body, or you may just be looking for simplicity.

NATURAL FAMILY PLANNING

You get pregnant if sperm meets egg, and this can only happen during the two days in every cycle when there is an egg ready for fertilization. Sperm can lie in wait in the fallopian tube for up to five days waiting for an egg to drop by, so essentially, you need to avoid intercourse, or use contraception, for a period of at least seven days in each cycle. To be able to do this you must know exactly when you are ovulating. You can use the chart on page 55 to estimate when your fertile time might be, but training is essential before practising this method.

ADVANTAGES This natural method is free of side effects. Used carefully and taught by experienced teachers to highly motivated couples, it is as effective as barrier and progestogen methods. See pages 187–88 for training centres.
DISADVANTAGES The natural method needs cooperation from your partner, as you may need to exercise restraint during your fertile periods. You must have a thorough knowledge of your cycle, and, if it is not regular, you will have to recognize the changes in your cervical mucus and chart your temperature. This method is therefore not suitable for women who have erratic cycles and spontaneous love lives. It also offers no protection against STDs.

STERILIZATION

Sterilization involves a minor operation under general anaesthetic to block the fallopian tubes by cutting the tube and then damaging it by heat treatment, or by sewing, clipping or tying it. The usual method is by laparoscopy, where a tube is inserted through an incision in the abdomen, close to the navel. The tube contains a fibre-optic filament that allows the surgeon to see your fallopian tubes, which are sealed with an instrument inserted through another small incision.

ADVANTAGES Following sterilization there is no need to think about contraception at all once you have had your next period. After the initial period of recovery – you may feel discomfort for the first week or two – there are no side effects. Sterilization does not affect libido or your menstrual cycle.
DISADVANTAGES Sterilization is rarely reversible and should not be considered unless you are absolutely sure you do not want to get pregnant. Few doctors would be prepared to sterilize a young, childless woman. If you think you could be pregnant, see a doctor immediately as there is an increased risk of ectopic pregnancy (the result of the blockage in the tube), which can be dangerous. If you are sterilized, you are still vulnerable to infection and should use a barrier contraceptive if you are not in a long-term, committed relationship. Sterilization does, occasionally, fail. Get a test if you suspect pregnancy.

ABORTION

Some people see pregnancy as a voluntary act; they believe that a woman should decide whether to allow a baby to grow inside her. Others see women as the temporary containers of new human beings whose rights must be preserved above hers. But for each pregnant woman faced with an unexpected pregnancy, the dilemma is a new and deeply personal one, because a woman is not merely giving her body to another, she is considering the whole of her life and the life of her potential child. It is not a decision to be made lightly, nor is there evidence that it is ever taken lightly.

ABORTION AND THE LAW

The laws concerning abortion vary widely, depending on where you live. For specific information see page 186.

THE SAFETY OF ABORTION

Abortion has been practised everywhere throughout the ages, often as a primary method of birth control. Until very recently, illegal, and often insanitary, methods of abortion were a major cause of deaths among women of childbearing age. Today, where abortion is practised legally, it can be obtained relatively easily in a medical setting in the first 12 weeks of pregnancy.

METHODS OF ABORTION

MIFEPRISTONE WITH PROSTAGLANDIN This method can be used in the first nine weeks of pregnancy. It involves taking two separate doses of the drugs which, after a few hours, induce contractions and empty the uterus. This may cause nausea, vomiting and pain. Some women find this method very unpleasant.

VACUUM ASPIRATION This method is used during the first 12 weeks of pregnancy. It involves gently opening the entrance to the uterus and removing the contents, under local or general anaesthetic, through a tube by vacuum suction. Women may experience some of the following side effects:
* If the uterus is not opened gently, it can be painful under local anaesthetic.
* There is a risk of infection if the womb is not entirely empty, or instruments are not properly sterilized, or there was a pre-existing infection in the vagina that is transferred to the uterus. Signs of infection can include a rise in temperature or an unusual odour and should be reported to a doctor immediately for treatment with antibiotics.

LATE ABORTION After the first 12 to 14 weeks, abortion can be performed either by dilation and evacuation (D & E), which involves dilation of the uterus under general anaesthetic and surgical removal of the foetus, or by chemically inducing labour using prostaglandin. Late abortions are rarely necessary when early abortion is easily accessible, except in the case of a foetal abnormality. Again, there are some side effects:
* D & E involves a risk of infection, of damage to the cervix and of accidental perforation of the uterus. Any of these consequences could affect future pregnancies.
* Chemical abortion involves no greater risk than childbirth, but it can be very distressing for the woman involved.

LOOKING AFTER YOURSELF
*Gentle exercise will keep your
body supple.*

PREGNANCY

PREGNANCY IS TIMED from the first day of your last menstrual period (LMP). In fact, conception occurs halfway through the cycle (see page 55) when sperm and ovum meet in the fallopian tube. Two weeks later you may notice slight spotting as the embryo implants in the womb, but for most women the first sign of pregnancy is a missed period.

FOUR WEEKS TO TWELVE WEEKS
This is the period of the fastest, most complex development: by 12 weeks there will be a recognizable embryo with a head and spine. It is also, for many women, the worst part of a pregnancy. You may feel nauseous (or you may actually be sick), and you may be very tired and emotional. Give in to your need for sleep and eat little and often. You should feel a great deal better in a few weeks.

TWELVE TO SIXTEEN WEEKS
You start antenatal visits and will be offered tests to monitor your health (blood tests to check iron levels, urine tests to look for infection, and blood pressure checks) and others to check your baby's development. The checks on the baby are a fast-developing field aimed at spotting signs of foetal abnormality. Some parents prefer not to know. They have decided to love and care for their child whether or not it has a disability. Others prefer the chance to end a pregnancy if there seems to be a serious problem. The choice should be yours to make with informed support.

SIXTEEN WEEKS TO TWENTY-EIGHT WEEKS
If all is well, this is the best time, despite the ever-present minor physical complaints of pregnancy. Your energy should have returned, sickness should be long gone, and your pregnancy is starting to show. By the end of the 28th week, your baby is almost fully developed. If you are at work, take advantage of this time to make plans, make sure you know the maternity regulations, and to think about whether, when and how you want to return to work (see page 145).

TWENTY-EIGHT WEEKS TO TERM

You will probably start to slow down now. Your baby is gaining weight and your body may feel clumsy and uncomfortable. You may start to have difficulty sleeping as your baby kicks and wriggles. Try to give yourself plenty of opportunities for contemplation and rest; your life is about to change utterly and you need time to charge your batteries ready for that challenge.

THE BIRTH DAY

You will be alerted by either a rush of amniotic fluid as your waters break, or by early contractions, which are usually light to start with, gathering momentum and coming closer together as labour progresses. The whole process of labour can take many hours with a relatively short, intense period (known as transition) toward the end when your cervix opens to its full extent, followed by the second stage when you push your baby out.

READY FOR THE BIRTH

"Term" is the name for your estimated date of delivery, usually 40 weeks after the first day of your last period. Many women give birth weeks before this date, and many after 40 weeks. Few babies arrive on their due date.

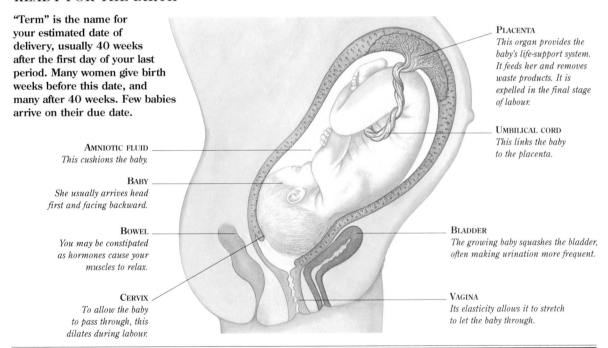

PLACENTA
This organ provides the baby's life-support system. It feeds her and removes waste products. It is expelled in the final stage of labour.

UMBILICAL CORD
This links the baby to the placenta.

AMNIOTIC FLUID
This cushions the baby.

BABY
She usually arrives head first and facing backward.

BOWEL
You may be constipated as hormones cause your muscles to relax.

BLADDER
The growing baby squashes the bladder, often making urination more frequent.

CERVIX
To allow the baby to pass through, this dilates during labour.

VAGINA
Its elasticity allows it to stretch to let the baby through.

PREGNANCY ALERT

Be aware of any warning signs in pregnancy, the following in particular:
- Bleeding or pain. This should always be reported to a doctor. Bleeding in pregnancy is not uncommon, but (particularly if accompanied by pain) it could herald a miscarriage or, in late pregnancy, a problem with the placenta.
- Sudden swelling of the legs or hands, or sharp headaches, particularly in late pregnancy. Seek immediate medical advice.

ESSENTIAL HEALTH SCREENING

- EYES • TEETH AND GUMS • BREASTS • SKIN CARE
- BLOOD TESTS • YOUR HEART • YOUR LUNGS
- YOUR BONES

EYESIGHT

Eye tests show whether your vision can be improved by glasses or contact lenses. As you get older tests can reveal many disorders at an early, treatable stage. If you have high blood pressure, diabetes or glaucoma in the family, or if you suffer pain, headaches or vision change, have a test. See pages 68–69.

TEETH AND GUMS

Dental checks reveal early tooth decay or gum disease and monitor wisdom teeth. Visit your dentist once or twice a year, or if you have pain or other problems. See page 69.

BREASTS

Breast examination can sometimes detect breast cancer in the earliest, treatable stage. Check yourself monthly after a period. Mammography should be offered every three years after the age of 50, or annually if you have had breast cancer or your mother or a sister has had breast cancer. See pages 70–71.

SKIN

If you notice a new mole or if an existing mole grows, bleeds or changes colour, visit your doctor. This could be a symptom of skin cancer. See page 72.

COLON

If you have a family history of bowel cancer or of multiple polyps of the colon, talk to your doctor about screening. A blood test for screening is currently being developed. If you notice any sign of blood in your stools, consult your doctor. See page 73.

REGULAR HEALTH CHECKS detect signs of disease before you feel symptoms. This gives you time to adjust your lifestyle or take any other necessary action to prevent a minor abnormality growing into a major health problem. The type and the frequency of checks will vary at different stages of your life. Some regular monitoring is offered routinely at birth control and antenatal clinics. Older women should also undergo regular health screening.

CERVICAL SMEAR
This check reveals abnormal cells that could develop into cervical cancer. You should have the first test as soon as you become sexually active, another a year later and thereafter every three years up to the age of 65. You will probably be advised to have a smear more regularly if you have had previous abnormal smears or a history of vaginal warts. See page 76.

URINE TESTS
These screen for urinary or kidney infection and for warning signs of diabetes. You will be tested routinely if you are pregnant, if you attend a sexually transmitted diseases clinic or if you have symptoms of urinary infection. See page 77.

SEXUALLY TRANSMITTED INFECTION SCREENING
Checks are important for sexually active women. They can detect sexually transmitted infections which, if untreated, can cause pain and possibly infertility. Get checked if you, or your partner, have had unprotected sex (without a condom) with someone else, if you have symptoms (see page 81), or if you are having problems getting pregnant. See page 77.

WEIGHT
Many people are obsessed by weight gain, though weight loss is just as serious. Once you reach a stable, adult weight there is no need to weigh yourself unless you are concerned about rapid weight loss or gain. See pages 38–41.

BLOOD PRESSURE
A blood pressure check monitors the health of your heart and circulation. You should have it tested once at secondary school and then every three years, or every six months if you are on the pill or hormone replacement therapy, and at regular intervals during pregnancy. See page 74.

BLOOD TESTS
These check iron and cholesterol levels and detect other symptoms of hormone imbalance or defects of the immune system. Ask for a test if you have a family history of high cholesterol, or symptoms such as persistent tiredness, heavy blood loss, erratic periods or unusual growth of facial hair. See page 73.

SEE ALSO
• **PAGE 74** Your Heart
• **PAGE 75** Your Lungs
• **PAGE 75** Your Bones

EYES

The eyes are the windows of our souls but, unlike most windows, they have a remarkably efficient system for cleaning themselves. Eyelashes trap dust and dirt, eyelids provide instant protection by closing very fast if something dangerous approaches and, if anything does get in, eyelids and tear ducts provide a gentle wash and wipe. Sometimes, however, these defence systems do not work.

EYE PROBLEMS

FOREIGN BODIES Do not rub your eye as you may scratch the cornea. Put your face in a bowl of water – or use an eye bath or eggcup full of water – and blink rapidly to allow the water to clear the object away. If the object is washed down to the lower lid, pull the lid away gently and wipe it out with the corner of a clean cloth. If this does not work, seek medical attention.

STYES A stye is a painful reddening and swelling of the eyelid caused by an infection at the root of an eyelash. It may help to apply gentle heat with a damp cotton wool ball or to soothe the eye by bathing it in an eye bath. A stye will either burst and release pus or dry up within a week – if it doesn't, consult your doctor.

CONJUNCTIVITIS This is an infection of the conjunctiva that makes the eye pink and sticky. It may be caused by hayfever, a cold, or by failing to clean contact lenses properly. Check with your doctor who may prescribe antibiotic drops or cream. Be scrupulous about hygiene; this can be a highly infectious condition.

EYE EXERCISES

This quick sequence will relax your eyes, particularly if you work at a computer. Keep your head still; only move your eyes.

1 Raise your thumb directly in front of you, at eye level and about 50cm (18in) away. Stare at your thumb, then look into the distance. Repeat 5 times.

2 Open your eyes wide and look at the opposite numbers of an imaginary clockface. Repeat this exercise 10 times.

3 Cup your hands over your closed eyes; the fleshy part of your hand should fit neatly into your eye socket. Relax your eyes for about 30 seconds.

VISION DISORDERS

Abnormalities can normally be corrected by spectacles, contact lenses or (in the case of short sight) laser surgery. It is essential to have your eyes tested by a qualified optometrist who can find out exactly what is wrong and who may be able to detect other problems, such as glaucoma and cataracts, which are usually associated with ageing. An inaccurate prescription can cause headaches.

SHORT-SIGHTEDNESS (MYOPIA) The most common form of vision disorder, this varies in severity from person to person, from those who can see little but blurred shapes, to those who just have difficulty reading numbers on the front of a bus.

LONG-SIGHTEDNESS (HYPERMETROPIA) Sufferers can see in the distance but have difficulty focusing close-up, for example, when reading. A similar condition (presbyopia) may start to appear in mid-life, causing difficulty in close focusing.

ASTIGMATISM This is caused by irregularity in the shape of the cornea, which creates problems in focusing. It can be completely corrected by lenses tilted at the right angle. An inaccurate prescription can cause headaches and difficulty concentrating on reading or close work.

COMPUTERS AND EYESIGHT

Working at a computer screen for long periods of time can affect your eyesight. A good employer should provide for an eye test when you start work and regular annual tests thereafter. Take frequent breaks (at least every hour) to rest your eyes and try doing some eye relaxation exercises (see left). Check the latest regulations for the correct positioning of the computer monitor and the distance between your eyes and the screen (see page 186).

TEETH AND GUMS

The major cause of tooth decay is the consumption of refined sugar in sweets, canned foods and fizzy drinks. Sugar coats the teeth as plaque, providing a breeding ground for bacteria. Bacteria then produce acid, which rots the teeth and causes gum inflammation. People (and animals) who do not eat sugar never get tooth decay.

Make regular visits to your dentist every 6–12 months for check-ups; she will be able to detect problems and treat them promptly, and can also advise on the best brushing technique. A toothbrush with a small head and soft, rounded bristles reaches difficult areas most effectively, and daily flossing will help remove plaque from between teeth and under the gums, where your toothbrush cannot reach. Your dentist should also monitor the development of wisdom teeth.

PROTECT YOUR TEETH
- Avoid sugary foods.
- Strengthen your teeth by using fluoride toothpaste.
- Clean your teeth after every meal to remove the sugar and gently massage the gums.
- Clean between your teeth every day using dental floss.

A HEALTHY SMILE
Make the most of your teeth by looking after them.

BREASTS

The development of breasts is a powerful symbol to the outside world of the change from child to woman. It is a transition that is not much helped in Western cultures by the obsessive use of female breasts to sell everything from motor cars to beer. However, breasts are not the body's advertising hoardings. Though our lovers may appreciate them, they are primarily important for the satisfaction they give to us. They are exquisitely sensitive – some women can come to orgasm just through having their nipples sucked or stroked – and, in time, breasts can be used for something that is almost as satisfying: feeding a baby. There is no right shape for a breast, only a right feel, and the right feel is whatever makes you feel good.

THE STRUCTURE OF THE BREAST

Inside your breast, a layer of pectoral muscles lies against the rib cage. Most of the rest of the breast consists of fat cells and a milk-producing mammary gland. The gland is made up of milk ducts that produce milk and carry it out through the nipple, which is surrounded by an area of darker pigment, the areola. The amount of glandular tissue in the breast increases at puberty and again during pregnancy, but differences in breast size depend on the amount of fat.

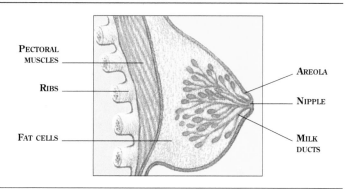

PECTORAL MUSCLES
RIBS
FAT CELLS
AREOLA
NIPPLE
MILK DUCTS

SELF-HELP FOR CYCLICAL BREAST PAIN

■ Improve your diet by cutting out excess fat and sugar and increasing your intake of vegetables, fruit and water.
■ Wear a properly fitted, supportive bra with wide straps.
■ Improve your posture.
■ Spray or splash your breasts with cold water to boost blood circulation.

CYCLES OF CHANGE

Breast buds start to develop any time between the ages of eight and 13. They will usually have finished growing by the age of 17. The size of the breast makes no difference to sensitivity or the ability to produce milk, and since breasts contain no muscles, they cannot be increased in size by exercise. They do contain fat, however, and so will fluctuate according to your weight.

Hormone fluctuations affect the breasts. They tend to increase in size in the second half of the menstrual cycle (after ovulation) and during pregnancy. They reduce in size at the start of a period and after the menopause. Often the increase in size is accompanied by acute sensitivity or even pain. Some women cannot bear to be touched in the few days before a period, and may also find that their breasts feel lumpy.

BREAST PROBLEMS

PAIN If you suffer breast pain that does not come and go with your periods, see a doctor. In most cases there is nothing seriously wrong, but it is wise to check.

LUMPS Most breast lumps also come and go with your cycle; if not, consult your doctor. The vast majority of breast lumps turn out to be benign, but they may also be an early warning of breast cancer, which can only be effectively treated if it is diagnosed early. If you are over 50, most breast experts recommend examination by mammogram at least every three years, annually if there is a history of familial breast cancer. Before the age of 50, such a screening test is not likely to be useful.

BREAST CANCER

Breast cancer rates are highest in countries with a high-fat intake, such as Britain and the US, and lowest in countries with a low-fat diet, such as Japan. Women who start their periods early and end them late are at higher risk, as are those who have no children or have their first pregnancy late. Other factors include breast cancer in a relative (fewer than 10 per cent of cancers are thought to have this link, and then only when a mother or sister has been affected) and pesticide pollution, although little research has been done to establish these chemical links.

EXAMINING YOUR BREASTS

You are the best early-warning system for breast cancer. If you examine your breasts after each period, when your breast tissue is least likely to be swollen or lumpy, you will be able to feel any lumps that do not go away with the changes in your body during your menstrual cycle. If you are past the menopause, examine your breasts monthly.

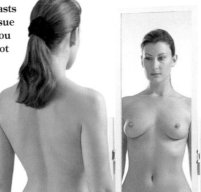

1 Start by standing upright and naked and look at yourself in the mirror. Get to know your shape so that you will be aware of any changes. Nine times out of ten a lump will be nothing to worry about, but it is always worth making sure.

2 Raise both arms above your head and turn side on so that you can see the outline of each breast. Check for dimpling or puckering. Look carefully at your nipples; unless you are pregnant or breastfeeding, there should be no discharge from the nipple.

3 Lie flat and using the right hand for the left breast (and vice versa), move the flat of your hand over your breast firmly and smoothly as if you were ironing the skin; go right up into the armpit on each side. If you note any changes, lumps or bumps, consult a doctor.

CLEANSING

An occasional face pack will clean your skin, stimulate circulation, and give you an excuse to relax and pamper yourself.

SKIN CARE

One of nature's nastiest tricks is to give the most beautiful skin to people who are too young to care about it. When puberty hits, that perfect, smooth outer coating develops spots, open pores, greasy patches and then ... wrinkles! We cannot reverse the process, but we can prevent it speeding up by keeping the skin clean, drinking plenty of water and protecting ourselves from the effects of the sun, which is responsible for most of the effects we associate with "ageing".

SKIN PROBLEMS

ACNE This skin condition usually occurs around puberty. The spots can become infected and, if scratched, form permanent scars. It helps to drink plenty of water, keep hair, skin and hands clean, and avoid touching spots. In extreme cases, your doctor may recommend a low dose of antibiotics to reduce bacteria.

WRINKLES Skin is kept smooth by the presence of fat in the lower layer and water in the middle layer. The outer layer of skin is made up of dead cells and no amount of moisturizer can turn them into live ones, although face creams do have some value as a protection against wind, weather and (if containing a UV filter) the sun. For better protection against dehydration, drink plenty of non-alcoholic fluids. The best anti-wrinkle treatment is to avoid:
• Continual dieting, which depletes the layer of fat in the skin.
• Too much sunbathing, which forces the outer layer to thicken.
• Smoking, which depletes oestrogen supplies.

RASHES Some rashes are the result of contact with an allergen (the metal in earrings, or the gum in sticking plaster), and will resolve when the allergen is discovered and removed. Conditions such as eczema or psoriasis, both of which can be triggered by contact with (or ingestion of) allergens, may be caused by stress in people who are susceptible. The standard medical treatment is with steroid creams, although many people prefer alternative treatments such as acupuncture.

SKIN CANCER This disease is on the increase among light-skinned people. Factors may include the depletion of the ozone layer, the fashion for suntanned skin and the increase in tourism that takes far more light-skinned people to sunny countries.
The best advice is to stay out of the sun or to cover up. If you must tan, do so gradually, making sure that you do not burn. If you are exposed to the sun during sports or walking, or in the water where the sun will be reflected, use a high sun protection factor sunscreen (SPF 15+) that screens out both UVA and UVB rays. Although there seems to be a connection between sunburn and skin cancer, there is no evidence as yet that sunscreens, which protect against burning, also protect against skin cancer.

BLOOD TESTS

High blood pressure rarely produces symptoms in itself, but it makes you more prone to a heart attack or stroke, which can kill, and serious complications in pregnancy. Having your blood pressure checked is simple, non-invasive and should be done routinely, every three years from adolescence onward, and annually after the menopause. If you are on the pill, your risk increases and a reading should be taken every six months. This is particularly important if you also smoke or are overweight. During pregnancy, blood pressure is checked at every antenatal visit.

A normal blood pressure (BP) reading will show two numbers. The top number (systolic) should not be higher than 140 and the bottom one (diastolic) not higher than 90. In pregnancy, a somewhat raised BP is normal, but should always be monitored. A high reading should be double-checked as transient stress can push blood pressure up temporarily.

To help reduce high blood pressure, you can restrict salt in your diet, lose weight (if advised by your doctor) and try lowering your stress levels (see pages 90–91).

DEFICIENCY ANAEMIA

If you feel abnormally tired and lethargic and your skin seems paler or duller than usual, you may be suffering from a lack of iron or vitamin B, components of haemoglobin (Hb). Haemoglobin is the red pigment that carries the oxygen in your blood. Normal Hb levels are around 14g of haemoglobin to 100 decilitres of blood. Women are four times more susceptible to deficiency anaemia because we lose blood regularly through menstruation.

A simple blood test will show whether your Hb level is below the normal range of 12 to 14. If your level is low, you may want to take supplements. However, the best treatment for anaemia is to improve your diet by adding foods rich in iron and vitamin B (see page 35). Vegetarians may need specialist advice, particularly about sources of vitamin B12, which is normally found only in meat. Lack of vitamin B12 may cause pernicious anaemia (a severe form of anaemia), but it may also result from an abnormality in the way the body absorbs vitamin B12.

HORMONE CHECKS

Simple hormone tests to establish, for example, whether you are ovulating or to check your thyroid function (see page 52) can be organized by your doctor or clinic. For more complex tests to establish the relationship between different hormones you will need to be referred to an endocrinologist. Tests to check hormone levels in the blood can look into:
- Ovulation: whether it has taken place and whether your ovaries are functioning properly.
- An imbalance of hormones and whether this may be contributing to severe premenstrual symptoms.
- An unusual growth of body hair.
- Difficulties in getting pregnant.
- A possible reason for depression.

CHOLESTEROL TESTS

High levels of cholesterol in the blood may be inherited or, in some cases, due to a diet rich in saturated fats. You may want to have your cholesterol checked after you reach 30 if you have a family history of heart disease.

YOUR HEART

The heart is a muscle that contracts regularly at the rate of 70 to 85 beats per minute throughout your life. Like any other muscle, it works better if it is regularly exercised. To do so, you should exercise moderately (until you are slightly warm and out of breath) for 30 minutes five times a week. During our fertile years, oestrogen in the blood provides some protection against a sedentary lifestyle, but after the menopause, the risk of heart disease in women rises rapidly to almost the same level as a man of equal age. Women who have diabetes or a family history of heart disease are at higher risk.

HEART DISEASE

Rates of heart disease vary widely across the world, and the variation in the rate points to some of the ways in which we could prevent this debilitating, painful and often fatal condition. Countries with a high consumption of fats and a low consumption of fresh vegetables and fruit have the highest rates of heart disease – second only to cancer as the major cause of death. The rates of heart disease in Scotland, for example, are 12 times higher than in Japan, which has a very low rate; while countries bordering the Mediterranean, where fish and fresh vegetables are staple foods, have far lower rates than northern European countries. There are two ways to monitor your heart:

CHOLESTEROL LEVELS The average level for blood cholesterol in women is 5.9mmol per litre of blood. Any level above 6.5mmol per litre is considered too high. Your cholesterol level can be checked by blood tests (see page 73). You can lower blood cholesterol by reducing saturated (animal and dairy) fats in your diet.

HIGH BLOOD PRESSURE Blood pressure checks provide an early warning of narrowing of the arteries which can lead to a heart attack or stroke. Blood pressure can be lowered by increasing exercise and reducing alcohol consumption and salt in the diet. Women with high blood pressure should not take the contraceptive pill.

PREVENTING HEART DISEASE

These are measures you can take to safeguard yourself against heart disease:
  • Do not smoke. It is estimated that 11 per cent of deaths from heart disease in Britain can be attributed to smoking cigarettes. Women who smoke and take the pill have a risk of heart attack 10 times higher than women who do not.
  • Moderate alcohol consumption. Studies suggest that alcohol may be protective, but more than two to three units a day increases the risk.
  • Get plenty of exercise. Thirty minutes of moderate activity, five times a week is protective. Only 4 per cent of British women reach this target, and only 30 per cent are active enough to give themselves any protection at all.
  • Eat well. Increase your consumption of fresh fruit and vegetables.
  • Avoid excessive stress; stress raises blood pressure. Many women increase their risk by smoking, drinking and bingeing as a way of alleviating stress.

SEE ALSO

•PAGES 34–37 Food and You
•PAGES 42–51 Exercise and You
•PAGES 86–87 Pinpointing
Sources of Stress

YOUR LUNGS

Lungs provide a system of exchange in which oxygen is passed into the blood and carbon dioxide is passed out. If this exchange is interrupted, irreversible damage can be done very quickly, particularly to the brain. There are three likely causes: choking, asthma or respiratory disease (including lung cancer).

ASTHMA

Asthma is a response to an allergen that causes the bronchial muscles to contract suddenly, obstructing the airways. The sufferer will start to wheeze and may increase the distress by panicking. The level of childhood asthma is rapidly increasing, probably as a result of pollution, particularly from road traffic.

EMERGENCY ACTION Most diagnosed asthma sufferers carry an inhaler which should bring the attack under control. If it is a first attack, or there is no medication available, the discomfort may be temporarily relieved by inhaling steam from a saucepan or kettle. (Be very careful to prevent scalding.) If the attack is severe and the inhaler is ineffective, call an ambulance.

LUNG CANCER

Lung cancer is the second most common cancer in women, and smoking is the major cause. If you smoke 20 cigarettes a day, your risk of developing cancer is 20 times higher than that of a non-smoker. Passive smoking also increases the risk. Smoking damages the lining of the lungs so that they are unable to clear efficiently. The smoker's cough is the body's response to this damage.

REDUCING THE RISK The earlier you start smoking, the more damage you can do to your lungs because you actually impede the development of the air sacs – a process that should continue into your twenties. If you stop smoking, your lungs can recover, but it will take about 10 years to reduce your risk of lung cancer to half that of a smoker. It is far better never to start. To give up, see page 40.

YOUR BONES

Women need to take special care of their bones because of the risk of osteoporosis (brittle bones) in later life. Brittle bones create a far greater risk of fracture, from even a small fall. Osteoporosis can affect the bones in the spine, sometimes creating a humpback and back pain. Bone mass starts to decrease from the age of 35. Fair and slender women with a delicate bone structure are at most risk, as are those who have an early menopause. There are preventative measures you can take to protect yourself against osteoporosis:
  • Get a good supply of calcium and vitamins C and D throughout life.
  • Take regular weight-bearing exercise (running or walking rather than swimming), which will help to build bone mass.
  • Hormone replacement therapy (HRT) can provide protection by artificially postponing the menopause.

SEE ALSO

•PAGES 36–37 The Rules of Healthy Eating
•PAGE 57 Hormone Replacement Therapy

66 After years of treatment for pelvic infection I discovered that my partner, who had never been tested, was reinfecting me. 99

SEXUAL HEALTH

• GYNAECOLOGICAL PROBLEMS • INFERTILITY

THERE ARE MANY OPPORTUNITIES for regular health screening: when you go for contraceptive advice or check-ups, when you are pregnant or if you suffer menopausal symptoms. If you are not sexually active, it is tempting to forget all about your sexual health, but regular checks are recommended at least until you are 65 (longer if you have had a positive smear or treatment for cancer).

CERVICAL SMEARS

A cervical smear is a means of checking the cells of the cervix (the neck of the womb) to detect signs of cell change that may herald the onset of cervical cancer. Cervical cancer, if it is not caught in the early stages, is life-threatening, but with regular smear testing no woman need die from this cancer.

Every woman who is, or has been, heterosexually active, should have a cervical smear test within a year of first sexual intercourse, again a year later, and then every three years. Even if you are no longer active heterosexually, you should continue to have smear tests because some cancers are very slow growing. Avoid sexual intercourse for 24 hours before having a test and do not have one during your period. For the clearest results, go around the time you ovulate (see page 55).

You should be contacted with your results but, if you have not heard within a month, call and ask for them. A positive result does not mean you have cancer, but you will be recalled for a second test. If this is positive, and only a very small number are, you will be sent for further diagnosis, usually using colposcopy, a process in which a special microscope is used to view unhealthy areas. A small piece of tissue may also be taken for examination. If abnormal cells or cancer are diagnosed, they can usually be successfully treated at an early stage, but you will be asked to return for annual or six-monthly repeat smears.

WHAT HAPPENS IN A CERVICAL SMEAR TEST?

The doctor or nurse will insert a speculum into your vagina. A wooden spatula is then used to scrape a few cells from the entrance to the cervical canal. These are then put on to a glass slide and sent to the laboratory for analysis. The more relaxed you are, the less likely it is that you will find this procedure uncomfortable.

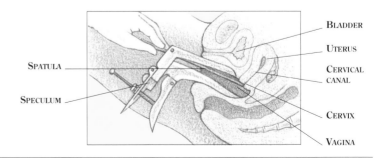

SPATULA

SPECULUM

BLADDER

UTERUS

CERVICAL CANAL

CERVIX

VAGINA

PELVIC EXAMINATION

A pelvic examination is routinely performed when you go for a smear. The doctor inserts one or two fingers inside your vagina and places the other hand on your abdomen. This way any abnormalities in your uterus, ovaries or fallopian tubes can be felt. You might have a pelvic examination in the following circumstances:

- If you experience bleeding problems.
- When you have a cap, diaphragm or IUD fitted.
- If you have unexplained abdominal pain.
- If you think you may have a vaginal infection.

You may discover, during a routine examination, that you have fibroids (see page 79) that you were unaware of. There is no need to worry about this. If you cannot feel them, and they are not causing you any distress, they can simply be left where they are.

URINE TESTS

Urine can be tested for the presence of protein (which would indicate infection), and also for the presence of sugar (which is an early sign of diabetes). Tests are routine in pregnancy, but you should also have a urine test if you have any of the following symptoms:

- Stinging, burning or pain when you urinate.
- Unusual frequency of urination.
- Unusual quantity of urine, accompanied by thirst, often a warning of diabetes.

VAGINAL INFECTIONS

If you have unprotected heterosexual sex with a new partner, it is wise to get checked. Even if you have a partner of long standing, it is possible that he could have picked up an infection in a previous relationship that may lurk, unsuspected and symptomless, until you stop using condoms and he then passes his infection on to you. Have a check-up before if you decide to stop using condoms.

Most health education these days focuses on AIDS (acquired immune deficiency syndrome), but it is the old infections, such as gonorrhoea and chlamydia, that pose the greater health risk for most women. Unlike AIDS, these are rarely life-threatening because they are curable with antibiotics; they are, however, potentially dangerous because, although early symptoms are mild, the infection can spread to the fallopian tubes, causing damage, and pain, and threatening fertility. Most doctors are alert to the importance of screening for these infections, but you may prefer the anonymity of a specialist sexually transmitted disease clinic where all the necessary tests can be done on one premises. Swabs are taken from the cervix and urethra and tested for signs of infection.

Gonorrhoea can be treated with penicillin, but chlamydia responds only to tetracycline (or related antibiotics). Of the other more common infections, vaginal warts will cause you no bother, but the virus may be associated with the development of cervical cancer so treatment and follow-up screening are vital. Herpes is not curable but, with medical advice, you can learn how to minimize the distress of symptoms that, over time, will fade. Less serious, though irritating, infections such as trichomoniasis or thrush can also be treated.

SEE ALSO

- PAGES 70–71 Breasts
- PAGE 73 Blood Tests
- PAGE 81 Gynaecological Trouble-shooting Chart

GYNAECOLOGICAL PROBLEMS

Those parts of us that are uniquely female may work all our lives without giving us the slightest concern, but they can also be the source of chronic health problems that are not always easy to solve. The chart overleaf may help you to link any symptoms with some of the following conditions.

CANDIDA ALBICANS (THRUSH)

This fungal infection results in a harmless, thick white vaginal discharge that makes the vulva extremely itchy. Thrush is caused by an overgrowth of the fungus that lives naturally in the vagina, and is commonly brought on by the use of antibiotics, which kill off the bacteria that keep this fungus under control. It can also be caused by anything else that upsets the delicate balance of the vagina, such as chlorine in swimming pools or tight clothing.

TREATING YOURSELF Thrush develops when the acid/alkali balance of the vagina is favourable to it (in particular when you have a period), so the best preventative treatment is to alter this balance. It is easier to make it acid: put a cup of vinegar in the bath or a couple of drops of dilute vinegar on a tampon during your period. If attacks still recur, use a vinegar douche (one tablespoon to a pint of water) or acigel capsules from a pharmacist, every other day for two weeks up to and during your period. This can be enough to break a cycle of recurrent infection.
MEDICAL TREATMENT Pessaries (such as nystatin) can be bought over the counter. If this is your first attack, see a doctor to make sure it is thrush and not a more serious infection. The doctor will prescribe pessaries or oral anti-fungal agents.

CYSTITIS

This inflammation of the bladder or urethra may be caused by an infection (possibly transferred from the vagina or rectum), or by some other irritation, such as bubble bath, detergent or hot, tight clothing, even sex. The symptoms are an urgent and frequent need to urinate, often accompanied by stinging or pain.

TREATING YOURSELF Cystitis often recurs, but you may be able to curb an attack by drinking 300ml (½pt) of clear fluid every 20 minutes throughout the day; avoiding spicy foods, alcohol and caffeine (all irritants); avoiding tight underwear; and by urinating frequently, and *always* before and after sex. Do not use a diaphragm.
MEDICAL TREATMENT Take a urine sample to your doctor for analysis. Broad-spectrum antibiotics will usually be prescribed to relieve symptoms in the meantime. If untreated, infection may spread to the kidneys and require hospital treatment.

ENDOMETRIOSIS

Endometrial cells, which should line the uterus, sometimes escape into the abdominal cavity, attaching themselves to other organs and behaving as if in the uterus – building up monthly and shedding. This can cause cyclical pain if there is nowhere for the tissue to escape to. Many women suffer from endometriosis unknowingly but, for an unlucky few, it is painful and distressing.

SEE ALSO

• PAGE 81 Gynaecological Trouble-shooting Chart
• PAGE 57 Hormone Replacement Therapy

MEDICAL TREATMENT Since endometriosis can be confused both with pelvic inflammatory disease (see below) and inflammation of the colon, correct diagnosis is important. If endometriosis is confirmed, treatment usually involves preventing ovulation through the use of the pill, progestogens or the drug danazol. Pregnancy is also effective in relieving symptoms.

Some women find the treatments difficult to tolerate and may contemplate surgery to cut out the growths, or hysterectomy to remove the uterus. Neither treatment guarantees an end to symptoms, which can continue until ovulation stops at menopause.

FIBROIDS

These are benign (non-cancerous) growths in the uterine wall. You may have fibroids for years and experience no symptoms other than a bulky womb, which may increase your waistline. You may also suffer distressing symptoms such as heavy menstrual bleeding and a dull, heavy sensation in the abdomen or back pain. Large fibroids can make it difficult to become, or remain, pregnant.

MEDICAL TREATMENT If you are under 40 and fibroids are causing real distress, or if you hope to get pregnant, it is possible to have them removed surgically, though they often grow back again. If you are not experiencing symptoms, you may prefer to leave them alone – they will shrink anyway after the menopause. If you are over 40 and have distressing symptoms, you may want to consider a hysterectomy, the only effective long-term treatment.

OVARIAN CYSTS

Sometimes a follicle develops, grows, but fails to release an egg. Instead it fills with fluid, becoming a cyst. Most cysts simply disappear without any symptoms. Some continue to grow and harden, causing anything from mild abdominal discomfort to very acute pain. If you regularly produce ovarian cysts (polycystic ovaries) you may have unusual hair growth or erratic periods and your fertility could be affected.

MEDICAL TREATMENT If pain is acute and doesn't resolve, surgery will be required to remove the cyst. If cysts recur, you should be referred to an endocrinologist.

PELVIC INFLAMMATORY DISEASE (PID)

Untreated vaginal infection may lead to PID, which can be a painful, debilitating and fertility-threatening disease. Symptoms include pelvic or lower back pain and a low fever or general feeling of illness. You may also notice an abnormal vaginal discharge or frequent urination.

MEDICAL TREATMENT Swabs from the cervix, vagina and urethra should be taken. If the infective organism is found early, antibiotic treatment may clear the infection completely. If it has been left for a long time or is misdiagnosed, the infection may require hospitalization and intravenous antibiotics. It is essential that any regular sexual partners are also tested and, if necessary, treated, or you risk reinfection.

HYSTERECTOMY

Hysterectomy, the removal of the womb, is carried out if cancer has been diagnosed; if there is an emergency during childbirth; or as the final option for a debilitating, chronic problem, such as fibroids, prolapse (when the womb drops into the vagina) or PID.

■ For a woman who is still fertile, or has had no time to adjust to the idea, or was not given a good explanation, hysterectomy can be traumatic.

■ For women who have suffered debilitating symptoms, such as persistent heavy bleeding, the removal of the womb may come as a welcome relief.

■ It is good medical practice to leave the ovaries intact unless there is a definite threat of further disease. This is particularly important for premenopausal women who will continue to benefit from the oestrogen released by the ovaries. You should also discuss hormone replacement therapy with your doctor (see page 57).

FACTORS AFFECTING FERTILITY

In up to one third of infertility cases no cause can be identified.

Female factors affecting infertile couples:

■ **Age** After the age of 35, female fertility starts to decline.

■ **Blocked tubes** Past pelvic infection that was not promptly treated, endometriosis (see page 78) or previous surgery may have blocked or damaged the delicate fallopian tubes.

■ **Hormonal problems** An imbalance may prevent ovulation.

Male factors affecting infertile couples:

■ **Sperm damage** Sperm can be affected by environmental factors, such as heavy smoking or workplace chemicals.

■ **Blockage** Damaged tubes can stop sperm being released when a man ejaculates.

■ **Hormonal problems** These may affect sperm production.

Joint factors affecting infertile couples:

■ **Infection** Couples re-infecting each other may damage sperm and fallopian tubes.

■ **Antibodies** Men and women can create antibodies to sperm.

■ **Physical problems** Sexual difficulties or ignorance of the menstrual cycle (see page 55) may mean that sperm and ovum never meet.

INFERTILITY

The average couple takes around six months to start a pregnancy. Even two young, healthy and fertile people stand only one chance in four of starting a pregnancy in any cycle. For women over 35, the chances are lower. Most doctors would not consider initiating sub-fertility investigations for a year unless there is already evidence of impaired fertility (see below). However, if you have not conceived after two years of trying, your chances of doing so (without assistance) are substantially reduced. For the average couple, studies show that 8.5 per cent fail to conceive after one year of unprotected intercourse. Of these:

- 3–5 per cent will conceive, some with, and some without, medical help.
- 3–5 per cent will fail to have children even after treatment.

INVESTIGATIONS

As well as a physical examination of both partners to check for obstructions and for infection, doctors may do the following tests:

- Sperm test to check the quantity and quality of sperm.
- Blood test to check progesterone level and hence evidence of ovulation.
- Postcoital test to check for presence of infection or antibodies that can attack sperm, and whether the man's sperm can survive the woman's cervical mucus.
- X-ray investigation of fallopian tubes (hysterosalpingogram) and laparoscopy if blockage is suspected due to infection or endometriosis (see page 78).

TREATMENTS

No treatment should be started without proper investigation. Invasive treatments and investigations are very stressful and a self-help group may provide useful support (see pages 187–88). Remedies might include:

- The treatment of joint infections in both partners with appropriate antibiotics. Steroid treatment may be successful when either partner is producing antibodies to sperm, but it must be used only for short periods and be carefully monitored.
- In the man, improved diet, general health and a reduction in stress may improve sperm count; blockages can sometimes be surgically repaired; artificial insemination of sperm can ensure that a higher concentration gets to the right place at the right time; artificial insemination by an anonymous donor may also be considered. Drug treatments are only rarely appropriate.
- In the woman, improved diet and stress reduction may trigger ovulation without further intervention. Failing that, drugs to induce ovulation may be prescribed. These should not be used without correct diagnosis and careful monitoring because they are associated with a high level of multiple births and there has been no long-term follow-up of their effects on women's health. Surgery may clear blockages. In-vitro fertilization, where an egg is removed from the ovary, mixed with sperm until the egg is fertilized and then replaced in the womb, may achieve pregnancy. So too might gamete intra-fallopian transfer (GIFT), where the egg and sperm are mixed together and placed in the fallopian tube, but this route is stressful, usually expensive and may take many cycles if it is successful at all. Egg donation may be appropriate if the woman fails to produce them herself.

GYNAECOLOGICAL TROUBLE-SHOOTING CHART

Symptom	Possible cause	Action
Bleeding problems		
• Bleeding between periods	Pregnancy	See pages 64–65
	Early menopause	See page 57
	Fibroids	See page 79
	Endometriosis	See page 78
	Progestogen-based contraceptives	See page 60
	Uterine cancer (a remote possibility)	See your doctor
• Heavy bleeding during periods	Impending menopause	See page 57
	Fibroids	See page 79
	Endometriosis	See page 78
• No bleeding	Pregnancy	See pages 64–65
	Anorexia (starvation)	See page 39
	Over-exercising	See pages 32–33
	Menopause	See page 57
	Stress	See page 86
• Bleeding with pain	Excess prostaglandin	See page 56
	Endometriosis	See page 78
	Pelvic inflammatory disease	See page 79
	Bowel problems (blood in stools)	See your doctor
Abdominal pain		
• With bleeding	Miscarriage	See page 65
(See also Bleeding problems above)		
• Associated with menstrual cycle	Endometriosis	See page 78
	Pelvic inflammatory disease	See page 79
	Ovarian cysts (mid-cycle)	See page 79
	IUD	See page 61
	Excess prostaglandin	See page 56
• With urination	Cystitis	See page 78
	Herpes	See page 77
Sore, itchy genitals		
• General	Thrush	See page 78
	Trichomoniasis	See page 77
• Lumps, sores or warts	Herpes	See page 77
	Genital warts	See page 77
Vaginal discharge		
• Unpleasant smell or unusual discharge	Sexually transmitted infection	See page 77
Frequent urination	Cystitis	See page 78
	Pregnancy	See pages 64–65
	Sexually transmitted infection	See page 77

❝ It was like
moving from
a positive into
a negative. ❞

MENTAL HEALTH

- COMMON REACTIONS TO MENTAL DISTRESS
- PINPOINTING SOURCES OF STRESS
- MAKING ANGER WORK FOR YOU
- STRESS-REDUCTION TECHNIQUES • SURVIVING A CRISIS

OST OF US, MOST OF THE TIME, take our mental health for granted. We get on with our lives, eat and sleep, laugh and cry, work, talk to our friends, travel, shop and cook. But there may come a time, perhaps very briefly, when the ordinary patterns of living become oddly distorted. Perhaps we cannot sleep, or we feel anxious, we may be afraid to go out, lose all feeling of hope and optimism, or swing wildly from peaks of furious activity to periods of deep gloom.

TEMPORARY DISTURBANCES

It is very common for mental health to be disturbed now and again. Most people have experienced an occasional attack of "the blues". It is part of being human. Sometimes these attacks come in cycles, affected by menstruation (see page 56), or by the seasons. You feel low for a while and then bounce back up again. If you learn to recognize the reason for gloom, you can usually learn to wait it out, then circumstances change and life seems to get better again.

SEASONAL AFFECTIVE DISORDER (SAD)

Winter mood drops could be the effect of cold, dark weather and a resulting increase in melatonin levels.
■ Melatonin is produced by the body to lower your level of functioning at night to enable you to sleep. Overproduction can cause anxiety and depression.
■ To combat SAD you will need regular exposure to daylight, either the real thing or a special daylight lamp.

NAME: **Janet Lee**

OCCUPATION:

Photographer

AGE: **25**

"It was like moving from a positive into a negative. Overnight, everything that had been light became dark. It felt as though the world was against me. There was no point in asking for love because I was unlovable; no point in going anywhere or doing anything. I was sunk inside my own head, glowering at everyone. Then just as suddenly the mist seemed to clear and life was worth living again."

Occasionally people get submerged, stuck inside misery. You need to ask for help to find a way out and back into the light again, but you may feel too low to make the first move, and sink into a cycle of feeling sad and uncared for. There may also be the fear of being considered weak, or perhaps of being labelled "mad". You may hope that by ignoring your pain it will magically go away by itself. Maybe it will, but you will almost always feel better for a little support. You may believe that you can pull yourself together, but the more you force the lid on your feelings, the more difficult it will become to deal with them and learn, first to accept them, and then to move on (see pages 86–87).

NAME: **Grace Jordan** OCCUPATION: **Bar worker** AGE: **32**	*"I couldn't talk about any of it with friends. I don't like burdening people with sad stories and I always felt that it was a sign of failure if you couldn't cope. I had always coped and I thought I had put the past behind me. Now I realize you cannot bury the past."*

For some people the distortion of everyday reality becomes frightening – either to them or to the people they are with. They may see or hear things that others are not aware of; behave in ways that friends find disturbing; threaten, or actually attempt, suicide. Janice Galloway in her novel *The Trick Is To Keep Breathing*, describes such a feeling:

"Cold spots dripped on my upturned palms but I didn't feel it was me crying. I could find no connection between these splashes and me. I connected only with the words. They swelled and filled up the whole room. I was eaten and swallowed inside those words, eaten and invisible."

When reality has slipped too far away, others may need to intervene and help you find a route back, or a way of living that decreases the stress and pain. It is not uncommon to have a breakdown, but nor is it uncommon to recover completely. The sooner you find help, the faster the process of recovery will be, and you can learn to find ways of keeping yourself out of the abyss in the future (see page 93).

COMMON CAUSES OF MENTAL DISTRESS

There may be many reasons for a temporary disturbance to mental health. Some are well documented – bereavement, divorce or moving house – while others may be less obvious:

A REACTION TO IMMEDIATE LIFE EVENTS The death of a loved one, the birth of a baby, the loss of a job, a serious accident or illness will throw most people, at least temporarily, off course.

STRESS Overwork, interrupted sleep, isolation, racism, sexual harassment, difficult, demanding or violent relationships all cause stress. Some stress is useful, but if we have too much to cope with, we may "break down" under the strain.

A REACTION TO PAST LIFE EVENTS Children tend to submerge or suppress memories of particularly traumatic events, or simply create a new explanation for the event, that makes the pain explicable. Buried pain may come back to haunt us in ways we find hard to recognize, affecting the way we feel and behave and making us more vulnerable to stressful life events.

A BIOCHEMICAL IMBALANCE Some mental health problems may be biochemical in origin. It is hard to tell whether this is genetic (we are born that way) or whether exposure to harmful life events has caused a kind of biochemical reaction similar to the effect of an allergen on someone susceptible to allergies.

SEE ALSO

•PAGE 92 Coping with a Crisis
•PAGE 93 Talking Treatments
•PAGES 90–91 Stress-reduction Techniques
•PAGE 39 Allergies

COMMON REACTIONS TO MENTAL DISTRESS

When you are distressed, unlike when you are physically ill, it may be difficult to give your symptoms a name, but these are a few of the more common reactions.

ANXIETY

HOW IT FEELS We are all familiar with butterflies in the stomach or a sudden feeling of nausea that may attack before a driving test or a date. Sometimes anxiety can make us keener and sharper, but if the feelings take over, even when there is no special reason to feel anxious, they will start to interfere with the way we function. Muscle tension may cause headaches or chest and neck pain. It may slow down the digestive system, or create a knotted feeling in the stomach or cause diarrhoea. Disturbing thoughts may lurk at the back of the mind. Panic attacks may be accompanied by a pounding heart, sweating, chest pains and rapid breathing, which can cause weakness, faintness or dizziness. If these symptoms persist, the effect of stress on the body makes it more vulnerable to disease.

GETTING HELP Your doctor may prescribe minor tranquillizers or sleeping pills for a short period to calm your fears and help you relax. Tranquillizers are not recommended as long-term therapy because of the danger of addiction, but they may provide a respite in which to look at the underlying causes of your anxiety (see pages 92–93). Try also the stress-reduction techniques on pages 90–91.

DEPRESSION

HOW IT FEELS You dislike yourself and others; you feel tearful, inadequate or unable to cope; you see the worst in everything; you feel numb, empty and despondent; you blame yourself or feel unnecessarily guilty about things; it is an effort to do the smallest task; it is hard to concentrate; you are unusually irritable and impatient; you sleep fitfully, or you sleep too much; you eat all the time, or not at all; you smoke or drink more than usual; you cut yourself off from others rather than asking for help; you feel unlovable and unable to love.

GETTING HELP Women seem to be particularly vulnerable to depression. It may be because we are trained from our earliest years not to express anger: depression is often described as anger turned inward. Most of us have had some experience of feeling depressed, perhaps before a period (see page 57), or when a relationship ends. Usually the feeling lifts of its own accord. If the depression deepens, you may benefit from help and advice (see pages 187–88) or possibly medical treatment. Reducing stress may also help you to keep your life in perspective. If you are severely depressed, you may need a short period in hospital where you can be taken care of and given treatment to get you on your feet again.

PHOBIAS AND OBSESSIONS

HOW IT FEELS A phobia is an extreme panic reaction to a particular situation. You may suffer symptoms of acute anxiety as well as depression. A phobia may be quite specific and affect you in a relatively limited way. For example, fear of

---

BEATING INSOMNIA

Sleeping problems are a common companion to anxiety and stress: just when you most need to get a good night's sleep, you find you cannot. Try these strategies to help you relax before bed:

■ Do not be tempted to stay up late in the hope of tiring yourself out: it is often harder to drop off when you are overtired.

■ Get up at the same time each day, even if you have had a bad night. If you regularly sleep late in the morning, you will find it even harder to sleep at night.

■ Don't panic. Remind yourself that you will get through the next day, however bad you feel, and that tomorrow night is only hours away.

ANTI-DEPRESSANT DRUGS

Anti-depressant drugs are the most common medical treatment for depression. They can be prescribed by a doctor and they work by changing the chemicals in the brain to lift your mood. They may provide a short-term respite during which you should take long-term action to find the cause of your depression (see pages 187–88).

spiders may only be a problem on the rare occasions when a spider finds its way into the bath, but a fear of open spaces (agoraphobia) could imprison you in your home, and social phobia (fear of meeting people) may cut you off from the human contact that could provide you with comfort. If you find yourself reacting with panic to life events that others seem to take in their stride, you may need specialized help.

Obsessive behaviour may also be a symptom of anxiety and it seems most likely to strike people who would describe themselves as perfectionists. A very mild obsession may simply be seen as extreme tidiness, unless you live with other people who are relaxed about their environment and find your behaviour irritating. A serious obsession can become quite disabling. You may find yourself checking the locks on your doors over and over again, or washing your hands until they are raw to rid them of imaginary bacteria.

GETTING HELP Relaxation techniques (see pages 90–91) may help you to avoid, or lessen, attacks. Your doctor may be able to arrange behaviour therapy to help you to explore your fears and overcome them. In the long term, if your fear is disabling, psychotherapy may help you to find the underlying cause and to come to terms with it (see pages 92–93).

PSYCHOSIS AND MANIA

WHAT PSYCHOSIS FEELS LIKE The British Association for Mental Health (MIND) gives the following explanation: "Perhaps you have woken up in the middle of a dream and, for a few moments, not known what is real and what is the dream. Imagine not being able to stop dreaming after you have woken. That will give you some idea of what it is like to experience psychosis: a state of mind in which people cannot distinguish between what is real and what is in their imagination. Often what they imagine is frightening and causes them to behave in strange ways."

WHAT MANIA FEELS LIKE You may feel euphoric and whiz around impressing everyone with your brilliant ideas. You may be unable to sleep, or talk like a steam train without realizing that no one is listening, possibly because they have understood that you are not really connecting with them. Often people experiencing a manic swing will become hugely extravagant, building up debts they cannot hope to pay. After mania comes a downward crash into a chasm as deep as the euphoria has been high.

GETTING HELP You may be unable to get help for yourself, but you do need it. This may be a one-off event, a reaction to extreme stress or to a drug you have taken but, if attacks recur, you may need support from people you trust to help you find ways of avoiding or recognizing early signs of an attack and getting medical help before it takes over. Drug treatment and/or hospitalization may stabilize you in the short term. Self-help groups can provide support from people who have also experienced these frightening symptoms: they will understand your fears and help you to cope with them. Psychotherapy may be useful in helping you to find hidden reasons for your reactions.

SEE ALSO
•PAGES 187–88 Useful Addresses

PINPOINTING SOURCES OF STRESS

Some people seem to thrive on stress. They may even create it by leaving work until the very last minute and then using the adrenalin that goes with panic to help them achieve what could have been done at leisure. Others find that even the smallest disruption to routine is unbearable and induces a panic attack. Most of us lie somewhere in between and our mental health depends on keeping the balance right. If you can recognize situations that wind you up, you may be able to learn how to avoid them or how to manage them so that they cause you less stress.

PUTTING YOUR HOUSE IN ORDER

Anxiety and stress may be caused by external factors – the loss of a job, the end of a relationship, bad housing or illness – but they can also be self-induced. The way we live, the state of our room, house or desk is often a reflection of how we feel inside. We may be obsessively tidy, imposing order on the physical world to prevent the threat of chaos overtaking, and we may be creating additional stress by worrying about tasks that do not really need to be done. Alternatively, we may allow our lives to become a physical reflection of our inner chaos: letters and bills in unsorted piles, clothes on the floor, phone numbers on scraps of paper, confirming what we already know – that we are not in control.

It will almost certainly help to try and work out why you are obsessed with ordering your life or why it is that you prefer not to take control of it. Perhaps you are still waiting for someone to do it for you. Maybe you spend your life preparing to do tasks as a way of avoiding actually starting them. Of course everyone is different, but when your physical world is swallowing up time and creating stress, it is time to take a look at how you run your life. Try the exercise below:

TASK PLANNING

JANE'S TASKS

1 **Write a list of the tasks you need to accomplish.**

2 **Separate the list into two: pleasant and unpleasant tasks.**

3 **Place the tasks in each list under three different headings: urgent, necessary, unimportant.**

4 **Make a list with the most urgent tasks at the top and the least important at the bottom. Try to cross off any tasks that you do not really need to do.**

Finish the report for the sales department	**PLEASANT TASKS**	**UNPLEASANT TASKS**
Sell my desk at auction	**Urgent** *Book my holiday*	**Urgent** *Finish the report for the sales department*
Find the birth certificate I lost	**Necessary** *Book theatre tickets for the 6th*	**Necessary** *Find the birth certificate I lost*
Book my holiday	**Unimportant** *Sell my desk at auction*	**Unimportant** *Clean the car*
Book theatre tickets for the 6th		
Clean the car		

• Use this list to plan your day, allowing time for the pleasant tasks, even if they are not urgent: they are your rewards. Do all the less pleasant tasks in order of priority.

HOW DO YOU REACT TO STRESS? HOW WOULD YOU RESPOND IN THESE SITUATIONS?

The train stops for no apparent reason. Do you:

1 Enjoy the opportunity to read a book.

2 Try to hold down the feeling of panic at being trapped.

3 Worry about being late for work.

4 Walk to the door, try to look out, mutter about the state of the railways, and feel yourself getting tense.

Your annual holiday is due. Do you:

1 Phone a travel agent at the last minute to see if there are any cheap seats.

2 Think about going away, but can't decide where to go. You could not leave the cat, and think you wouldn't enjoy it anyway.

3 Revel in the fact that you booked a holiday six months ago. You have been packing clothes all week.

4 Dread the holiday you booked for ten people. Your stomach is in knots with panic.

How Did You Score?

If you picked mainly 1s
You are so laid back you are practically horizontal. The only thing that creates tension in your life is the trouble you cause by leaving everything to the last minute. You might drive everyone around you crazy, but you are unlikely to need stress-reduction exercises. But perhaps you leave everything to chance because you are incapable of confronting problems. If this is the case, you may even feel scared and out of control beneath your casual front. It might help to talk to friends or family about ways of creating a little order in your life.

If you picked mainly 2s
You are under a great deal of stress already and may find that even the smallest inconvenience tips you over into panic or tears. You try to keep a brave face and cover up the misery you feel inside. You need to relax more, to try to find ways of reducing your tension, but you also need to find out why you have so little self-belief. Stress reduction will help (see pages 90–91), but you may also benefit from longer-term counselling or therapy (see pages 84–85).

If you picked mainly 3s
You are a little obsessive about the way you live your life. The more rigidly you keep yourself under control, the less you are able to tolerate even the smallest changes in routine. When you do feel angry (which is probably often), you bottle it up and stew on it, possibly using drink or drugs to calm down. You will probably never thrive on stress, but if you can find a way of expressing anger and learn to relax, you may find you can let go of the reins just a little and enjoy life more.

You are meeting a friend for lunch and she is late. Do you:

1 Assume she has been held up and order a drink.

2 Convince yourself that she has either forgotten or never meant to come.

3 Feel angry about waiting two minutes after the appointed hour because you were 10 minutes early.

4 Phone to check that she has left, and when she arrives you tell her how angry you are at being kept waiting.

Someone cuts you up at the traffic lights. Do you:

1 Ignore it and carry on driving, unperturbed.

2 Assume you are to blame and park so that you can calm down.

3 Fume angrily for much of the day and bore your workmates with it.

4 Hoot, make obscene gestures, or accelerate after the car so that you can beat him at the next set of lights.

You have some important work due in next Friday. Do you:

1 Enjoy the week and stay up all night on Thursday.

2 Cancel all engagements, but then find that you are writing and rewriting, and still not finished by Thursday evening.

3 Start work a week in advance and have it ready several days early, neatly typed and stapled.

4 Find that you already have three other deadlines and sit up every night working.

If you picked mainly 4s
You drive yourself and others at breakneck speed and explode at the drop of a hat. You are probably a high achiever and get a great deal done, but you may not stop for long enough to enjoy what you do. If you keep this up, you may find you have pushed yourself at the expense of your health in later life; let up a bit.

MAKING ANGER WORK FOR YOU

Anger that is stewed over turns inward to make you hate yourself or, eventually, it explodes all over someone else. Anger that is expressed at the slightest pinprick of frustration will exhaust you and everyone around you. Making anger work for you requires learning not to care so much about things you cannot change and learning how to act on your anger and change what you can, rather than exploding or becoming hopeless and depressed. This exercise may help:

WHOSE PROBLEM IS IT?

SUSANNAH'S PROBLEMS

1 Write down a list of the things that make you angry or frustrated.

2 Now cut the list into separate items.

3 Sort them into three piles: not my problem, my problem, our problem.

4 For analysis of each type of problem, see below.

Not my problem	My problem	Our problem
The office manager shouts at me when she feels fed up – not my problem, her problem.	*I spent an hour looking for a lost document – my problem, I should be more careful.*	*I have had to reorganize my work because someone else changed their mind.*
There is a traffic jam on the way to work – not my problem, I cannot control the traffic.	*I've just bought a new pair of trousers – now I'm overdrawn again.*	*My brother has broken my CD player.* *People are starving in refugee camps.*

NOT MY PROBLEM

Learn to let go of these. It might help to write down the problem and then tear it up and throw it away. Or imagine the driver who just swore at you tied to an air balloon. You cut the string and he just floats up into space. You have expressed yourself without damaging anyone. Sometimes something is "not my problem" but it still hurts. This is particularly likely if you work with sick or unhappy people, when it may be tempting to take on their troubles and turn them into your own. Your feelings are understandable, but it is very hard to help others if you descend to their level of depression. They need someone on the outside to help them through. If you know that you have taken care of your responsibilities and done everything in your power to make things better, then you have to learn to let go. This does not mean that you will not feel pain. You still need the opportunity to talk to others about your work and to cry if you need to.

MY PROBLEM

It is futile to be angry with yourself, but we all are from time to time. If it helps to yell and curse, do (but try not to do it *at* anyone else) – you may feel better for it. Sometimes "my problem" becomes so great that you are no longer able to cope. You may feel submerged and start putting off trying to sort things out; your anger with yourself may soon turn into panic or depression (see page 84). "My problem" will not disappear if you ignore it. It will just get bigger. If things seem to have spun totally out of control, you may need advice, perhaps from a trained counsellor, to help you to prioritize and get things back on track (see pages 187–88). Tackling the things you have been avoiding will disperse the tension inside.

OUR PROBLEM

These problems are hard to tackle because you have to act rather than store up your rage, pretending it doesn't matter. Here is a rough outline of things to do:

FEEL Anger stimulates the production of adrenalin, which in turn prepares your body for fight or flight, making you physically prepared for action. This response creates stress. You should not sit on all that stress, so pass some of it on. *Talk* to someone, preferably someone who is completely unconnected, and tell them all about it. If this is not enough, *write* it down, telling the person concerned exactly how you feel (but do not send it to them). If you are still steaming, go to the gym and *punch* it out on a punch bag (not on the person concerned); go for a run – stand in a large empty field and *yell*.

THINK If you feel calmer, sit down and think about what has happened. Use the "Whose problem is it?" exercise again. Does the problem really matter? If it does not, then let it go – it does not really matter who is right and who is wrong. If it does matter, make sure you know whose problem it is. Perhaps you lost an important memo, forgot an appointment, tried to do too many things at the same time, left it too late. If so, blaming someone else will not help. Accepting responsibility may be hard, but it is more fruitful than apportioning blame when none is due. If the problem really is due to someone else, even partly, and if it really does matter (for example, if it will affect your relationship with someone or interfere with your work), do not sit on your anger, do something about it.

ACT Each situation is different. If you feel angry with your boss or a colleague for failing to pass on vital information, write a memo, not accusing him or her of undermining you, but pointing out that communication systems are not working as well as they might and asking to discuss it. If you feel angry with your brother for breaking your CD player, ask him to work out a way he can repay you, if not in cash, then in kind. If you feel angry with a foreign power for the massacre of innocent civilians, find ways of acting on your anger: write letters, join a pressure group, demonstrate. If you are being bullied by someone with power over you, then you will feel trapped because you may feel you cannot take action. The first step is to talk to someone. The simple act of sharing your feelings will empower you. You may then find that you can act and change the situation.

TALKING TOUGH

It is very hard to act if you cannot express yourself clearly, and the temptation is either to swallow your anger and pretend it didn't happen, or to let rip and start a row. Indeed it may be your fear of a row that stops you from doing anything at all. A useful assertiveness training trick is always to start with the word "I", and to make a statement rather than an accusation.

■ Do not say: "My project has been ruined because you forgot to order the raw materials". Do say: "I am pretty upset that my project has been cancelled. Please can we discuss our planning systems so that it doesn't happen again?"

■ Do not say: "You have broken my CD player you little rat, and I am never going to lend you anything again as long as I live". Do say: "I am really angry that my CD player is broken. It would help if you could come up with a way to pay for it".

STRESS-REDUCTION TECHNIQUES

You can do exercises on your own to reduce feelings of stress and help you relax, or go to a class to learn techniques such as yoga and meditation (see right).

RELAXATION EXERCISES

Try to make time every day to do the simple exercises on these pages. If you have had a bad morning, try to find a private space where you can relax in your lunch break. If you are at work, follow the steps sitting in a comfortable chair that fully supports your back. You might prefer to lie down if you are at home. Start with the breathing exercise below.

FREE YOUR MIND

Often anxious thoughts, chasing around your brain, make it difficult to relax. It is hard to empty your mind if there is a constant ticker tape of worry hammering away in the background. It may help to put something else in your mind to occupy the space, such as a warm beach or a pool, and chase out the negative thoughts. To start with you may find this difficult to achieve. Reality will keep slipping through and jerking you out of your reverie. It may help to make a tape for yourself, describing your special place in a quiet, slow voice and repeating, "The sun is warming me", or "The water is holding me gently". Practise until you are able to take yourself off to this special place and stay there as long as you want.

BREATHING EXERCISE

A simple breathing exercise can be used for an instant "pick-me-up" when you find yourself getting wound up. You can repeat the exercise at the end of the day to calm yourself ready for sleep. Five minutes will usually be enough to dispel feelings of tension and anxiety, or at least to reduce them.

◄ 1 Sit comfortably. Put one hand flat on your upper chest and the other on your diaphragm, just above your navel. Watch your hands as you breathe. Your upper hand should be still and your lower one should rise with each inward breath and fall with each outward breath.

2 Take a deep, slow breath in and hold it to a count of five. You should be able to feel your diaphragm rise as you do this.

3 Breathe out slowly to a count of five. Take as long as you can to expel all the air.

4 Relax for a couple of seconds and then repeat the exercise.

TENSION-RELIEVING EXERCISE

Allow yourself at least 5 minutes to de-stress and relax your body. You may not have even realized that you were frowning, clenching your teeth and tensing **your shoulders. If you work at a computer, try to do this exercise several times a day. Make sure you are comfortable and that your back and legs are supported.**

1 Shut your eyes. Think about the muscles of your head and face. Squeeze your forehead into a frown and then relax. Move to your mouth. Open it wide, then relax. Now squeeze all the muscles in your face, and relax. Can you feel the release of tension in your forehead, the loosening in your jaw? Move down to your neck. Stretch your head backward, hold the tension for a few seconds and then relax. Press your chin on to your chest, hold it, and then relax. Turn your head slowly from side to side, and relax.

2 Check your shoulders. Are they up near your ears? Pull them up as far as you can and then let them drop heavily. Now pull them back, as if you wanted them to meet, and then release. Can you feel the muscles relax where you have been holding your head in place? Check your arms and hands, stretching them and then tensing your hands into a fist. Let the tension go, letting your hands dangle heavy and loose.

3 Stretch your legs and circle your ankles. Stretch your toes. Let your legs flop heavily on the ground. Now sit, or lie, for at least five minutes, mentally checking each group of muscles and making sure they have not begun to tense up again.

VISUALIZATION EXERCISE

Make sure you are in a warm and comfortable place. Start with the exercise **above, relaxing your body, and then focus on your mind.**

1 Close your eyes and search for an image that makes you feel happy. It may be lying on a beach in gentle sunshine, floating in water surrounded by lily pads, or lying on a cloud swaying gently in a breeze. It does not have to be real, but it must be a place where you would feel totally supported and at ease. ▼

2 Allow the image to fill your mind. Feel the sun on your body, the swaying of the water as your limbs lie supported, or the soft embrace of a cloud. Feel your head and neck and imagine the warm, soft sand that supports them.

3 Tell yourself, "I am warm through and through". Allow the heat to penetrate right into your bones and hold you there. Now drift off; you may even fall asleep. Allow yourself 20 minutes of total relaxation, then open your eyes, stretch and get up slowly.

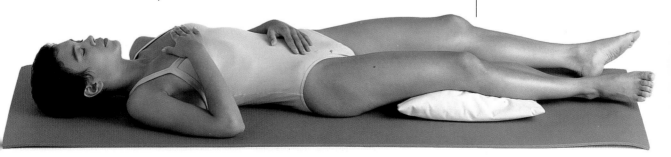

SURVIVING A CRISIS

A change is not as good as a rest. Any change, whether positive or negative, creates stress. Some events, such as the death of someone close to you, divorce or separation, financial collapse or personal injury, are almost always stressful, but so too are life's positive changes. Marriage, pregnancy and childbirth, or a change of job or house, involve both change and significant loss – the loss of a way of living that you are used to. If the stress is isolated and you are well supported, you will probably avoid reaching crisis point. If you have no support, and if the stresses come together, they can build up to an intolerable level.

KNOWING WHEN YOU HAVE HAD ENOUGH

A crisis for one person may be only a minor irritation for another. The issue is not so much what happened, as how you feel about it. You may feel any of the symptoms listed on page 86. You may feel that it is not worth getting out of bed in the morning; you may keep trying to work but find that you are doing the same thing over and over again, going around in circles and getting nowhere. You may feel your palms sweating, your heart beating faster; you may be unable to sleep and eat; you may feel pain in your chest or stomach, or find it hard to breathe. You may think that you can no longer differentiate between the frightening thoughts in your head and the real world outside. You may believe that the only way out of the situation is to kill yourself, or that any action, small or extreme, is beyond you.

COPING WITH A CRISIS

You can ask for help in some of the following ways:

TALK TO SOMEONE *"I couldn't get close to my baby. I think now that I was afraid of loving her in case she died like my last baby. Everyone tried to push her on me and that just made it worse, but I didn't dare tell anyone how I felt in case they took her away from me."*

The simple act of telling your worries to another person can have an almost magical effect. They seem to shrink in the telling. Very often the worst thing about a problem is the fact that you have been too frightened to look at it. By telling someone else, you have to put your fears into words and you may find that they do not look nearly as big as you thought they were. You may also find that something that seemed to you quite monstrous turns out to be a great deal less terrible than you expected.

ASK FOR PRACTICAL HELP *"Everything has built up. I owe money to everyone and it goes up every week. I am afraid of answering the door. I just lie in bed waiting for them to come and get me."*

If there are concrete reasons for your crisis, you will need specific advice to deal with the underlying problem, and the sooner you get it, the better. Most practical problems can be alleviated, no matter how bad, and just by tackling them, with appropriate help and support, you will feel less powerless and be better able to find a way out of your crisis. If you do not know where to get help, ring a crisis line (see pages 187–88).

Divide a big problem into smaller ones *"I have two essays that are overdue, I haven't started my dissertation, I will have another essay to hand in by the end of the month, and I am still working all day every day on my practical project. I know I am going to fail so there is no point in even trying anymore."*
Failure to pace yourself and prioritize your work can easily lead to a crisis. All you can see is a mountain of undifferentiated tasks. If you go through them with someone else – a friend, a colleague, a teacher – you may find it easier to set yourself a number of small tasks that will, in the end, reduce the mountain. If you find yourself getting into crises regularly, you may need to think about how you organize your life. Write yourself a list of tasks, with the most important items at the top. Work through them in order; and you may discover that the least important tasks do not really need to be done at all. If you still have too much to do, you need to find ways of reducing your load.

Ask for medical help Drug treatments can be highly effective at providing a short-term respite from your feelings, but it is important to use this period constructively to find the long-term help that you need.
  • Anti-depressant drugs can help to lift you out of a state of hopelessness. They are not addictive and are usually prescribed for a short period of time.
  • Minor tranquillizers may provide short-term relief from terrifying feelings, but they should not be taken for long as they are addictive.

TALKING TREATMENTS
Often you can talk your way out of a crisis. See pages 187–88 for helpful contacts.
Individual counselling This may help you find a way of tackling problems. Counsellors listen and provide general guidance rather than giving advice. Your doctor may refer you or you can ring a counselling advice line.

Individual psychotherapy Usually a longer-term process, this is aimed at helping you arrive at a deeper understanding of your own motivation and, through understanding, changing the way you feel and behave. Some people start psychotherapy because they feel unhappy, others want help with a specific problem, such as compulsive eating or a phobia. There are many different psychotherapeutic disciplines. Find a practitioner registered with the relevant professional body.

Psychological treatments Behaviour therapy will help you deal with specific difficulties like phobias. Cognitive therapy is aimed at recognizing your thought patterns and learning to change them, as is assertiveness training.

Self-help or support groups These are for people with a shared problem, such as alcoholism or depression, or a shared situation, such as new motherhood. Members are encouraged to talk about common experiences and support each other in learning from them. Group therapy is lead by experienced group psychotherapists who help people to share and learn, both from their individual experiences and from their interaction within the group.

66 It got so bad I was afraid of going to the shops for a bottle of milk. I would feel sick, the pavement would feel as though it was moving independently. 99

Forging friendships

Exploring sensuality

Considering parenthood

Resolving quarrels

YOUR RELATIONSHIPS

Human beings need other people as much as they need food. Indeed, without loving care, a baby may stop eating and quietly fade away, and without affection it is very hard for a child to develop and grow. Our early relationships do not only give us the will to live, but for better or worse, they mould our future behaviour as surely as the genes with which our parents give us life. To understand our present, we have to look back to our past. The pages that follow offer interactive exercises and constructive support to help interpret the past and forge successful new relationships.

FAMILY AND FRIENDS

• MAKING AND SUSTAINING FRIENDSHIPS

FOR MOST OF US, OUR FIRST RELATIONSHIP IS WITH OUR MOTHER. It is the warmth of her body that first calms us and it is her eyes that first make contact with ours. Hers may have been the first voice ever raised in anger, and it is the realization that she is not part of us, but a separate person who can come and go at will, that gives us the first taste of our own separateness. Fathers have always come second (if they are there at all), but being second does not make them less important. The relationship with a second loving adult provides a safe bridge to the outside world. Children who have only one close adult in their lives may live with a fear of loss that undermines their confidence in personal relationships.

THE LINK THROUGH THE GENERATIONS

The relationship chain does not begin and end with our parents. Good and bad patterns of behaviour pass down the generations in an endless chain. Some of the messages we receive from our parents are explicit, some are hidden. Your mother may tell you that you have a temper "just like your Aunt Sally". She may be labelling you to avoid dealing with the reasons for your anger. Perhaps your anger reminds her of the frustration she felt when her little sister Sally hit out with a spade but was not to be hit back.

A TWO-WAY AFFAIR

Even the tiniest baby contributes to the personality that makes her. One baby may cry and be rewarded with attention, while another is left alone until she stops. The first baby may turn into an optimistic child who expects the world to come when she calls. The second may have learned to rely on her own resources and seem self-contained or withdrawn. They may each have a sister who was a quiet, peaceful baby and demanded a very different response from her parents. Though their parents are the same and their circumstances similar, they may approach the world in very different ways.

Where a child comes in the family order has lasting repercussions. Every first child is an experiment. She will get more individual attention than her younger siblings, though her parents are more likely to be anxious, which may affect her self-confidence. She may also suffer jealousy if other children come along.

Younger siblings have the advantage of having parents who have already been "broken in". These later children may be calmer and better at negotiating relationships. Middle siblings may find that they are being crushed between the demands of the oldest child, who still wants all the attention, and the youngest, who gets it. A middle child often needs to make a very particular mark in order to establish her place in the family.

NO FAMILY IS AN ISLAND

We are all affected by the circumstances of our birth. Whether our parents are rich or poor, come from comfortable stable families, or have suffered traumatic change in their lives, all these factors affect the way they behave. They may be used to talking about every detail of their emotional lives, or they may have learned to sweep problems under the carpet in an effort to cope with difficulty. But unpleasant or disturbing experiences that are hidden rarely stay there; ghosts return to haunt us as we get older.

One way to get in touch with familial patterns of behaviour we might not even be aware of is to write a life history and look for patterns. People (not necessarily family members) and events can have significant influences on our lives and the way we develop.

WRITING YOUR LIFE HISTORY

MARGARET'S LIFE MAP

1 Write down the significant events in your life. This is Margaret's life history.

2 Underline the names of the people involved. You may want to do the same with your parents' lives, and then move on to your grandparents and any other notable family members. Continue back as far as you are able.

3 Take each name in your map and write about that person. How did you feel about them at the time and how do you feel about them now? Write freely or just jot down words that you associate with these people or situations.

4 Now look for patterns. It is possible to identify a pattern in Margaret's life, for example. She has lived through a cycle of loss and she is hanging on to a relationship that makes her unhappy because she is afraid that if she loses Jack, she will never find anyone else. The sense of being left by everyone she cares about has undermined her belief in her own importance.

Significant events in my life	People in my life
• *Moved house about every four years from birth to the age of 16.* *I lost touch with* **Mary**, *who used to look after me; with* **Josie**, *my first best friend; with* **Diane**, *my second best friend; and with the gang I hung out with at school.*	**Mary:** *I feel good when I think about her.* **Josie:** *She was a good friend. We shared all our most intimate secrets.* **Diane:** *We used to have fun together. She was quite naughty at school.*
• *When I was 16 my parents divorced and I moved again. I really missed my* **Dad**. *My* **Mum** *was very unhappy and cried all the time.*	**Dad:** *When I am with him I feel happy, but the minute he leaves I feel empty and very angry.* **Mum:** *Guilt! I feel responsible for her and don't ever feel that I give her what she needs. I sometimes go for weeks without seeing her because I can't stand the nagging in my head. When she rings she always sounds so sad. I wish she would get her own life and I feel terrible about feeling such mean things about her when she is the only person who has always been there for me.*
• *I was depressed for most of my last years at school and I did badly in my exams.*	
• *When I was 19 I met* **Jack** *and moved in with him after three months. We have been together three years.*	**Jack:** *Love and misery. I have tried everything to make him happy. Sometimes I think I should leave him, but I would fall apart without him.*

Conclusion

You may not be able to spot the patterns in your own life at first. It takes time. The next few pages may help you to see them more clearly. If you feel that you need help to sort out your feelings, consider seeing a counsellor (see pages 187–88).

HOW DID YOUR RELATIONSHIP WITH YOUR PARENTS AFFECT YOU?

Life events are important in shaping your character, but so too are the ways in which your parents helped, protected and guided you. These relationships set patterns that govern the way you behave toward others. The questions below may help you to recognize the patterns in your life, but be aware that your interpretation may be coloured by the way you feel at the moment. If you are going through a difficult patch, for example, you may judge your parents unkindly. If you are getting on well, you may be inclined to remember only the rosy moments. If your parents treated you harshly, you may find it hard to face the truth because every child wants to believe her parents were the best – it is part of the foundations of self-belief. Facing the fact that they were not perfect may be hard, but you can learn to rebuild those foundations once you recognize that they are shaky.

THINK ABOUT HOW YOUR MOTHER REACTED IN THE FOLLOWING SITUATIONS.

If you fell over in the playground, did your mother:

1 Always pick you up, cuddle you and make sure you were alright.

2 Comfort you if you cried, but otherwise ignore it.

3 Brush you down and tell you not to cry.

4 Scold you for your carelessness.

If you did badly in a test at school, did your mother:

1 Comfort you and say, "Don't worry, I know you can do better next time".

2 Offer extra help so that you could do better next time.

3 Become quiet and disapproving.

4 Shout at you and say you must be stupid.

If your friends were mean to you, did your mother:

1 Always support you and say you should stay away from that friend.

2 Listen to what had happened and suggest ways of healing the rift.

3 Never hear about it from you.

4 Say you should think of some way of getting back at them.

As a teenager, did your mother:

1 Always seem anxious about your safety and worry if you were a minute late home.

2 Make clear rules for you to keep, but forget odd lapses.

3 Seem not to show much interest in anything but your performance at school.

4 Lay down the law and get very angry if you were a minute late home.

If you bought a dress that you weren't sure about, did your mother:

1 Tell you that you looked a million dollars (even if you were sure you didn't).

2 Say you shouldn't wear it if you felt uncomfortable in it.

3 Say you looked a complete mess.

4 Make a fuss about the money you would waste if you didn't wear it.

Looking back, do you feel that your mother:

1 Was always 'there' for you – even when you didn't want her to be.

2 Was usually 'there' for you when you needed her.

3 Was only 'there' when her programme allowed.

4 Was rarely supportive at all.

HOW DID YOU SCORE?

Our analysis is no blueprint; your parent may have combined the best from several categories.

Mostly 1s
Your mother bolstered your feelings of self-importance, but you may find it difficult to believe that you are capable of managing without someone to keep your life together.

Mostly 2s
Your mother provided support which enabled you to find your own way in the world. But you may wish sometimes that you could relinquish control to someone else for a while.

Mostly 3s
Your mother did not provide enough for you on an emotional level. You may be prone to depression or anger and to bottling things up. You may have difficulty expressing good feelings too.

Mostly 4s
You may feel unsupported and angry with your mother. Perhaps you come across as independent, even bolshy, but you are probably quite unsure of your capabilities and are inclined to be aggressive when really you want to ask for help. Friends can help to build your self-esteem.

MAKING AND SUSTAINING FRIENDSHIPS

Successful friendships are often more flexible, more sustaining and more enriching even than relationships with parents or lovers. Good friends support you, forgive you when you make mistakes and provide life-long pleasure. But if you are to have good friends, you must be a good friend.

Our first real friendships start between the ages of three and six. Children, and girls in particular, often develop one intense relationship in which they play out the scenarios of their adult lives: love, jealousy, betrayal and forgiveness. Ideally, this first love teaches children to lead as well as to be led, to stand up for themselves, but also to forgive and forget, to stand up for each other and to recognize the other person's point of view. Good, sustaining, early friendships make the best possible basis for later partnerships, but not everyone starts out so well. You may have had some of the following difficulties:

- Changed schools very frequently.
- Were bullied.
- Had difficulties with your work that made you feel bad about yourself.
- Had trouble at home which made you turn inward, away from other children.
- Felt different because of the colour of your skin, your clothes, your religion.
- Learned that "strangers" are always dangerous.

As a result, you may still be afraid of new people and hypersensitive to criticism. People who cannot make friends often believe that the world is hostile to them, but all too often it is they who are sending out go-away signals. Think, for example, about the effects on others of the following:

- Only smiling at others if they smile at you first.
- Avoiding casual conversation with people you do not know for fear that they will "take advantage".
- Avoiding eye contact when someone talks to you and answering any questions with the shortest possible response.

If this sounds like you, it may not be easy to change, but it will be worth it.

BEING A GOOD FRIEND

Practise being friendly. Start with someone easy – the person you buy your newspaper from, for instance – and see how people begin to respond positively to you. Be the first to smile when greeting someone. You may have to push yourself to start with, but it will gradually get easier. Remember that friendship, like all good relationships, must be worked at.

If you have been isolated for a long time, you have probably not yet learned how to give as well as how to take friendship. Above all, it is important to learn not to judge too harshly. A good friend should be able to:

- Forgive your absence when you fall in love, but will be hurt if you never phone.
- Listen to hours of misery when you lose your job, your love or your figure, but expect you to listen to her misery too.
- Listen to you babbling on about your baby as long as you also make time to see her alone.
- Tell you when you are making a fool of yourself without making you feel worse.

66 Friendships last so long because they are flexible. They can ride out periods of separation but they need sustaining too. **99**

POSITIVE SIGNALS

■ Talk to people at the supermarket, in trains and at work. Initiate conversation – don't wait to be talked to.
■ When someone talks to you, look them in the eye and give a full answer, then ask them a question in turn.

LOVE, PARTNERSHIP AND SEXUALITY

- SEXUAL ATTRACTION • HOW SEX WORKS
- DISCOVERING YOUR SEXUAL FEELINGS
- ASSERTIVE SEXUALITY • COMMON SEXUAL DIFFICULTIES

CONNECTION, INTIMACY, ECSTASY: our drive toward sexual love is almost as strong as our need to eat. It is the underlying theme of most of our literature as well as our lives. But for most of us, sexual fulfilment is not enough on its own. It is a means of moving into a deeper connection with another human being, a way of breaching the walls of our separateness. It is this, as well as the desire for intimacy and the fear of rejection, that often makes sexual love feel as dangerous as it is delightful. According to psychoanalyst Michael Balint, sexual love is about needing to be loved "always, everywhere and in every way, my whole body, my whole being – without any criticism, without the slightest effort on my part".

SEARCHING FOR THE OTHER HALF

While our unconscious desire may be for unconditional love, deep down most of us understand that this is really only possible between parents and children. If we go into relationships looking for unconditional love, we will almost certainly be disappointed. A partnership in which each person is looking for a parent is likely to collapse the first time that either one really needs support. Small children do not want to support their parents; they want to be the centre of their parents' world and may scream until they get what they want. In an equal, adult relationship, each partner needs to be honest about their needs and expectations.

NAME: **Michèle Roberts**
OCCUPATION: **Novelist**
AGE: **46**

"Our relationship is about allowing both of us to be what we want to be. About pleasure, and work, and a commitment to each other. And it is an adventure in itself. Going deeper and deeper into the other person. It's been fantastic to feel so loved. I have never felt that before. My marriage isn't a wall around us, it is a safe place from which to go out into the world. It satisfies a deep need for intimacy and love and at the same time encourages me to be more daring as a writer."

FEAR OF LONELINESS

While some of us demand too much from a relationship and are unable to give back in equal measure, others may demand too little and rush into the arms of the first person who asks, in case no other opportunity comes along. Fear of being alone in a world of couples is not a good reason for getting into, or staying in, a relationship. The fear of being alone is, above all, fear of your own company, and if you really do not feel that you are good enough company even for yourself, then you cannot expect to be valued by anyone else (see pages 12–13). This fear-induced caution is probably keeping you from the very thing you most want. We use the words "falling in love" advisedly. To love someone wholeheartedly is like falling from a cliff believing that, at the bottom, there will be someone to catch you. To fall this way takes courage, trust and a belief that life is fundamentally good. It is a risk worth taking and to settle for less is to cheat yourself.

SEXUAL ATTRACTION
A good sexual relationship should be based on mutual love and trust.

SEXUAL ATTRACTION

The spark that lights up a relationship and separates it from friendship is sexual attraction. It is not something you can knowingly control or even understand. For some, the spark will come slowly, when you have already started to know the other person and have begun to find out whether there is enough trust and understanding to take things further. Often, however, it is the power of sexual attraction that comes first and you have no way of doing a reality check – deciding whether this person really does share your outlook or understand your faults – until you are already deeply involved. If you are a head-over-heels type of person, you owe it to yourself to take care, not just of your body, but of your emotions too.

DECIDING ABOUT SEX

The decision you make about sex will be influenced by far more than the feelings of the moment. Each of us carries around ideas and inhibitions implanted by our parents, religion and the social expectations of the time and place in which we live. Often these shared beliefs provide a useful framework to help us make decisions about sex. But there may be times when desires are in conflict with convention and decisions have to be made without much help. At some point in life we all discover that sexual freedom comes with responsibilities. Pleasure is only one side of the sexual coin; the other side is pain. If you value yourself, learn to play carefully (see right).

NEGOTIATING SAFE SEX

■ Go as slow as you want. You are giving another person access to your body and nobody has the right to take, or touch, what has not been offered.

■ Take responsibility for the way you feel. If you want to have sex, be honest with yourself. Do not blame your partner for going too far.

■ Be responsible toward your partner. Sex opens people to difficult emotions. Be honest and expect honesty in return.

■ Protect your body and your partner's body too. Sexually transmitted infections are very common and can infect anyone. Use condoms in all new sexual relationships (see page 76).

HOW SEX WORKS

Our bodies are wired for sex. Feelings of sexual arousal are transmitted to our brains by a complex web of nerves encouraging us to do more of what excites and stimulates us. In response, the slower, cruder, physical matter of muscles and blood get moving, leading, if we let it, to a climax of feeling. Knowing how we work can help that process and can heighten pleasure.

FEMALE SEXUAL AROUSAL The whole body is an erogenous zone. The right hand on your arm or breath in your ear can be enough to bring you out in prickles of anticipation. Most women find that their breasts are particularly sensitive, but the centre of all this sensation is sited in the pelvis and most specifically in the clitoris. Found at the top of the labia and protected by its folds, the clitoris is the nerve centre of sexual feelings. It behaves just like the penis during sexual arousal and orgasm (see below). However, the network of veins and nerves in the pelvic region makes the whole vaginal area extremely sensitive. For some women, pressure on the G-spot (located about halfway up the front wall of the vagina) can be sufficiently stimulating to trigger orgasm without the clitoris being touched. Other women prefer direct stimulation of the clitoris.

SEXUAL ANATOMY

THE VULVA
The clitoris contains a bundle of nerves that connect to all other parts of the pelvic area. The inner lips (labia minora) swell and change colour during sexual arousal. The outer lips (labia majora) open as you become aroused. The vaginal entrance can be particularly sensitive. Many women find that the vagina becomes more sensitive after they have had children.

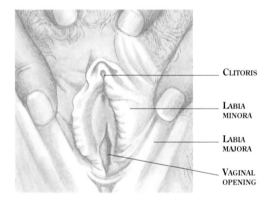

CLITORIS

LABIA MINORA

LABIA MAJORA

VAGINAL OPENING

THE PENIS
The penis, like the clitoris, contains erectile tissue that fills with blood during arousal, making it larger, harder and darker. The head (glans) is very sensitive to stimulation from tongue, hand or vaginal walls. During ejaculation, muscle contractions squeeze semen out of the penis. This contains sperm produced by the testes (in the scrotum) and seminal fluid produced by the prostate gland, which is near the bladder.

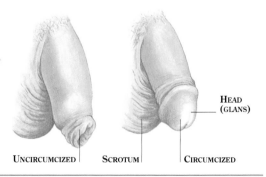

HEAD (GLANS)

UNCIRCUMCIZED   SCROTUM   CIRCUMCIZED

FEMALE SEXUAL RESPONSE

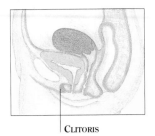

| CLITORIS

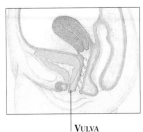

| VULVA

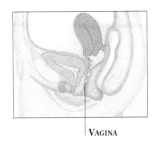

| VAGINA

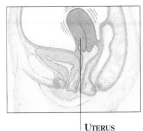

| UTERUS

1 It may just take a glance, or the touch of a bare arm against yours. Your clitoris starts to swell and lengthen, sending out rippling signals along the length of its complex system of nerves throughout the pelvic region.

2 If stimulation increases, the clitoris continues to swell until it is erect, and the vulva and vagina deepen in colour as blood begins to fill up the tissues in the whole pelvic area. Your vagina starts to feel wet and your uterus rises up inside the pelvic cavity.

3 If the clitoris is stimulated with a tongue, finger and/or penis (for most women a penis thrusting does not provide enough direct stimulation to achieve orgasm), the tissues of the vagina swell and the head of the clitoris might draw back and disappear. Don't stop now, you are on the verge of orgasm.

4 If the right stimulation continues, you may reach orgasm – a series of involuntary, rhythmic contractions of the vagina, uterus, anus and urethra, during which tension is released in waves that echo through your body. Then the blood flows back out of the pelvic area, leaving you feeling relaxed.

MALE SEXUAL AROUSAL This follows a very similar pattern to our own. It starts with some kind of stimulation. For some men, the sight of a breast (even under a thick winter coat) is sufficient to send blood rushing to the penis, making it stiffen, thicken and become erect. Other men may need to be touched and stroked to achieve an erection, and even then may not always respond. Men vary just as much as women in what they like. Some seem to feel only with their penis. Others like to be caressed elsewhere: the nipples, inner thighs or around the anus are common areas of sensitivity. Some men prefer touching to being touched, and others will enjoy it best when their partner takes over. Experimentation will help you to discover what excites you both (see page 104).

Whole books have been written about the embarrassment caused by the apparently uncontrollable penis, and most men, and women, will have some experience of an occasion when the lights were low, the opportunity presented itself and nothing happened. While it is true that men have little conscious control over erections, it has never been true that a man with an erection has no control over his behaviour. There is no point at which a man cannot stop, even if he does not want to.

Once an erection has happened, continued stimulation is usually necessary to reach orgasm, though some (usually young) men may reach orgasm without even making contact (known as premature ejaculation). Most men can get the right stimulation from moving the penis in and out of the vagina, but many also like to be sucked or stimulated by hand. At the point of climax, orgasm occurs: a series of rhythmic contractions during which sperm is ejaculated. Afterward the penis becomes flaccid again.

DISCOVERING YOUR SEXUAL FEELINGS

Tiny children touch themselves without inhibition. Then they grow a little older
and learn to keep their hands away from "down there". Some seem to forget that
it feels good to touch until the hormones of puberty switch the electric current
of sexual feelings back on. Unfortunately, by this time, many young women have
developed inhibitions about touching themselves at all and, instead of exploring,
they wait for a Prince Charming to kiss them awake. Sadly, Prince Charming is
likely to be too busy sorting out his own new feelings to act as teacher and, as
most women soon discover, if you want a job well done, it is better to learn how
to do it yourself. Start by looking at the pictures on the previous page, then find
a time when you can be completely alone and undisturbed.

SEX IN YOUR HEAD

Sexuality is not just physical; it starts in the imagination. Think about the people
and situations that arouse you. You may want to read something (women tend to
be more responsive to ideas than pictures) to get you going. Let your imagination
go and enjoy the feelings that your thoughts arouse.

EXPLORE YOUR BODY

Find out what you like. Allow yourself to enjoy the feeling of stroking your own
bare skin. Explore inside and feel the ribbed walls of your vagina. See what feels
good for you. Some women like to rub quite hard on their clitoris; others prefer
a lighter touch.

   You may find you can intensify the sensations by putting a finger inside your
vagina or you may find that it distracts you. When you discover something that
feels right, keep going. You may reach orgasm quite quickly or you may feel that
you will never get there. On the first few occasions it can take a very long time
to reach the necessary level of stimulation. Once you know how to reach orgasm
you can find ways of intensifying the sensations so that it is easier in future.

TEACH YOUR PARTNER

Once you have let yourself think about and feel your own sensuality you will be
more confident about what you really want. For example, if your mind and body
tell you that you love women, not men, you are less likely to blame yourself for
not responding to a man's desire. We are all different. Not only are we attracted
to different people, we enjoy different things. Your own explorations will help you
to guide your partner so that you both get as much as you can from making love.
According to Shere Hite, in her ground-breaking book, *The Hite Report*, only a
minority of women achieve orgasm with male partners through intercourse alone.
Some prefer manual stimulation before (or instead of) penetration, and most like
to be stimulated, or to stimulate themselves, during penetration. You need to take
time to find out what you like and to let your partner know. But the idea is not to
learn how to be an A+ lover; there are no exams in lovemaking and no amount of
technique can take the place of feelings. Love will transform even a fumbling first
time into a magical experience.

ASSERTIVE SEXUALITY

Good sex is not just about love and sharing, it is also, ultimately, a bit selfish. To get the most out of sex you need to be able to ask for what you want, to allow yourself to linger and to open yourself up entirely to sensation. And you will want to give your partner the same opportunity because it is deeply satisfying to make love with someone who is lost in the sensations you are creating together.

EXPLORE POSITIONS　If you want your partner's penis inside you during orgasm, it might help to find ways in which either he, or you, can touch your clitoris at the same time. This is least likely to happen if he is lying on top of you. Try sitting astride your partner or position yourselves like "spoons", side by side, with your back tucked against him. This position helps if, like some women, you can only reach orgasm with your legs together.

NON-VERBAL COMMUNICATION　You do not have to issue a stream of instructions. You can tell your partner what you want through the sound of your pleasure, or by guiding his (or her) hand.

> 66 A hand under the skirt can create much more heat than the same hand in the same place when you are naked in bed. 99

USE YOUR WHOLE BODY
Find a time when you are both relaxed to explore each other's bodies slowly.

COMMON SEXUAL DIFFICULTIES

We are surrounded by sex. Books, films, television, advertising hoardings – everywhere we look we see people in various states of pretended arousal. Indeed, there is now so much information to be had about sexual behaviour and sex that you could be forgiven for assuming that it is something very difficult to do, for which we all require lessons. Seeing sex everywhere can also lead to feelings of inadequacy. As one woman explained, *"I spent much of my life feeling inadequate because, according to the book, I didn't 'do it' properly. I have felt so ashamed about it. I still fear that you will all despise me and think me odd. I have never masturbated. That took a great deal of courage to type"*.

There are really only five issues concerning sex that may lead to difficulties:

FIVE QUESTIONS TO ASK YOURSELF

DO YOU WANT TO HAVE SEX? If you do not want sex and are worried about it, you might like to consider why. Perhaps:

• You are very young and not physically ready for a sexual relationship. If this sounds like you, then wait, you have the rest of your life for falling in love.

• You have recently had a baby. Some women find that sexual desire falls off in the early months because they are tired and satiated with the physical closeness of the baby. Your feelings will come back; give yourself time.

• You are preoccupied with other things. As long as there is no one around who is expecting you to have sex, this should not cause problems.

• You feel you ought to be interested in men but aren't. Some women find it so hard to admit to themselves that they are attracted to their own sex that they cut off their feelings completely. If you can come to terms with your preferences, you may find that you are interested in sex after all. There are organizations and helplines that you can contact in confidence which may be able to help you clarify your preferences (see pages 187–88).

• You have had a very bad early experience of sex and you are afraid of opening up to another person. Women who have been raped or sexually abused may cut themselves off emotionally and physically from sexual contact. If this is your experience, counselling or therapy may help you to come to terms with your past and open up to sexual pleasure (see pages 187–88).

IS THERE SOMEONE YOU WANT TO HAVE SEX WITH? Why is it that some women fall into a new relationship within minutes of leaving the last, and others never seem to find Mr or Ms Right?

• You may have convinced yourself that it is because you are not sufficiently attractive, but whatever you might see on television, in real life it is not only the beautiful people who have mates. Long-term emotional connection is not achieved by wearing the right colour lipstick, and you can see that by taking a look around you. It is much more about being open to other people and not being afraid to show your feelings (see page 100).

• You may be hiding away so that you never meet any likely partners. If this sounds like you, think about making some changes to enable you to go out into the world and create opportunities.

• Perhaps you have closed yourself off from possible encounters because you are afraid of such a level of intimacy or you are not ready for a committed relationship. In this case, you will know when you feel ready, but don't wait too long for that knight on a white charger to sweep you off your feet.

DO YOU BOTH HAVE AN EQUAL DESIRE TO HAVE SEX? Incompatible levels of sexual desire are likely to be a feature of any long-standing relationship – don't panic.

• It is absolutely normal to go through periods in a relationship when one or other partner is less interested than usual. "Giving in" for the sake of your partner is unlikely to work because it will make you feel resentful. Furthermore, a male partner may be physically incapable of having intercourse when he is not "in the mood".

• What is most important is to keep the channels of communication between you open and to deal with any underlying anger and resentment that may be fuelling your feelings (see page 116). The partner who is still interested will almost certainly feel neglected and need some reassurance that lack of sexual interest does not mean lack of love.

• You may decide that you want to give your partner physical satisfaction even when you do not feel aroused yourself. Your partner can do the same, but this needs to be something given willingly, not something that is demanded.

• Perhaps this is just a seasonal change in desire, a switch from the passionate intensity of the early months to something deeper but less electrifying.

• Be honest with yourself. Are you sufficiently committed to each other to make an effort to find a way of rebalancing your sex life so that both of you feel loved? Or is it time to consider calling it off?

DO YOU TRUST YOUR PARTNER TO TAKE CARE OF YOUR BODY AND FEELINGS? Some people feel that risk adds to their pleasure in sex, but most of us prefer to feel relaxed and safe.

• It will be very difficult for you to let go and enjoy sex if, for example, your partner is unwilling to use condoms and you fear pregnancy or a sexually transmitted infection; if he, or she, pressurizes you into having sex when you are not ready or not relaxed; if you are afraid that he will hurt you, or simply roll off and lose interest when you are only halfway there.

• You need to be able to talk about these things to your partner and if you cannot, you may be better off without him or her.

ARE YOU BOTH ENJOYING THE SEX YOU HAVE? You may be hopelessly in love, feel aroused at first sight and have plenty of opportunity for sex, but still not be enjoying it. Look back at pages 100–107 and consider whether:

• You know enough about your own reactions to tell your partner what you like.

• You are able to talk about what you like without feeling embarrassed and that your partner is able to listen to you.

• If this is early in your relationship, it may be that your partner is in too much of a hurry or that you are just not relaxed enough to enjoy it – or both.

EARLY EJACULATION

You can help your partner to control his ejaculation by putting your forefinger and thumb around his penis, high up, where you can feel a bulge all round. As he comes close to orgasm, squeeze firmly, pressing underneath with your thumb. His penis may start to go soft, but the erection will come back again. If necessary, repeat the action. Between you, you will learn to co-ordinate your responses.

PAINFUL PENETRATION

If you are not fully lubricating and opening up, it may be painful when he tries to insert his penis.

■ It may simply be that he is in too much of a hurry to get inside you and that more time for sexual arousal is needed.

■ Some women prefer not to be penetrated at all and to be stimulated by their lover's hands, mouth or some other part of their body. Since sex is about pleasure, it makes sense only to do the things that feel pleasurable.

■ If you both want to have penetrative sex, but you find you are closing up every time he tries, slow right down. Find every other way you can of giving each other pleasure. It may take time to build up the necessary trust. If he is insensitive and demanding, he will make the situation worse.

CONSIDERING PARENTHOOD

- FROM PARTNERS TO PARENTS
- BEING A LONE PARENT • MOTHER, LOVE YOURSELF
- STEPMOTHERS

THE DECISION TO HAVE A BABY IS RARELY RATIONAL. We have all heard about the bad nights, financial hardship and lack of freedom parenthood can bring, and yet a clear majority of women are still prepared to take the risk and opt for children. Fortunately, few of us are ever asked to explain our motives or even to explore them. We would find it hard to do so because the impulse to be a mother is tied to deeply submerged memories of our own childhood. Sometimes we are impelled to reproduce by the desire to recreate those memories, and sometimes in the hope of correcting them, but we rarely try to understand what is driving us. Those who decide against motherhood are not often any more rational in their decision-making than those who decide in favour.

Yet today women are finding, increasingly, that they are forced to rationalize. They recognize that it may be very hard to be a top-flight lawyer or war correspondent, flying around the world at the drop of a hat, while at the same time giving their children the care and attention that they need. Where men have always been able to rely on women to provide the consistent caring while they rule the world, the reverse is rarely possible. Some women deeply resent this double standard, but for others the choice to be child-free has brought new freedom.

NAME: **Josephine Ward**

OCCUPATION:

Civil servant

AGE: **48**

"I was the oldest of four. My parents were completely thrown off course by my father being made redundant. They simply couldn't provide stability and security for a family. There was no malice there. They just couldn't cope. As the oldest I was held responsible for the younger children but it wasn't a role that I sought, or accepted. At 12 I remember looking at my mother and thinking, 'I am not going to let this happen to me'. I felt sorry for her. She did not have a happy childhood and nor did her mother; I didn't want to perpetuate a pattern. I've been married for 15 years and we are very happy alone."

KNOWING WHEN YOU ARE READY

Even if we do not know why we want children, we can decide when we want to have them. Your desire to have a baby may be so strong that you just want to go for it. Often things turn out fine. Some partners seem to want the decision to be made for them and, if you are alone, you may feel secure in the support of family and friends, but think carefully. If you are thinking about getting pregnant, or are faced with a *fait accompli*, consider the following:

WILL YOU WANT TO CONTINUE WORKING? You will certainly want to go on being an autonomous individual, but deciding to have a baby will totally change your life.
• Could you combine a major commitment outside work with your job?
• Do you feel confident enough at work to say, "No, I won't work overtime tonight. My child needs me at home"?
• Would your work colleagues support your right to put your children first?
• Do you feel that you have got as far as you wish to get at work and that a temporary lull will do no harm?
• Would you welcome a period out of the workplace to reorientate your life? Would it be possible to do that now?
• Financially, can you afford to devote less time to work, or give up altogether for a while?
• Would you be able to get back into work easily if you did take a break?

HOW WILL PARENTHOOD AFFECT YOUR LIFE AND YOUR RELATIONSHIP? There are some issues that you can try to tackle in advance, but do not set your decisions in stone. Be prepared to change your mind when babies arrive.
• If you and your partner live together, have you discussed having children?
• Have you decided who will provide primary care or whether you will share it?
• If your partner will take primary responsibility, have you jointly considered what this would mean if you decided to part?
• If your partner is ambivalent, have you given him a chance to explain why?
• If you do stop work, would your partner support you happily or would this be a point of contention?
• If you do not have a permanent relationship, will you be able to cope with the emotional, financial and practical problems of lone parenthood?
• If you have been tempted to force a decision by getting pregnant and facing the consequences afterward, have you considered that your partner might feel angry and leave? He might feel that since it was your decision he does not need to take any responsibility and might find it difficult to trust you in future. If you feel strongly enough about having a baby to cope with these possibilities, perhaps you should discuss the strength of your feelings in advance.
• If you have not felt able to talk this through with your partner, what chances do you think you have of an open, honest relationship after the baby is born?
• If you are not living together or are not in a long-term relationship, what kind of relationship do you hope your partner will have with your child?
• If you have no relationship with the father, do you believe you have the right to take this decision alone? Will you be able to explain this to your child?

66 My partner and I planned to have children but I am now bringing them up alone. It was something very strong driving me. I made no sensible plans. I had no idea what motherhood would mean. I just wanted it. 99

SEE ALSO
•PAGE 111 Being a Lone Parent
•PAGE 146 The Cost of Working

FROM PARTNERS TO PARENTS

The baby arrives. You may be captivated, you may be devastated, you may be numb or just plain exhausted. In the first weeks you will have little time to think and even less time to talk to your partner, and you may find that you are drifting apart. You may resent him leaving for work in the morning and feel jealous of his attachment to the adult world. He may feel excluded from your charmed circle. Of course it helps to talk, but it may seem impossible, not just because of the lack of time, but because each of you is afraid of what the other is thinking.

You may be afraid that he is not really interested in the baby, but he may be hanging back because he is afraid of his incompetence. You both need the courage to say what is on your mind and the courage to listen to what the other person is saying without feeling threatened by it.

Too often the unsaid little things are pushed down because both of you are being careful with each other's feelings. Then something will set you off and they will come tumbling out. The exercise below will give you a chance to deal with negative feelings as well as positive ones in a calm and unhurried way.

MAKING TIME TO TALK TO EACH OTHER

Choose a time when you will have at least one hour undisturbed. You may need to ask someone to look after the baby. Make sure you are feeling comfortable. Promise that you will not interrupt or correct each other, even if you feel what is said is unreasonable. You are finding out how the other person feels, and the feeling is valid even if the facts are not.

1 Each of you should write down three positive things that you feel about being a parent.

2 Now write down three negative things you feel about being a parent. Tell each other what you have written down, keeping something positive to end with.

ALLOW FIVE MINUTES TO THINK ABOUT WHAT HAS BEEN SAID BEFORE RESPONDING.

3 Make at least one suggestion to each other about something that you could do to make the other person feel better.

4 Make at least one suggestion of something you could do to make things better for yourself.

• If you find writing things down too awkward, you may prefer to take it in turns to talk, five minutes at a time, promising not to interrupt or to correct, but only to talk about the way you feel. Again, offer each other something to take away that shows you have been listening.

HER RESPONSE

Positive
1 *When she falls asleep in my arms I feel I could burst with happiness.*
2...
3...

Negative
1 *Every morning when you go I feel abandoned.*
2...
3...

HIS RESPONSE

Positive
1 *I feel really grown up for the first time in my life.*
2...
3...

Negative
1 *Feeling incompetent when she cries and you take her away.*
2...
3...

HER RESPONSE

For you
1 *Trusting you to look after her and not taking over the minute she cries.*
2...
3...

For myself
1 *I could join a mother and baby group.*
2...
3...

HIS RESPONSE

For you
1 *I could ring you from work to tell you how much I miss you both.*
2...
3...

For myself
1 *I could read a book on childcare.*
2...
3...

BEING A LONE PARENT

Some women choose lone parenthood, but for most it is an unwelcome outcome to what should have been a joint venture. You may feel resentful, you will often feel physically and emotionally tired, and you will almost certainly be under financial pressure, but lone parenthood is not all bad, it can be very rewarding too.

THE UPSIDE

Being a lone parent means that you will do everything your way. You will never have to argue about who puts the children to bed, what time bedtime should be, or whether it is alright to watch television while eating. With only one set of rules in the house, you should be able to provide clear and consistent boundaries for your children. Young children are tremendously loyal; they will return your love even if they are missing their father.

THE DOWNSIDE

If you are the only person to enforce the rules, you will be the only person to feel the force of your children's rage and that can be hard. If you are the focus of their love, it will be up to you to help them disengage as they grow up, which can be painful. It takes strength to be the only person in your children's lives and there are times when you will not want to be strong. You will miss having an adult to give you a hug at the end of the day and remind you that you are important too.

SUPPORT FOR YOU

To get the most out of being a parent you need time for yourself as well as time with your kids and, as a lone parent, that means creating a network of support from friends and relations. A support network is not just good for you, it is also good for your children. They will feel more secure if they know that there is a circle of adults whom they can trust and who care for them.

If you are lucky, your family will step in. If you have no close family to rely on, a circle of friends can provide the same kind of support. Other lone parents are often the most reliable source of friendship because you all know how much you need each other. Your children can help you to make friends. Many a firm friendship has grown between mothers of children who met at nursery school.

SUPPORT FOR YOUR CHILDREN

You may be the best mother there is, but your children will benefit from spending time with other people. Children learn about themselves and their place in the world from the people around them and it helps if they have close relationships with a variety of adults. By creating support for yourself you are also creating support for them. You might:

- Join a mother and baby group; many of them grow out of antenatal classes and keep going until the children start primary school.
- Find out if there are organized lone-parent groups in your area.
- Organize a lone-parent group yourself with the help of local health workers.
- Let children break the ice; where they are, parents are never far behind.

LEARN TO LISTEN

Fear of strangers has become a major worry for all parents, but you will do your children more harm by teaching them fear than by teaching them trust. Children know if a relationship is wrong, so listen to what they tell you. If there are lots of people in your children's life, they will avoid the ones who make them feel bad and move toward those with whom they feel safe. Experiences of good relationships will enable them to recognize and turn away from bad ones.

Mother, Love Yourself

"Once there was a princess and anybody who went near her would cry. They would cry because she was so sad and because she held the power of sadness."

This is the opening of a story written by a nine-year-old. In the story all the people get weak and ill because they are too sad to eat, but in the end, the princess is given the power of love and all the sick people get well.

Children's stories are full of queens and princesses because children are acutely aware of the power that adults have to make life good or bad. If Mother is in a good mood, the world is a benign place. If she is miserable, life is sad. But mothers are not supernatural and it is hard to generate happiness when you feel like hiding. If mothers are to wield the power of happiness in their homes, they have to feel happy and that involves taking their own needs as seriously as they take the needs of their families. If you are feeling swamped and used up by the needs of others, sit down with a friend and make a plan. It does not need to be too ambitious, you just need to set some time aside for yourself.

CREATING TIME FOR YOURSELF

ELICE'S IDEAS

1 **Draw three boxes.** In the first, write down something you can do for yourself this week.

2 In the second, something you can plan regularly.

3 In the third, something you plan for the future.

This week	**Regularly**	**In the future**
I will send the kids to a friend's house and have a hot, candle-lit bath with aromatherapy oils. I will lock the door and put my favourite music on.	*I will go for a swim or to an aerobics class once a week, on my own.*	*Go back to college. I will find a course that really interests me and I will be disciplined about attending and completing the work.*

NEW MOTHERS

SURVIVAL STRATEGIES

If you are exhausted, do not be afraid to ask for help.

■ If you are alone, sleep whenever your baby sleeps, ignore the housework and accept any offers of help.

■ If your partner or a friend can cook a meal and wash up while the baby sleeps, you, too, will be able to rest.

■ If you have a partner, share the night feeds. If you are bottle-feeding, you can alternate nights. If you are breast-feeding, your partner can look after the baby after the early morning feed so that you can get a couple more hours of sleep.

New motherhood is like a big dipper ride. One moment you are on top of the world, the next moment you want it to stop so that you can get off. The arrival of a baby can herald pleasure and delight, but also stress, strain and anxiety. Your mood will probably stabilize with your baby's sleep patterns.

Periods of depression are common in the early days, but if the feeling persists you may need help. Signs might include some of the following feelings:

• You will never be any good as a mother.
• You should never have had a baby.
• You care about nothing and no-one.
• You will never stop crying.
• Life will never get any better.
• You are alone.

If extra help (see left) does not seem to shift your mood, talk to your family doctor. Postnatal depression can be treated (see pages 187–88) and the sooner you get help the better for all of you.

THE PRESCHOOL YEARS

If you enjoy playing, these can be some of the best years of parenthood. You will get enormous pleasure from stimulating your children and they will reward you with their growing creativity. On the other hand, you may find sandpits and potato prints boring, and long for the moment when you can sit your offspring in front of the television and get some time to yourself.

If this sounds like you, don't torture yourself. Your children know when you are happy being with them. They also know when you are not and would rather be somewhere else. Look for a playgroup or nursery (or even a friend's) where your children can cover themselves in paint in the company of people who really enjoy it and you can read a book, go to the gym or meet a friend. Then make the time to do the things that you like doing with them, such as cuddles and stories and walks in the park.

THE TERRIBLE TEENS

The early school years are often the easiest. It is when children reach their teens that the difficulties of the early years return – magnified. Once again you will be woken at night, only this time it will be to rescue them from a party at 1am.

Again there will be tantrums, only it is much more difficult to hold a tall 16-year-old in your arms until he calms down. This time you will have to cope with the fact that your child has to find some way of separating from you and yet still needs you as much as he or she has ever done.

It will be a time of turmoil for your teenager, but perhaps also for you. Pulling up the roots you have nurtured for so long hurts. You will feel unloved, you will be constantly challenged, you will compare your fading colour and thickening waist with your daughter's growing beauty. You will need, more than you have ever needed, people around you to remind you that you are doing okay. If you have a good relationship with your partner, you can help each other through this onslaught. If you are alone, or unhappy in your relationship, you will need to draw strength from elsewhere. Old friendships will be invaluable, but make a point of meeting the parents of your children's friends if you can. You will have much in common and can give each other a lot of support.

TEENAGERS
Moving on into lives of their own.

STEPMOTHERS

Stepmothers have always had a bad press. Cinderella's turned her into a kitchen slave; Snow White and the Babes in the Wood were nearly murdered by theirs. There is more than a kernel of truth at the centre of these fairytales; step-relationships are hard. It takes patience and a great deal of understanding, but it is possible and very rewarding to build a good relationship with your stepchildren.

NAME: **Susan Adams**
OCCUPATION: **Solicitor**
AGE: **32**

"At the start I felt unreasonably jealous of Jim. I knew that this five-year-old had a hold on his father that would last forever and always take precedence over me. Gradually, as I became more secure about my relationship with his father, I was able to relax and get to know Jim. Now I can honestly say that I love him and that I think he really likes me. I am not a mother to him, I am a friend and that is a very privileged relationship to have with a child."

STEP-RELATIONSHIPS
You can establish a mutually satisfying relationship.

If you want a good, mutually satisfying relationship, you will have to do the building yourself. It might help to consider the following:

• There is no reason why your partner's children should love you (or even like you), you have to earn their respect.

• You have no rights over your partner's children. If you are likely to be left in sole charge at any time, the limits of your authority should be agreed, among all of you, in advance.

• Stepchildren do not have the right to be rude to you. Your partner can be understanding, but he should always stand up for you.

• You may feel that your partner indulges them, but keep your feelings to yourself until you can discuss them calmly when the children are not there.

• If you have children of your own, try to agree on basic house rules.

One of the biggest barriers to a good step-parenting relationship is the baggage left behind by separation or divorce. Adults often underestimate the power of a child's feelings. It may be convenient to assume that the ex-wife is poisoning the children against you, but it might not be true: children can be angry in their own right. When a six-year-old says, "I'm going to take my Daddy away and lock him up and put you on the rubbish dump", it is difficult not to feel rejected. If instead of comforting you, your partner starts cuddling the child and saying how much he loves her, it is hard not to feel jealous or even angry. Yet this six-year-old is only saying out loud what she feels inside: that you have stolen her father. You have to find a way of letting her know you accept her relationship with her father and do not want to interfere with it. You might wish you could have your partner to yourself, but how much could you really respect a man who abandoned his children for you?

NAME: **Hannah Jones**
OCCUPATION: **Journalist**
AGE: **25**

"She was a witch. We were absolutely beastly to her for about ten years. Mostly we just ignored her. It wasn't hard to do because she is the kind of person who would do anything to avoid conflict. She seems to have only one emotion and that's jolly. It's horrifying. Even now we see our father's wife, not as a person, but as 'the other woman'. Quite honestly, I still can't see what he saw in her. Though I suppose that underneath we resent her for the fact that he would so obviously rather be with her than with any of us."

GRANDMOTHERS

Your first child is the ultimate rite of passage; a definitive marker of the end of childhood and the start of something new. It is a time to re-evaluate so many things, not least of which is your relationship with your mother and hers with you. It is a time when the rifts of adolescence can finally be repaired, when relationships that may have got stuck in old patterns can be changed. Mothers and daughters who have hardly spoken for years find that they have a common bond through the baby. You may feel that it is only in having a child that you are able to convince your parents that you have grown up. But this change can bring with it new and unexpected uncertainties, particularly for your mother, in a culture in which maturity in women is not valued. Unresolved fears and anxieties can clutter up attempts to forge new relationships on both sides. It may help both of you if you can understand some of the unspoken undercurrents:

• Jealousy. To be a mother is to have a certain kind of power. Now that power is being passed on to a new generation, your mother has to take a step back.

• Loss. A new child may remind your mother that her own mothering days are over; if motherhood was the centre of her life, she will feel loss.

• Insecurity. If your mother is used to being the centre of family life, she will now have to work out how to fit into the family that you have constructed. She may feel unsure about how to do so, or even whether you want her to.

• Uncertainty. Should she offer help or wait to be asked? Rushing in with advice that is rejected can lead to hurt. Hanging back for fear of being thought interfering may be interpreted as unhelpfulness.

• Anxiety. She may worry about your ability to manage – especially if you are young or the new baby is unwell.

• Worry. She may feel that she is expected to go back to her previous mothering role and that the responsibility for the care of the child will fall on her and threaten her independent life.

If you are used to talking to your mother about sensitive issues, this period of transition may be uncomplicated and you can look forward to deeper friendship and loving support. If not, you may feel that you are either being swamped or starved. Try to find the words to tell her what you want, rather than leaving her to guess. You are unlikely to find more willing help.

POSITIVE SUPPORT

It may help to keep the following in mind:

■ Every child will benefit from having extra, loving adults in his or her life.

■ An enduring relationship between grandparents and grandchild is important for its own sake.

■ It is good to share some childcare with the grandmother: she may well be the only person you trust to care for your child.

■ If a grandmother offers help or advice that you disagree with or think wrong, explain that you need to do things your way, but that you do value her support.

■ Every grandmother has a right to her own life. Set boundaries and be clear about what she is willing to contribute in order to lessen the chance of families taking advantage.

DEALING WITH CONFLICT

- JEALOUSY • VIOLENCE IN A RELATIONSHIP
- CONFLICT RESOLUTION • WHEN A RELATIONSHIP ENDS
- PROTECTING CHILDREN • CREATING A NEW LIFE

CONFLICT WITHIN A RELATIONSHIP is not always bad. It can be stimulating, and resolving a conflict can lead to a new and deeper understanding. But repetitive cycles of conflict that go nowhere can kill a relationship. If you can identify what triggers an argument and change your habitual responses, it is possible to break the cycle. Sometimes misunderstandings between men and women arise not from differences of opinion, but because men and women communicate in different ways. Men, for example, are more likely to be combative than women, and respond more positively to direct questions. Women often find it impossible to break into male conversation because their own style encourages participation and they don't know how to claim space in a more competitive arena. As a result, men accuse women of being imprecise and women find men aggressive.

PATTERNS IN CONFLICT

Cycles of conflict follow patterns. If one person is able to change the pattern, it can break the cycle. It is easier to change your own pattern than someone else's. The following suggestions might help:

- Do not expect other people to guess what you want. Make your intentions perfectly clear. Use language that cannot be misunderstood.
- To some people an indirect, or open-ended, question is a positive invitation to conversation; to others it feels like a trap.
- An aggressive response may be a defence against a perceived attack from you. Do not respond in kind – it will only escalate the aggression – simply rephrase the question.
- If you find the other person intimidating, tell them so calmly, after you have resolved the matter and no longer feel wary.
- If you feel like bursting with rage, take time out. You should both leave the room for a specified period, then start again. Do not analyse your behaviour or emotions; return to the issue.
- Try to monitor your body language. If you stand, your partner might feel threatened. If you remain seated, this could work to reduce the tension.
- Speak firmly and quietly. Shouting and ranting are rarely useful in resolving conflict, though they are frequently the initial response.

HOW MEN AND WOMEN COMMUNICATE

- Women often seek consensus, using indirect questions to stimulate discussion. They tend to equalize relationships by matching experiences, for example, by saying, "It happened to me too".
- Men tend to dominate mixed conversation because they expect resistance and so keep talking to wipe out opposition. They prefer to ask questions that will elicit specific responses.

SEE ALSO

• PAGE 98 Making and Sustaining Friendships
• PAGES 122–23 Conflict Resolution

ANNA AND BRAD'S ARGUMENT

Anna and Brad have lived together for two years, but their relationship is now in danger of breaking up due to constant, meaningless quarrels. This argument is a typical example that illustrates their patterns of conflict. Anna would like to book a holiday with Brad. She is afraid of a fight so she avoids eye contact with him and approaches the subject indirectly.

THE ARGUMENT

Anna – *"What are you doing tomorrow, Brad?"*

ANNA wants to book a holiday, but broaches the subject with an indirect question and doesn't state what she wants.

Brad – *"Why do you want to know?"*

BRAD feels the open-ended question traps him into giving the "wrong answer".

Brad – *"Stop trying to control me. I'm going out."*

BRAD responds as he did when, as a child, his mother told him off for upsetting his sister. He storms out, leaving the issue unresolved.

Anna – *"No need to bite my head off, I was only asking."*

ANNA interprets Brad's response as a rejection and retorts in a defensive way.

Anna – *"You never tell me what you're doing."*

ANNA starts to whine. She has still not said what she actually wants.

Brad – *"I wasn't biting your head off. Why are you so sensitive?"*

BRAD is reminded by Anna's tone of his little sister, who always got her own way by crying. He feels manipulated and fights back.

RESOLVING THE ARGUMENT

Anna does not need to change her style completely to avoid conflict. She needs to be aware of the potential traps, and deal with them accordingly.

Anna – *"Shall we go out to book the holiday tomorrow?"*

Brad – *"Can I check what I'm doing and let you know?"*

ANNA'S direct question clearly states her intentions. Brad knows what he is responding to but may not react as she wants.

BRAD, by putting her off, disempowers Anna. Subconsciously, he needs to feel in charge.

Anna – *"I want to make plans for tomorrow, so can we decide now?"*

ANNA can feel irritation rising and the cycle of conflict starting again.

Brad – *"Stop nagging. I'll let you know when I'm ready."*

BRAD is feeling pressurized and retaliates by holding his ground. If Anna responds to this attack, they will argue. She must stick to the issue, and avoid both the attack and Brad's attempt to take the initiative. She leaves the room to collect her thoughts. On returning she says what she wants.

Anna – *"I really want to do this together. If you can't make tomorrow, can we fix a date that suits us both?"*

ANNA not only states her intentions, but sounds as if she means it.

CONCLUSION

Anna has given Brad a concrete proposal and offered him space to state his views. If Brad follows the suggestions opposite, next time he could be the one who breaks the cycle.

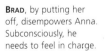

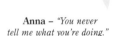

JEALOUSY

Jealousy is the reason why you sat down and cried or lashed out with rage when another child was given an ice cream and you were told to be content with an apple; the misery mixed with anger when you heard your best friend whispering about you with your arch enemy; the suffocating anguish you recognize as an adult when you suspect that the one you love is with another. Jealousy is a nasty, mean emotion; we all feel it and we feel bad about it, and because we feel so guilty about feeling it, we find it hard to acknowledge. If we let jealousy grow, it can destroy the relationships we most treasure.

When we are on the receiving end of jealousy, we are equally likely to ignore its real meaning. We are all familiar with the taunt, "you are just jealous". Why *just* jealous when we know from our own experience that jealousy is so painful?

WHERE JEALOUSY STARTS

In the beginning, an infant believes that she is the centre of the universe and that her mother belongs exclusively to her. The first jealousy of all is said to be the feeling a child has for the father who walks in and takes the mother away. The second time jealousy overwhelms us may well be the moment when a younger sibling arrives and moves into the love and the lap that we have occupied alone. The more secure we felt in the love of both our parents, the better insulated we are against the fear of loss in the future, but even the most devoted parents cannot insulate us entirely.

TRANSFORMING JEALOUSY

It doesn't take long for us to learn that jealousy is bad, but like many other emotions that we cannot simply cut out of the psyche, we learn either to submerge the nasty feeling and turn it against ourselves or turn it against the object of our feelings.

Jealousy turned inward becomes self-loathing. We feel that we are unworthy of love or unable to get what we want in life so we stop trying and turn ourselves into victims expecting to get kicked.

Jealousy turned outward becomes anger. We take the bad feelings inside and project them on to the person who we believe has robbed us of our love. Jealous rage can fuel murder or destroy friendship.

DEALING WITH JEALOUSY

If your partner really is having an affair with your best friend, you have a right to feel angry with them for betraying you, but if you live in constant fear that he is philandering, you may be making your life a misery for no purpose. Consider whether your jealousy might not be rooted in your own insecurities and feelings of inadequacy (see page 14). If you turn your fear into anger and destroy his CD collection, you will lose your dignity and will probably lose him too. Since jealousy is based on fear of loss, the best antidote to it is reassurance from loved ones, and you will get further by asking for reassurance than by turning your fear into anger and dumping it on the ones you love.

THE GREEN-EYED MONSTER STORY

Jean and Tandi had been friends since college. They lived together, shared each other's clothes, friends, confidences and dreams of promotion. When a plum job came up at Tandi's office, Jean encouraged her to apply, helped her choose the right clothes to wear, coached her for the interview, but never dreamed she would actually get the job. After the celebrations came the war.

JEAN AND TANDI'S STORY

Jean – *"From day one she was off into her new world. She never talked about anything else. She never thanked me for the help I gave her."*

JEAN was insanely jealous, but instead of recognizing why, she felt so upset that she projected her misery on to Tandi. So, rather than wholeheartedly joining in with her friend's pleasure, she looked for opportunities to find fault in an effort to create excuses for her own bad feelings.

Tandi – *"I was nervous and excited. The job meant longer hours, but when I got home longing to talk about it, Jean was never there, or if she was there, she would snipe at me and say she was tired."*

TANDI was high on her own success and didn't stop to ask herself why her friend was behaving like this. Had she been able to recognize Jean's pain and sense of loss, she might have been able to offer her reassurance.

Jean – *"How dare you have a go at me because I haven't washed up? You may think you're special, but I'm not going to wait on you."*

JEAN had left the dishes in the sink as a symbolic gesture – "I was here eating without you, please notice me" – but it made the situation worse, rather than better, and gave Jean an excuse to express all her bottled-up, infantile rage.

Tandi – *"This is the final straw. I invite this guy back from work and the sink is overflowing. It's really embarrassing."*

TANDI should have realized how upset Jean was, but it would have taken a saint to ask the questions that needed to be asked at this point: "What is the matter; why are you angry with me; can we sit down and talk about it?" By taking her friend's rage at face value, Tandi was throwing away a relationship that could have grown deeper and stronger.

Jean – *"We used to be such good mates. When something funny happens at work I think, 'I must tell Tandi about that', then realize I can't. It really hurts."*

JEAN, initially riddled with jealousy, now feels real sadness, but she still hasn't understood that it was her jealousy, not Tandi's new job, that caused the rift between them. She is unable to reach out to her friend and ask her to forgive and forget.

Tandi – *"We just aren't getting on any more. We don't speak to each other. I feel sad about it because we used to be so close. I am looking for a new place to live, but I haven't told her yet."*

TANDI is now compounding Jean's feeling of being deserted. She has made no attempt to find out what is wrong and is now proposing to leave her without even discussing their difficulties.

ANALYSIS

JEAN was understandably jealous, not just because Tandi had landed the job they both dreamed of, but because she was losing her friend's company, the mutual support of someone "in the same boat" and the comfort of a shared dream. Jean was also facing up to the possibility of her own failure because, by making her dream a reality, Tandi had shown up the unreality of the vision that had comforted them both. Rather than examining her own feelings, Jean simply projected them on to Tandi.

TANDI could have helped Jean to cope with her feelings by being a little more sensitive toward her. The child who eats her sweets in front of her friend and never offers to share is partly responsible for the friend's anger. Tandi could have made more effort to help Jean feel included in her new life. By excluding her (perhaps inadvertently), Tandi compounded Jean's feelings of failure and loss. She could have made more of an effort to make Jean feel cared for and needed.

Violence in a Relationship

66 You learn to kick someone else when he is down just so that you can stay up. 99

All human beings are capable of being violent. Most girls learn that violence is frowned upon and that they are not strong enough to impose their will by physical means. They learn that they must rein in their rage and find verbal or other means of settling arguments. Boys often find that violent behaviour is excused and even expected as a part of their being male. In most societies a level of domestic violence is still tolerated, and in some, the men of a family can be excused for murdering women thought to have smirched the family name.

Boys too often see, by the examples of the adult men around them, that disagreements are solved by violence. They note that when they have done something wrong, someone bigger uses superior strength to slap them down. They may also learn that they can use their superior strength to slap down people who are smaller and weaker. At school they may find that violence is not only condoned but encouraged and that bullying is not challenged.

NAME: **Steve Jonson**
OCCUPATION:
Youth worker
AGE: **35**

"As a boy, I had learnt no way of expressing my feelings. If you aren't able to articulate frustrations verbally, or control or understand your emotions, you resort to whatever is available and men often resort to violence. Fathers are violent to their sons, and men are violent toward each other. It is a law that is never challenged."

While male violence is condoned by society and women continue to be seen as subordinate to men, it is inevitable that some men will feel that they have a right to impose their will against "their" women and "their" children. It is not until they start to recognize the damage they are causing, and to look for the help they need to control their anger, that they will be able to change. Often this will involve breaking patterns and unlearning lessons learned early in childhood.

FINDING THE COURAGE TO LEAVE

Women involved in relationships with violent men cannot alter their partner's behaviour themselves, either by avoiding conflict or by encouraging it; nor can they afford to wait for them to change. They need to protect themselves and their children. This requires finding the courage to leave, which can be very hard to do. Often women in this situation will come to believe that they are somehow to blame for the anger, or they may believe that they are so unlovable that this violent "love" is all they deserve. They may have nowhere else to go for shelter, and no money to live on; those who live in a religious or tightly knit community may also fear being ostracized for leaving.

Sinead grew up in a family in which violence was commonplace. Her father was verbally and physically abusive to her mother, and her brother was abusive to her. Male violence was accepted as normal and female subservience was equally normal. When Sinead married she found herself recreating the cycle.

Her husband was an alcoholic and before long she too was tip-toeing around their home, terrified of attracting his anger: "I kept asking myself, why am I in this terrible relationship when it is destroying me? But I felt helpless and powerless. I knew I needed help and I knew what the problem was, but I couldn't look at it".

A CATALYST FOR CHANGE

It was when she realized that her sons were following in their father's footsteps that Sinead found the strength to save herself. She talked to a counsellor and grew to understand that, only by learning to value herself, could she find the strength to change her life. When she told her husband she was leaving him he begged her to stay, but Sinead was strong and clear and knew that only by leaving could she save herself and teach her sons that she was not a doormat.

Sinead and her husband managed to forge a reconciliation, but on her terms this time. She says, "I didn't think I could ever go back to him, but now I know it will be alright because I know I can leave. I am no longer afraid of being on my own. He wouldn't dare treat me the way he used to because he knows that I would just walk out".

By changing herself, Sinead has become a catalyst for change within her family. Her sons were first confused, then angry. Now they treat her with the respect with which she treats herself. In a sense she has been lucky. Her husband was prepared to go into counselling in order to make changes and win her back. Many violent men are unable, or unwilling, to recognize that they can change.

WOMEN'S NEEDS

The right to be safe in your own home must surely be the most basic of human rights. No society should deny a woman the help and support she needs to rid herself of a violent man. A woman should have:

- Access to laws and a legal system that recognize her right to safety.
- The right to call on the police and the community to provide protection by removing violent men and ensuring that they are not able to return.
- Access to a place of safety, on demand, whenever she feels it necessary.
- Access to non-directive counselling which will help her to understand the effects of battering on her willpower and self-esteem, help to heal the emotional scars of living with violence, and help her to find the strength to help herself (see pages 187–88).

MEN'S NEEDS

Many men would welcome release from the prison of their own violence. They need:

- To have access to counselling and anger-management programmes.
- Support from their peers for their attempts to change.
- To know that violence will not be tolerated and that action will always be taken.

The only effective response to domestic violence will be the attainment of real sexual equality. When boys no longer grow up believing that they have a right to use their strength to control women, and girls grow up knowing that they have the economic means to leave violent men, we may not need places of refuge to protect women from the men who pretend to love them.

WHERE TO GO FOR HELP

■ Women's aid refuges or similar organizations are being established in a number of countries. There may be one near you that can offer help, advice, counselling or refuge (see pages 187–88).
■ Specialist counselling for men who need help to break destructive patterns of behaviour may be available near you (see pages 187–88).

> 66 I felt belittled by my parents and so when I finally left home, I was reluctant to return. I used to manufacture arguments and pass the responsibility for my absence back to my parents. 99

Conflict Resolution in the Family

There are times when conflict in a relationship becomes too explosive to manage without help and there is a danger that it will overwhelm and destroy the relationship itself. Rows between parents and children, or between brothers and sisters, can ruin family relationships and turn special events into dramas.

Although these feuds may appear to be triggered by a trivial incident, they are often rooted in misunderstandings and disappointments that have been festering for years. Parents and children may have problems as a result of separation; siblings may still be working out old rivalries. Resolving family conflicts can be particularly complicated because it is necessary for all concerned to be equally prepared to look at themselves critically.

NAME: **Kate Olaffson**	*"I used to invite my younger sister to parties and*
OCCUPATION: **Lawyer**	*social events but I have stopped doing it because she*
AGE: **28**	*flirts with my boyfriend. I can't explain why, it sounds too stupid, and I know she is upset by my reaction, but it's too bad. This time she isn't getting what she wants."*

FRIENDLY MEDIATION

Kate, whose story is told above, had no idea how her sister Kristen saw their relationship. She learnt from an aunt that both sisters were close to, that far from wanting to hurt her, Kristen had always admired her academic prowess. Since Kristen saw herself as insignificant compared to Kate, she had not realized that she had the power to hurt her. Finding out that Kate was in fact vulnerable brought them closer together. Sometimes a less-involved family member or a close family friend can bring angry family members together to talk a problem through. The person acting as mediator needs to set rules:

• Each person must first tell their version of the triggering event and then say how they felt about it.

• The feeling must be treated as of equal value to the facts.

• No one can interrupt.

• No one can insult others.

• No one can contradict another person's version.

• Everyone must speak in turn until they seem to have got out everything that they need to say.

• Each person must then suggest something positive that they could do to improve the situation and something positive that they would like other people to do to improve it.

FAMILY COUNSELLING OR THERAPY

A trained therapist, or counsellor, will see all of you together and help you to listen to the messages that are not being said out loud. She or he will gently guide you into areas of your relationship that you may have been afraid to talk about and provide the support you may need to help you cope with what you find.

CONFLICT RESOLUTION FOR COUPLES

We all have conflicts with those we love. Some of them can be resolved easily, others need working at, and some may benefit from the help of a neutral third person who will help both parties to stand back and see where changes need to be made. These are some of the most common areas of conflict:

- Feeling that you are growing apart but are unable to bridge the gap.
- Fearing that your partner is having an affair.
- Arguing over childcare or the sharing of housework.
- Finding your partner's behaviour irritating.
- Having difficulties with your sexual life.

Sometimes conflicts within a relationship are not genuine differences of opinion but reflect difficulties in your own life:

- They may arise from unresolved problems in a previous relationship or even in your childhood that you have brought with you into this relationship.
- You may feel unfulfilled and be projecting your feelings of irritation on to your partner rather than trying to resolve them yourself.
- If your partner has not fulfilled your expectations in some way, you may feel disappointed, but the problem may well lie in your expectations rather than in his or her behaviour.
- Unemployment or financial insecurity can be particularly hard to handle if you have fixed ideas about who is the breadwinner.

INFORMAL MEDIATION

It is difficult for anyone known by both partners to be genuinely neutral, which is why attempts by friends or family members to mediate may make matters worse. Talk to a trained counsellor. If you belong to a religious community, you may want to talk to a priest or a rabbi, but do bear in mind that a person who believes that divorce is a sin may be more concerned with welding together the relationship than with helping you to address any problems.

COUPLE COUNSELLING

A trained counsellor who is prepared to see both of you together may be the best solution. A genuinely neutral third person should allow you to say things to each other that you would feel afraid of voicing in a one-to-one situation, and can also provide a sense of security to the person who feels afraid to tell the truth (and there usually is one). Sometimes couple counselling can be carried out by two people who see you separately and then together. This can help if one of you feels the other is more powerful, or if either of you fears that a counsellor of the opposite sex may be biased. One-to-one counselling is more expensive, but it is effective for many couples so might be worth investigating.

You may find that airing your difficulties helps you to put them into perspective. You may discover aspects of your partner that you had never understood and which will help you get to know each other better. You may also find that there are unresolvable differences, in which case couple counselling can also help you to find a dignified way of moving apart.

FIRST HELP YOURSELF

Try to sort out how much of your anger is down to your own feelings and how much is due to your partner's behaviour (which will of course affect your feelings).

■ Put two pieces of paper side by side. Label one ME and the other MY PARTNER. Think carefully about all the things you feel angry about and assign them to the different pages.

■ Try to be scrupulously honest with yourself.

■ If you are feeling dumped on at work, that is your problem.

■ If your partner's refusal to help at home is affecting your work, that is for him to solve. You can ask for his sympathy for your work problems, but he cannot change them. What he can change is the distribution of work at home. Have you asked?

■ If you can clarify the issues at stake at this stage and talk about them, it will be easier to negotiate a change of behaviour (see page 116).

■ If you cannot clarify the issues or talk about them rationally, you may need outside help.

WARNING

If conflict involves violence, threats of violence, or sexual abuse, seek professional help immediately (see pages 187–88). Behaviour of this kind does not just stop; both abuser and abused need help.

SEE ALSO

•PAGES 187–88 Useful Addresses

WHEN A RELATIONSHIP ENDS

Separation hurts, and the longer you and your partner have been together the more it will hurt. It does not even matter much whether you initiated the parting or merely suffered it: any partnership that has weathered years of ups and downs will have woven itself inextricably into the lives of its members.

If your partner walked out on you without warning, the pain and shock can be quite paralysing – the agony of lost love mixed with the sharp pain of anger and hurt. Even if you were the one screaming abuse and throwing saucepans, the relief will still be tinged with loss when the din dies down.

NAME: **Charlene Lewis**
OCCUPATION:
Shop worker
AGE: **30**

"Just as a hurt child will crawl on to a friendly knee for a cuddle, I needed to find a way of comforting myself. I wanted someone to put their arms around me and tell me everything would be alright like my mother used to do. My misery seemed so huge, one person would have collapsed under the weight of it. I needed an entire regiment of mothers."

LOSING YOUR PLACE

When someone dies, the shared grief brings people together. In separation there is no shared grief. Friends and relations are either for or against, so you may find that, just when you most need support, the people you used to rely on have gone over to the other side. You are not just losing a partner, your life is being sliced in two. If you relied on your partner for your place in the world, this sense of dispossession will be overwhelming and may hurt more than the loss of your partner. It will take time to recreate a world in which you can feel whole again.

MOURNING

With many changes in life you will experience a period of mourning. With a change as big as the loss of a partner, the mourning process may be lengthy – perhaps much longer for one partner than the other. You may be desperate to numb the pain, but you may heal faster if you allow yourself simply to live through it. There are suggestions that may help the process on pages 126–27. The stages of mourning follow a similar pattern for most people:

• Shock. You can keep going because you have shut down your emotions – you feel less pain, but you may also find it very hard to think clearly.

• Yearning and anger. Once the clouds lift, you will feel the pain. You may want everything back as it used to be.

• Depression. When the anxious anger disappears, you will feel limp and low. If it is you who has left, this is the point at which you may feel regret, but also start accepting that your life has.changed forever.

• Resolution. One day you will notice that your life has changed. You no longer think of the past but have started to embrace the future. Life is again worth living. It may even be better than before.

PROTECTING CHILDREN

The long-term effects of separation and divorce on children have been studied in great detail and in many countries, and although every case is different, some unequivocal statements can be made.

The effect of marital conflict can be just as bad and may be worse than the effect of separation, but research confirms that children usually prefer their parents to stay together. Children generally do best when they live with the parent who already has the closest relationship with them. They adjust more readily if they have regular access to both parents and their parents are not fighting over their heads. This will happen more easily if both parents are genuinely committed to a regular access agreement. Even in an amicable separation, it can take at least a year for children to adjust (boys may take longer than girls). If the parent they are living with remarries, they will have to start adjusting all over again. If marital conflict continues after the marriage ends, adjustment will be far harder and take much longer.

UNDERSTANDING THEIR FEELINGS

The most useful thing you can do to make separation easier for your children is try to imagine how it feels from their point of view; this involves separating your feelings about your partner from their feelings. You may feel belittled, betrayed or just plain angry, but they have their own emotions, which might be quite different. They will suffer loss, just as any adult would, but they will also feel powerless. Their world is falling apart and they have no way of stopping it.

Children may believe that they are somehow responsible for the separation and that their parent is leaving because of something they have done. If they do not see the parent who leaves, they will feel rejected. If contact is impossible, try to reassure them that they are not to blame. Other common responses include:

FEAR Children may be afraid that if one parent can leave them, the other may leave too. They need reassurance from both parents that they are loved and that they can easily see, or speak to, either parent when they feel the need.

ANGER They may be angry with the parent who has abandoned them or the parent who (as far as they can see) has taken them away. If either parent establishes another relationship, they may transfer that anger to the new partner who, they feel, is taking their place (see page 114).

ACTING OUT Children and young people are often unable to articulate their feelings and may instead act them out by being difficult or withdrawn at school, arguing, having tantrums or refusing to be left. In this case:
• Do not try to get them on your side.
• Do not encourage their anger toward the parent who has left.
• Do not try to obstruct their relationship with the other parent.
• Be aware of their needs, recognize their fear, reassure them, give them time and encouragement and they will survive and emerge stronger and more aware.

CREATING A NEW LIFE

CHOOSING TO SEPARATE

Sometimes couples part but still do not separate. They are so emotionally enmeshed that there is no real possibility of starting again. If one tries to start a new relationship, the other will immediately find a way of stopping it.
■ Partial separation is particularly likely if you have children in common. You do not want to hurt the kids and you do not want to hurt each other, so you find yourself keeping all the old connections going – but in different houses.
■ You need to recognize that neither of you will be able to start a meaningful new relationship if you are still bound up with the old one.
■ You may be happy with this; if not, you may need the help of a counsellor to allow each of you to let go (see pages 187–88).

You may feel like retreating and hiding from the world, or even like throwing yourself at his feet and begging him to have you back. Neither course of action will help you to do what needs to be done.

You need the chance to express your grief, anger and misery. Friends will often give you that chance, but be wary of those who join in with the abuse, intending support but merely magnifying your sense of anger and betrayal. This may be the time to seek the help of a counsellor who can provide a safe place for you to pour out your feelings (see pages 187–88). Very often the thing you miss most is physical contact. You can find other ways of comforting yourself: steam baths, saunas, yoga or massage all provide soothing opportunities.

Once the mist has cleared, you may need help to recognize that you are not merely a victim. You have contributed to the end of this relationship. Your contribution may have been small, you may not be able to see it at first, but to deny any involvement is to deny your own power. You will only be able to recreate your life when you come to believe in your own power to act. If you continue to project yourself as a victim of your partner, you will find it far harder to make a new life for yourself.

POSITIVE ACTION

In order to act positively you have to see yourself positively. This is easier if it was you who left the relationship, or you have separated by mutual consent. Often, in the agony of a failing relationship, things will have been said, or done, that have utterly undermined your self-confidence. He may have mocked your competence as a person, sneered at your sexual attractiveness, called you stupid. This "slash and burn" technique for ending a relationship is devastatingly destructive, but it says more about the difficulty he felt in separating from you than about the person you really are. If he needs to reduce you in order to leave you, he finds leaving hard.

You may be tempted to rush into the arms of the next person who seems to fancy you as a way of proving to yourself that you are sexually attractive; or you may hide yourself away, fearing intimate contact with anyone because you have lost all faith in yourself. If you try the former, you may hurt yourself and set yourself up for more pain, because a relationship based on panic is unlikely to survive. If you opt for the latter, you may feel safer but you could cut yourself off so far that you are unable to start a new relationship at all.

REGAINING SELF-CONFIDENCE

Rebuilding the confidence you used to feel in yourself may require coming to terms with your life as a single person as well as, in time, renegotiating a new kind of relationship with your ex-partner. An unseen "bogey man" has the power to damage your self-esteem far more than someone you occasionally see. It may take years to achieve this, but when you can look at the person you used to cry over and see someone who does not appear special, you will know that you are no longer walking around with a bleeding wound where you used to be joined to your other half.

SEE ALSO
•PAGE 123 Couple Counselling

FRIENDS IN NEED

Few of us have the luxury of being able to wait for the grieving period to be over before we start making changes and facing a new life. Sometimes the effort and energy of reorganizing provides a welcome distraction.

Your friends are your greatest asset. Close friends will listen to you endlessly as you work out your feelings, but once the first pain is over, be sure to get in touch with the people you have inevitably neglected. Some of them will have been hanging back, uncertain how to behave; others may feel that their friendship with your ex-partner means that they can no longer be friendly with you. Let them know if you would like to stay in touch, but do not test their loyalty by expecting them to listen to your complaints about your ex-partner.

NAME: **Ingrid Thomson**   *"I always liked singing in the bath, but I would never* OCCUPATION: **Teacher**   *have dared sing in public. I heard an acquaintance* AGE: **28**   *talking about a jazz singing class she had joined. She just swept me along with her. The great thing about singing is that it forces you to relax and open up. I will never be terribly good at it, but singing along with the chorus was what I needed to feel a real lift."*

OPEN UP TO NEW PEOPLE

If you have shared a social circle with your ex-partner, this may be the time to strike out into pastures new. Going to parties without a partner can be lonely. Look for other ways of making new friends. It is old advice, but it may help to join a new club or evening class or take up a sport. If you have young children, your social life may be somewhat circumscribed, but if your children spend time with their father, use this time to branch out.

ENJOY YOURSELF
Friends are your greatest asset. They will help you to laugh again.

REDISCOVER YOURSELF

If you were together for a long time, bits of you will have grown rusty from lack of use. If your partner liked opera, you may have forgotten about listening to soul music. If he was the family gardener, you can rediscover your green fingers. If you have time on your hands, use it to develop the talents and the pleasures that you had left aside, and that will help you feel better about yourself.

If you still live in the home you shared, every time you walk into a room you will be reminded of the life you had together. If you cannot move house, you can at least move the furniture and redecorate to turn your home into something that belongs to the new you.

Your working life in perspective

Finding the right job

Making a career move

The working mother

WOMEN AT WORK

Women no longer have to fight for recognition as working people; we take for granted rights that have been fought for over two centuries. The new world of work offers a whole different set of challenges and women are uniquely placed to take advantage of them. For us, work has a far broader meaning than it has for men. Our working role may be as mother and homemaker, as wage earner, or more commonly as both, and it is our access to these two different working roles that provides us with the flexibility, both emotionally and in terms of our skills, to succeed. The pages that follow explore the different aspects of the world of work, offering practical strategies and pragmatic advice.

YOUR WORKING LIFE

• THOUGHTS ON EMPLOYMENT • STRATEGY FOR A WORKING LIFE • GETTING A JOB • FLEXIBLE WORKING • CHANGING DIRECTION • PROTECTING YOUR RIGHTS AT WORK • CONFLICT AT WORK

WHAT ARE THE THINGS that bring you most satisfaction in life? Relationships probably top your list, but according to research in the United States, most people rank work second, ahead of leisure activities such as sport and watching television. It seems that we feel happiest when we are achieving something in our lives, and leisure time that is undirected and aimless does not give us as much pleasure as a job well done.

Nevertheless, not all work is fulfilling. It can be boring, repetitive and tiring. Too often, women in particular have too much of it – splitting time between paid and unpaid work with little time for friends and family, or for resting and taking stock.

Work stresses are growing as the workplace changes. Employers are more able, and more inclined, to cut their work force and demand longer hours from fewer people, or alternatively, to get rid of permanent, full-time staff and replace them with people working part-time or on short-term contracts. These new forms of work add to the profitability of a company, but they also add to the insecurity of employees who may have to work much harder.

THOUGHTS ON EMPLOYMENT

Attitude surveys, like some of those quoted below, show that these new ways of working are beginning to affect the way people think about work. Some people seem to be sinking under the changes, others are resisting change, and a new, usually younger, group is turning the change to their advantage.

STRESS Work stress can be creative and stimulating, but too much stress can cause illness and misery.

"I suffer stress nowadays." Fifty per cent of British adults agree with this statement. Women are 10–20 per cent more likely to agree than men of a similar age and status.
(HENLEY CENTRE FOR FORECASTING, 1994)

"If you have a demanding job with little control and low rewards, particularly a blue collar job, your risk of a heart attack is two to four times as high as a person in a job with lower demands and high rewards and security."
(PROFESSOR JOHANNES SEIGRIST, DÜSSELDORF UNIVERSITY, 1995)

NAME: **Sylvie Prentice**	*"I left college determined to establish a career. I took*
OCCUPATION:	*every little job that came my way, building contacts,*
Event manager	*improving my skills, but still the big break seemed to*
AGE: **27**	*be elusive. I felt such a failure. Then a friend pointed*
	out that I do have a career. This is it. I am already
	there. Now that I have stopped trying to fit myself
	into a non-existent slot I have felt much better about
	myself – and I have felt far less stressed and anxious."

IN FOCUS
If your work is creative, stress can be challenging rather than debilitating.

WORKING HOURS For most of the twentieth century, reforms in the law regulating labour have succeeded in pushing the length of the working day downward. Then, in the 1970s, this process stalled and began to reverse.

"Over the last 20 years working hours have gone up, in the US, by the equivalent of one extra month a year; commuting time is up by 23 hours per year and vacation time down by 3½ days."
(BEYOND CERTAINTY, CHARLES HANDY, 1995)

FIGHTING TO PUT THE BALANCE BACK There is a growing resistance to this "burn-out" way of working. The buzz word of the moment is "balance", and many young people in employment are increasingly demanding the right to balance work commitments with their home and social lives.

"Among 18–34-year-olds almost 58 per cent are not prepared to let their commitment to work interfere with their lives."
(BRITISH SOCIAL ATTITUDES SURVEY, 1993)

"One third of Americans would accept a 20 per cent cut in income in exchange for shorter working hours."
(PREFERENCES FOR WORK AND LEISURE, F.T. JUSTER, 1995)

FINDING THE BALANCE

Balance will vary for each one of us according not only to individual temperament but to our differing needs at different stages in life. In order to achieve this balance, we need to learn skills that we can sell on the labour market, either as full-time employees or as contract workers or consultants. The better our skills are, the wider the range of possibilities before us will be, and the greater our chance of job satisfaction and of finding that elusive "balance".

The pages that follow will help you to think about who you are, what work means to you, and how you can get the most out of your own working life.

Strategy for a Working Life

I F WORK IS GOING TO BE AN ABSORBING PART of your life, and not just a means of paying the rent, you need to look for the kind of work that will suit you, not only in terms of skills, but also taking into account your temperament and the stage of life you are currently at. You may be a wonderful pianist, for example, but if you don't have the drive and the single-mindedness to beat the competition and rise to the top, you may be happier using your talents on a smaller stage, perhaps running a community music workshop or teaching. Answering the questions below may help you to understand more about your temperament.

WHAT KIND OF PERSON ARE YOU?

WHAT IS MOST IMPORTANT TO YOU?

1	Getting to the top and/or earning a lot of money.
2	Making something that works well and/or having good ideas.
3	Implementing good ideas and/or seeing things through from beginning to end.
4	Inspiring others and/or being useful to others.

ANALYSIS

1 You are a be'er.
You probably have a clear career trajectory already or you know you require one. You need to be assertive and single-minded, but must also recognize that you will be relying on doers to provide you with ideas and to carry things through. Learn to value creativity and creative people: you'll need them as much as they will depend on your determination to get things done. You will thrive in the driving seat of a project.

2 You are a doer.
You are more concerned with being absorbed and fulfilled than in making it to the top. Respect your preferences: doers find external recognition less important than the need to satisfy themselves (though appreciation from others may help boost your self-belief). You will have to recognize, though, that it will often be other people who make the money (and take the credit) for your creativity. You might find that you are forced to become more of a be'er just to get your ideas across. You might be happier teaming up with someone, or some organization, to do the managing for you.

3 You are a sustainer.
You are the kind of person every organization needs to carry a good project through. You will be happiest in a middle-management position, running an organization that is already on track, or providing the structure in which more maverick people can thrive.

4 You are a facilitator.
You will be happiest in a job that keeps you in direct contact with people: teaching, medicine, social services, the voluntary sector. Your desire to see everyone's point of view means that you will often be asked to mediate in disputes, but you are not likely to be the person who pushes unpopular policies through. Avoid jobs that will bring you into conflict with others.

WHERE ARE YOU IN YOUR WORKING LIFE?

PHASE ONE
Education: Work is changing fast and we all need to update our skills from time to time, but it makes sense at the start to set down educational building blocks that will allow flexibility. Look at the skills audit on page 134 to check whether you are learning the skills you need to succeed at work. If not, can you add courses or change direction? Are you using your vacations not just for leisure, but as an opportunity for work experience? Now is the time to make friends for life and also to establish the network on which your working life can be based.

"I did two weeks' work experience and then managed to stay on one evening a week the whole way through college. When I was ready to leave, my experience meant I was well ahead of the field."

PHASE TWO
Learning About Work: Your first job experiences offer an opportunity to increase your skills and to find out what kind of work suits you. Be prepared to trade a low salary and short-term contracts for an opportunity to try out work that really interests you and to find out about your chosen career from the inside. Your first contact may be a stroke of luck, but it takes judgement to turn a lucky break into a career opportunity. Read specialist magazines, look at job advertisements, ask questions, watch, listen and learn. Consider what you can learn from the job you are doing to help you land the job you want. Remember that even the humblest job can provide you with something new if you look for it.

"I bumped into a friend who graduated last year. She needed someone to cover for her while she went on holiday. I love the job and her boss has promised to introduce me to other people who may be able to offer me a more permanent position."

PHASE THREE
A Job Strategy: It is time to take stock. Draw up a skills audit (see page 134). Divide it into two sections: the skills you arrived with at this job; the skills you have learned since. Now make a list of the skills and experience you want to acquire. Can you make the changes needed to attain these in your current job? Are you working in the field that interests you? If not, this is the time to change trains (see page 140). Are you learning new skills? If not, can you ask for extra training or take an evening course to improve your skills? Do your working hours still suit you, and if not, can you change them (see page 138)?

"There was a lot of talk about mergers with a French company. I signed on to an evening course to brush up my French. Then, when it became clear that the merger was going ahead, I wrote a note to the manager asking if they would need someone to liaise with the French office. It was all a question of timing."

PHASE FOUR
Onward, Upward or Out?
Have you achieved your initial ambition? It may take you two years, or ten; much depends on the pace of your chosen industry as well as your personality and ambition. You now have to decide whether to continue at a steady pace, whether to sharpen up your act, perhaps get some extra training and go for promotion, or whether to leave and set up on your own. Re-do the skills audit (see page 134). Do you still score a high satisfaction rating for the work you are doing? Can you see a challenging path to take for the foreseeable future? Timing here is as critical as recognizing your own preferences. If you have reached the point at which you may decide to have children, consider whether you should prioritize job security or greater control of your own time (see pages 145–46). If you are considering starting out on your own, think about whether you would find this level of freedom exciting or terrifying (see pages 138–39).

"I was running a department and earning well, but I never seemed to see my children, so I decided to start out on my own. My salary plummeted, but I had control of my own time. I could knock off at 4pm if I wanted and start again at 9pm."

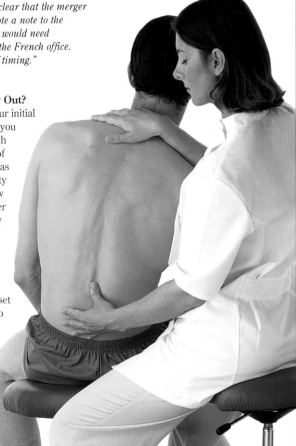

AUDITING YOUR SKILLS

This is the skills audit of a 22-year-old woman called Marie. It is designed as an example to help you to think not only about your skills and preferences, but also about the best environment for you to work in. Your preferences, like Marie's, may change with experience and circumstances; you can do a skills audit at any time during your working life.

1 Draw up three charts, as opposite. Label the first "Employment" and list every job you have had in the last few years. If you are just starting out, include holiday and Saturday jobs at school and voluntary work.

2 Label the second chart "Life Experience" and list holidays, plays you have acted in, parties you have organized, and so on.

3 Label the third chart "Education/Skills" and list skills learned privately, such as dressmaking or cake decorating, as well as formal education.

4 In each chart think about the skills you have acquired and classify them under the following headings:
• Communication
• Professional/Job
• Management
• Thinking.

5 Finally, head the last column "Satisfaction" and evaluate the level of satisfaction you derive as high, moderate or low.

EMPLOYMENT	COMMUNICATION	PROFESSIONAL/JOB
Working in a shop	Helped customers	Operated a till, credit card transactions
Painting and decorating	Very little	Learned how to handle paint and wallpaper
Freelance editing, working on an index	Detailed discussion at the beginning and end of the project	Being organized, learned how to index, used word-processing skills
Waiting tables	Explained menu options to customers and dealt with drunks and lechers	Gained knowledge about food and wine

LIFE EXPERIENCE	COMMUNICATION	PROFESSIONAL/JOB
Going on holiday with friends	Coped badly with conflicting demands of different personalities	Nil
Climbing	Co-operated with others	Nil
Travelling through France by train	Good for practising my French	A second language will be useful in many jobs
Teaching at a summer camp	Learned that it isn't easy to communicate effectively with a group of unruly kids	Learned negotiating skills and some understanding of children

EDUCATION/SKILLS	COMMUNICATION	PROFESSIONAL/JOB
English degree	Learned to write well and express my own ideas	Useful for publishing/ media work
Word processing	Learned basic layout and editing skills	Useful in most jobs
Dressmaking	Nil	Learned to understand and carry out written instructions
French language diploma at night class	Learned to speak the language and make conversation	Useful in jobs for travel and business
Voluntary work for housing charity in campaigns department	Participated in discussions about communication strategy	Learned about different modes of communication for different audiences

MANAGEMENT	THINKING	SATISFACTION
Nil	Assessed what help customers needed	Low
Managed my own time	Time by myself to think	High
Taught me to be independent and to take responsibility	A lot because some of the tasks were not obvious	High
Nil, except when dealing with tipping and asserting my rights	Observing who needed serving next	Low

MANAGEMENT	THINKING	SATISFACTION
Learned that I prefer to lead a group rather than work as a part of it	Planned the route we should take	Moderate
Learned that I co-operate well if the task is clearly defined	Had to concentrate on each move	High
Nil	Grappled with another language	Moderate
Managed a group of young people	Learned to consider the consequences of everything I said	Low

MANAGEMENT	THINKING	SATISFACTION
Learned to accumulate data and analyse it	Improved analytical and debating skills	Moderate
Nil	Learned different software programmes	High
Learned to organize time and materials	Developed design ideas	High
Nil	Worked through the nuances of another language	High
Nil	Helped devise a student recruitment campaign	High

ANALYSIS

You should be able to see from this exercise not only what you have learned from each experience, but also the direction you should be taking to exploit your strengths.

In Marie's case, though she is sociable, her skills audit shows that she is probably not going to be a great team worker. She would be happier in a job that allows her plenty of autonomy. Her academic qualifications do not give her as much pleasure as the practical skills she has acquired on her own. With additional training in, for example, on-screen editing and design, she could use her academic training in a practical job that would also give her a degree of autonomy, such as freelance work in publishing. Computer editing skills are useful in a variety of jobs right across the industry.

GETTING A JOB

It is never easy to get the job of your dreams, but there are many ways to approach it. Here are some surprising statistics from a British government survey that show how jobs are filled:
- 30 per cent of jobs were filled via advertisement.
- 12–23 per cent of jobs were filled by a temp agency.
- 12–18 per cent of jobs were filled through speculative applications.
- 8–10 per cent of jobs were filled internally.
- 5–8 per cent of jobs were filled by personal contact.

It pays, therefore, to check the national, local or specialist press every day and keep applying for every job that seems relevant, and to sign up with employment or temping agencies who, even if they do not find you the job of your dreams, may be able to locate work that will pay the grocery bills while you look. Then use every other means at your disposal to get to that all-important interview.

PERSONAL CONTACTS

Equal opportunities policies in many organizations ensure some level of fairness and have, to some extent, broken up the often discriminatory networks that used to provide the major channels for advancement in many areas of work. Nevertheless, it may still be a personal contact who gives you the very first foot on the ladder, whether in passing on information about an upcoming vacancy, or offering the opportunity to do some holiday replacement work. It also does no harm to be already well known by people you will be working with in the future: when colleagues make big career advancements, there is always the possibility that they will want to take you with them. Make a point of getting to know people who work in your field. Keep in touch with student colleagues (especially the pushy ones). Ask friends and relations to introduce you to their contacts or ask if you can use their names when making your first call about work.

Taking on part-time, casual, freelance or shift work, or even voluntary work, in an area that you are keen to get into may mean that when a job comes up you are well ahead of the field, just because you know the ropes.

SELLING YOURSELF

Self-advertisement is the single most successful way of getting a job. A large number of employers keep lists of prospective employees and then call them for interview when a vacancy arises; it is cheaper than advertising the position and takes less time. So it is very much in your interest to spend time sending out a curriculum vitae (CV), with a covering letter, to as many firms as you can. You may never hear from them, but just when you have given up hope, one of them may reach for your CV and give you a call.

Trawl through the national and local newspapers, specialist magazines and directories for the names and addresses of people you would like to work for. Do enough research to ensure that you send your letter to the right person and that you spell the name correctly (a phone call will tell you), and make it clear that you know what kind of job you want and that you think they can offer it.

CREATING A CV

Each time you apply for a particular job or course you should rewrite your CV, partly to update it, but also to ensure that it is relevant to the job you are applying for. It helps to keep the latest version on computer. There are a number of factors to keep in mind when updating a CV:

• Keep your CV to one sheet of paper. You can add relevant extra material, but it should be possible to take in your career history at a glance.

• If you have gaps in your career, or feel that simply listing the jobs you have done will not impress, it may be better to break the CV into skill areas, such as administration, computing, communication skills. Look again at your skills audit and use it to compile a comprehensive list of experience and responsibilities.

• Use voluntary as well as professional work experience. You may never have had a job, but if you were social secretary of the student union or organizer of a baby-sitting circle, you already have administrative experience.

• Make sure all the information is relevant to the job you are applying for and leave out anything trivial. Serving drinks at college parties may be useful if you are looking for a job as a waitress, but not if you are hoping to work in a bank.

• Be positive. Say why you want the job, not why they would be so lucky to have you. Be specific and make it clear that you know something about this field and the organization to which you are applying. Vague generalizations, such as "I get on well with people so I know I would be a good journalist", go straight in the bin.

• Make sure you have checked for spelling mistakes and that your page is clean and tidy. If you are sent a fill-in form, and you know you will make a hash of it first time round, photocopy it, retype it or do it on a computer. Sign all the relevant parts. State dates when you are on leave or unavailable.

• Never, never run yourself down, but do not talk yourself up either.

• You are under no obligation to state your sex, your age or your marital status if you are concerned about possible discrimination. Only mention children if you think it is relevant to the job.

THE INTERVIEW

Once you are eyeball to eyeball with your chosen future employer you have 10 or 20 minutes to let them know you are the one. These strategies may help:

• Take the initiative. If you are not being asked questions that give you an opportunity to expand, then try, politely, to change the direction of the discussion.

• If you do not understand, do not be afraid to ask for a question to be rephrased. A good interviewer is not out to trick you, but to draw you out. Give yourself time to answer each question. Do not rush or mumble.

• Be honest. Bluffing does not work. You will feel anxious about being caught out, and if you are caught out, you will not get the job. Be honest about the things you have not done and make it clear that you want to improve your skills.

• Make an impression. Pause and look at each person in the room when you arrive. Look the questioner squarely in the eye when you answer a question. When you leave, thank them for giving you an interview, looking them squarely in the face as you speak. If it is practical, offer your hand. Smile!

PREPARING FOR THE INTERVIEW

■ **Do your homework** Ring up beforehand and talk to the receptionist. If relevant, ask for a copy of the annual report, or any other material – and read it. Talk to friends in the field.

■ **Dress appropriately** Your clothes say a great deal about you, so use them to your advantage. If it is a high-status job, buy or borrow an expensive suit or jacket. If it is a job in a hospital or a school, look neat but not flashy. Avoid clothes with unnecessary pieces hanging off that you may fidget with, or anything that makes you feel uncomfortable.

SEE ALSO

•PAGE 185 Curriculum Vitae
•PAGES 16–17 Getting What You Want

FLEXIBLE WORKING

Economists and planners are predicting the death of the job as we know it. They suggest that the Industrial Age is now dead and that we are entering the Post-industrial Age. As with most predictions, this death is likely to have been exaggerated, but there is no doubt that fewer people can now expect to leave college, walk into a job at the bottom of a vast organization, and hang on in there until time and promotion move them to the top. Not that this pattern has ever been the norm for women. We have always been more likely to change our jobs and working hours according to the needs of family life, and these "new" alternatives have rarely benefited us either in terms of income or career.

However, with far more people moving out into the choppier seas of self-employment, and more employers attuned to the idea that jobs do not always have to happen between nine and five o'clock, it may be possible to use new job structures to our advantage. But be aware that these new ways of working were never intended to make our lives more convenient, only to maximize profit. Exploitation has never been easier.

ARE YOU FIT FOR SELF-EMPLOYMENT?

If you like the idea of working for yourself, you may be able to create a satisfying working life, but it helps to be aware of some of the pitfalls:

• Can you cope with the financial uncertainty? No matter how successful you are, there will always be times when the orders suddenly stop and you find yourself having to look for new markets while juggling the bills.

• Are you a self-starter and good at organizing your own time? You will need to be able to drive yourself hard, both in opening up new markets and in ensuring that work is finished on time.

• Can you sell yourself? If you do not feel that you can call a stranger and convince them that they should hire you, self-employment will be hard.

• Are you self-critical? As a freelance, you are only ever as good as your last job. If you mess up, you will not be hired again, so there is no room for mistakes.

• Do you have a marketable skill or product? Almost any skill can be marketed if you know who wants it. Firms are keen to buy in services rather than hiring staff, simply because it is cheaper to pay someone to do a few hours' work – even at a higher hourly rate – than it is to hire a full-time employee. Do your sums first. Your hourly rate must cover travelling time, holidays and sickness.

• Have you saved (or can you borrow) enough money to get you started and to keep you going until the bills are paid? Slow payment of bills is one of the major reasons why small businesses go bust.

• Will you be lonely? Companionship is one of the major advantages of going out to work for most of us. If you are self-employed, you are likely to spend long periods alone and only meet people fleetingly, which makes it hard to get to know them. You could consider a partnership or co-operative (see opposite).

• If you are considering going it alone, look out for courses and seminars on setting up a business and get as much advice as you can on areas that you do not know about, such as marketing, accounts and distribution.

PART-TIME WORK

The vast majority of part-time workers are women with families who are forced into low-paid and unskilled work because it is the only way of combining childcare and employment. Part-time work tends to be the area of employment in which employees are most exploited and have least control of their time, their income and the work they do. Legislation has gone some way toward protecting part-time workers by insisting that they share the same conditions as full-timers. Some firms, for example, will allow women to work short hours for a period after maternity leave, and in Sweden all parents have the right to work a shorter day until their youngest child is seven years old.

FLEXITIME AND JOB SHARING

Flexitime arrangements provide benefits to workers without taking away their control. Firms that allow flexitime recognize that people work harder when they are not worrying about their kids. They allow employees to establish their own hours, usually with a core of time when everyone must be in the office so that meetings can be arranged. This makes it far easier for parents to tie in their working hours with available childcare.

Job sharing also allows employees a degree of control. It can be done at any level in almost any job. The partners simply arrange to split the week, or to split tasks between them, according to their requirements. The employer agrees to split the salary. Before you enter an arrangement to job share, it helps to have an established job share policy setting out exactly what will happen when one partner leaves or wants to return to full-time working.

SHORT-TERM AND ZERO-HOURS CONTRACTS

It is becoming increasingly difficult, in some fields of work, to get anything other than short-term contracts. These contracts are usually tailored to ensure that you cannot clock up enough work to qualify for statutory employment rights. While this can be an insecure way of working, it is also a very good way of gaining experience in a number of different fields. You may also find that the level of responsibility is higher, and the work more interesting, than it would be in more secure employment. One thing your employer cannot expect from you is loyalty. Never skimp, or leave a job unfinished, but do not allow your employer to exploit you either. Use every job to your own advantage, to get new work, to make contacts and to further your own career.

A zero-hours contract is an agreement with an employer that you will be "on call" if and when you are needed. As an employee you have no regular income, you work erratic hours and you have no control over your time. Avoid zero-hours contracts if you have any choice at all.

SHARING THE RESPONSIBILITY

If you have a service to sell – anything from word processing to public relations advice or house cleaning – consider getting together with others who have similar, or complementary, skills (see right). You can share the cost of office space and someone to answer the phone and you will always have company at work.

PARTNERSHIPS

■ **A co-operative** This is a business owned and controlled by all its members. If you are likely to generate joint income, you should establish a legal partnership, or company, to regulate your relationship. In small co-ops all members are usually expected to participate in management decision-making. This works well if there are not too many decisions to take. If your meetings seem to be taking a disproportionate amount of working time, it might be better to delegate day-to-day decision-making to a manager.

■ **A legal partnership** This establishes a difference between those who own the organization and those who are employed by it. As a partner, you are an owner and liable for debts as well as profits.

■ **A limited company** This provides some protection against creditors, but as a company director, you must present audited accounts annually. In a very small business, the cost of auditors may outweigh the protection provided by forming a company.

CHANGING DIRECTION

In his book *The Empty Raincoat,* the management guru Charles Handy describes a Sigmoid Curve as *"the story of life itself. We start slowly, experimentally, and falteringly, we wax and then we wane. It is the story of the British Empire – and of the Russian Empire and of all empires, always. It is the story of a product's life-cycle and of many a corporation's rise and fall. It even describes the course of love and relationships".*

If every project follows this pattern, how are we to prevent ourselves, or our organizations, from sliding downhill into decline? The key, according to Handy, is to be aware of this rise and fall, and to start a new curve, not where energy is at its lowest ebb, at the trough of a first curve, but when energy is at its peak, when our first curve has borne us up and life is good. It is at this stage (point A on the curve below), that high energy gives us the impetus to look for new openings, take on extra training and make new contacts. The trick is to recognize and exploit point A as a jumping-off point for a new curve. Most of us will be able to recognize point A as a time when we analyse our employment and give it a high satisfaction rating.

CARRIE'S STORY

Carrie is in her late thirties. Her career shows the Sigmoid Curve in action.

Carrie has forged a solid career in the voluntary sector, heading and transforming a small organization.

On to the next curve, but the move is not easy.

Although she is successful, she feels it is time to move on.

Carrie starts to build a new and fulfilling career.

A

A

A

A

B

B

B

Carrie and her own organization are attracting positive publicity, but she feels the period of innovation is over and is ready for more responsibility in an organization with a career structure that will move her onward and upward. She is now at point A in her first career.

Carrie decides on a big career move into local government. This is the start of something new, and to begin with it proves very hard work. She is now on the downward part of the next curve, a learning period in which things feel wrong.

A year into the job, Carrie is doing well and gaining respect (she is on her way up the curve), but she now knows she has taken a wrong turn. She does not like the lack of autonomy, loathes the apparently limitless demands on her time and hates the politics. She does, however, enjoy the unexpected opportunities to learn about the growing field of electronic communications.

Instead of sliding down this rather shallow second curve to the doldrums of point B, where it would be hard to start going up again, Carrie decides to convert the experience into a jumping-off point for a third curve. She starts her own company with her newly gained experience of electronic communications, giving her a chance to innovate and experiment – something she has always enjoyed.

KICK-STARTING YOUR CAREER

In this example of a Sigmoid Curve, Carrie took the option of change as soon as she saw that the direction of her career was taking a wrong turn. All too often we do not save ourselves in time, as Carrie did; we slide down to point B when we know that work is going badly wrong, and we lack the energy to make any necessary changes. It is at this point that we need to kick-start a new curve. The following strategies may help:

RETRACE YOUR STEPS There are many reasons why people may end up at point B without anticipating it: redundancy, sickness and pregnancy can all dump workers off an upward curve. Perhaps a change of management has blocked off possibilities for promotion, or perhaps you have simply changed and a job that used to satisfy you has become dull and mechanical. It may help to try the skills audit again on page 134.

66 I started working as a volunteer with handicapped children. I felt needed, responsible, important, for the first time in my life. 99

NAME: Tabitha Potts	*"I couldn't work the long hours after I'd had my*
OCCUPATION: Mother/	*baby so I resigned. I stayed home with her for a year*
Community worker	*and then couldn't see a way to get back in again.*
AGE: 30	*I felt tired, dispirited and very broke. A couple of*
	friends persuaded me to help them set up a childcare
	co-operative. Suddenly I had time to think. As well
	as support, I now have something positive to be
	involved with."

IMPROVE YOUR SKILLS A new direction requires new skills. Look for training opportunities, find out about back-to-work schemes for those without jobs or with young children. Use your imagination. If you want a job that satisfies you, build it out of doing things you enjoy.

INCREASE YOUR ENERGY A new curve needs new energy. If you are at rock bottom, you will need even more energy. Paradoxically, human beings need to expend energy in order to create it. So consider the things that make you feel good and that will stir up your mind or your body. They do not need to have anything to do with your work, as the example below demonstrates.

NAME: Charlotte Dean	*"I started to write a novel. Soon the novel became*
OCCUPATION:	*more important than looking for a job. It took up all*
Administrator/ Novelist	*my time. It was like sitting in the middle of a storm*
AGE: 24	*with me as the calm centre. I let a friend read some*
	of it and she was very impressed. I began to feel like
	a writer – not a redundant administrator. I was high
	as a kite and at the next interview I knew I had got
	the job. By this time I didn't even know if I wanted it."

SEE ALSO
• PAGES 16–17 Getting What You Want

PROTECTING YOUR RIGHTS AT WORK

In every country, working relationships are governed to some extent by the law. At the very minimum it will state the age at which children are allowed to work, the employer's responsibility for health and safety, and such matters as your right to paid leave. The very existence of these laws is a recognition that an employee is not involved in an equal exchange: labour for pay. The employer has far more power, and it is this power that the law sets out to curb (or at least slightly temper). It is in your interests to be familiar with the basic laws governing workers' rights. Can your employer legitimately ask you to work through the night during a busy time, for example? Do you know if you have a right to paid time off if you are ill? Can you insist on a chair that properly supports your back while you work?

CONTRACTUAL RIGHTS

If you have a job, you should have a contract of employment that states the terms on which you have agreed to work. It is wise to read your contract of employment carefully and make sure you understand it. Some contracts include a job description. Make sure that it does describe your job. If it does not, ask to have it changed. Most of the time this will matter very little, but if you should get involved in a dispute, it will be crucial.

NAME: **Anna Patel**

OCCUPATION: **Television presenter**

AGE: **33**

"In my contract I was described as a producer. When I got pregnant my boss 'promoted' me to a presenter and got me to sign a new contract. It was only later that I discovered that he had done so deliberately. The change in contract was seen as a break in employment and I lost my contractual right to extended maternity leave."

TRADES UNIONS

Trades unions are changing so that they can better reflect the changing world of work. They often provide telephone advice on working rights and most will provide some level of legal support if you should get into a dispute. There seems to be a vogue among employers to try to prevent unions organizing in the workplace, and to insist on individual contracts of employment rather than collective agreements negotiated by a trades union. This is not likely to benefit employees unless they are at the very top of the wage tree and are particularly pushy about negotiating for themselves.

Research in Britain shows that women always do better with collective agreements in which wage levels are public knowledge, presumably because, even in the highest levels of management, women do not like asking for money. As a union member you will also always have an independent body to turn to for advice in the event of a dispute over, for example, sexual or racial discrimination or unfair dismissal.

CONFLICT AT WORK

Work conflicts can be particularly painful and difficult to resolve just because you spend so much time at work and your livelihood and career progress depend on smooth working relationships. Conflicts in the workplace may arise for some of the following reasons:

• Changes may have been brought in without sufficient discussion or support. Change creates anxiety, and people who feel anxious may take out their feelings on their colleagues.

• Someone has been promoted beyond their competence. Their insecurity can be manifested as aggression.

• A new arrival has shaken the existing hierarchy. Some people react by being very defensive of their position and refusing all suggestions for change or co-operation.

• There is overt or covert prejudice against individuals or minority groups.

ASKING FOR HELP

Take the problem to your immediate line manager. If there is an in-house counsellor, ask for an appointment or talk to your trades union representative. When you present your case, be very careful to present the problem fairly. Explain that you have a breakdown in communication, for example, not that you think Mary is an arrogant dinosaur who is refusing to do what you tell her or forcing you to kowtow to her.

Ask if someone can mediate between you and find out what the underlying problem is. You may have contributed to the breakdown even though you are not aware of having done so. Be prepared to listen and, if necessary, to apologize and change your own behaviour as well as expecting change from the other person.

> 66 As well as enduring advances, sexual innuendos, and put-downs, I was frequently asked to do photocopying, filing, and other clerical tasks that they would never have given to a man. 99

NAME: **Kerry Drew**

OCCUPATION:

Social worker

AGE: **29**

"My life was made hell. Men were advised not to work with me because I got a man the sack. I went through the right channels to ensure my assailant paid for what he did to me. He no longer works for the council, and I gave other women the courage to speak out about their experiences, but emotionally it left me less strong than when I started."

COPING WITH HARASSMENT AT WORK

If you are being sexually or racially bullied, keep a written record of events and speak to someone. If a superior is responsible for your predicament, ask to speak to his manager, to the personnel department, or to your trades union representative. Ideally your organization should have a clear policy for dealing with harassment which will protect you as well as discipline your harasser. If you feel you have no alternative but to leave your job, take legal advice; you may be entitled to compensation. This is not always an easy step to take; the case above was reported in a British national newspaper in 1995.

SEXUAL HARASSMENT

Sexual harassment can be defined as unwanted, uninvited and unreciprocated advances, verbal or physical, that make your working environment unpleasant and hinder your ability to do your job well.

66 The best thing is that I spent a lot of time with the children until they started school. The worst thing is that I have been through a total crisis of confidence because I was out of full-time work for nine years. **99**

THE WORKING MOTHER

• RETURNING TO WORK • THE COST OF WORKING
• LEAVING YOUR CHILD • THINKING ABOUT CHILDCARE
• CHILDCARE OPTIONS

WHEN YOU ARE PREGNANT, people react to the change in you. Although you may want to leave your sexuality, your vulnerability and your physicality behind at home, when you are pregnant your two worlds collide. Some women will welcome your pregnancy with generosity and offers of support. Some men will be unexpectedly solicitous and others will become physically aware of you in a way they have never been before. Some women will be jealous or feel threatened and may even use the opportunity of your leave to take over your job or sideline you. Your life is changing, but it is not closing in, it is opening out. Accept help from people who have been through this before; you will find it invaluable.

THE FIRST THREE MONTHS
You will probably feel emotionally confused, very tired and possibly sick. If you need time off, ask for it. This can be the worst part of a pregnancy. It is better to accept your vulnerability than to muddle through and run the risk of making mistakes. Pregnancy is a big event. You have every right to special treatment for the short time you need it. Make sure you know your rights to statutory maternity leave (see page 186), job protection and any locally agreed maternity policies.

THE SECOND THREE MONTHS
Most women find this the most enjoyable part of pregnancy. Use the energy of these months to plan ahead. Think about how you want to leave any projects you are involved in. Bring in people you trust to hold the fort while you are away. You will not be working at full stretch for a time after the baby is born, so organize your absence. Negotiate a sensible period of leave and, if possible, shorter hours after returning to work. Do not accept a leave period that seems too short.

THE THIRD THREE MONTHS
The last few weeks may seem endless. You will probably start feeling heavy and clumsy and long to have a midday nap. Start thinking about childcare and working arrangements for after the baby is born. Reduce social arrangements so that you can get to bed early. Stay at work for as long as you can cope to maximize your postnatal leave period.

Returning to Work

Becoming a parent is, more than anything else, about reconciling conflicting needs. In the end none of us has to be perfect, it is enough, as the childcare expert Bruno Bettelheim suggested, to be "a good enough parent". Being "good enough" means taking a round view of life: recognizing that children will not benefit from being home 24 hours a day with a mother who is frustrated and miserable, any more than they will benefit from spending all their waking hours with paid carers and never having the reassuring sense of coming first in their parents' lives.

When you do return to work, do not expect everything to snap into place immediately. Give yourself time to adjust and be prepared to make changes if you find that arrangements are proving too stressful. If you decide to stay at home with your children in the early months or years, look into free, or low-cost, training schemes that may be available locally to help you regain confidence and sharpen your skills.

MAKING CONTACT

Make contact with other working parents *before* you go back to work. There may be a working parents' support group at work or in your local area. You may have to rely on paid childcare while you work, but lone parents, in particular, may be very grateful for mutually supportive arrangements for those odd crises when work spills over into the evening, or just to get a breather at weekends.

INVOLVING YOUR FAMILY

If there are two parents in your household, try to ensure that you are both involved in the day-to-day care of children and home. Do not wait for your partner to offer. Make demands and make plans that include him. If your children are old enough, involve them in small tasks too. If grandparents live nearby, ask how much they are willing to help; they can provide loving continuity and crisis back-up.

EXPLORE ALTERNATIVE WORKING ARRANGEMENTS

Assume that you will not want to work long hours when you return to work. Try early on to negotiate something that will fit in with your needs. Do not be afraid to make these demands. If you go back to work and try to live up to unrealistic expectations, you will find yourself split in two directions and unable to give of your best at work or at home.

Look for ways in which you can cut down "face time", that time when you are at work but unproductive. Make clear work schedules that demonstrate that you can get the work in on time by working more intensively. Take work home and do it after your child is in bed rather than working late at the office and missing bedtime. If your job requires you to answer phones or field queries, suggest ways of sharing the load with others, perhaps by using telephone technology that automatically reroutes calls. You will be more productive if you are not worrying about leaving your child too long. If your work schedules are not flexible, and you have to be away for long days, consider cutting down on the number of days you work.

> 66 I felt so frustrated when I saw male contemporaries passing me by while I juggled childcare and work. But now, at fifty, they are burned out while I am full of energy and riding high. 99

THE COST OF WORKING

Good childcare is expensive, but like the cost of a mortgage or a pension, it needs to be set against lifetime earnings and in the context of your future employment prospects as well as what you are doing today. Consider all the following options before making a decision.

SHOULD YOU STOP WORK?

If your income is very low, it may seem better to stop work for a year or two, but be aware that you will be losing not only the actual money you are paid, but also the potential increases you might have expected at your current level of experience, as well as such benefits as pension contributions. Experience counts, and as expertise needs to be constantly updated, you may find it hard to return to the same kind of work in the future. The cost of childcare may seem prohibitive, but it may be worth struggling in the short term until your income starts to rise and the cost of care starts to fall.

WOULD IT HELP TO SWITCH TO PART-TIME WORK?

If you opt for part-time work, your childcare costs will be lower and you will find the conflicting demands of home and work less stressful, but your earnings will drop steeply. If you do decide to reduce your hours, try to do so with your current employer, rather than changing jobs. If you leave your full-time job and then look for part-time work, you will probably find that jobs pay less per hour, have a lower level of job security and restrict your chances of skills training or promotion. Over a lifetime, you may find that what you have lost financially is considerably higher than the cost of childcare in the short term, but the gains in other areas may be worthwhile.

SHOULD YOU BECOME SELF-EMPLOYED?

It is easier to tailor childcare to your needs if self-employed and to cut your costs by co-operating with other parents who work from home. But if your future is in management, or as someone who pulls the strings, you may find that your power and earning potential dwindle rapidly outside the power centre of the workplace.

NAME: **Sophie Browne**
OCCUPATION: **Freelance editor**
AGE: **31**

"I was working with Julie on a magazine when I got pregnant, so I left to freelance; it kept childcare costs down and I could spend time with my baby. Julie took maternity leave and went back to work. Initially, I was better off because she had to borrow money to pay for childcare; now I can't get a staff job and she is editor of her own magazine earning far more than me. I am glad I spent more time with my children when they were young, but I do wonder where I would be today if I had stuck in there like Julie."

Leaving Your Child

In spite of many theories generated to make us feel guilty about going out to work, there has never been a golden age in which mothers and children gambolled together throughout infancy and early childhood, untroubled by the need to generate income, prepare food, till the fields or develop their own minds. Indeed, a study by Barbara Tizard in 1986 looked at 186 contemporary, non-industrial societies and found only five in which "the child was looked after almost exclusively by the mother". Children can, and do, gain a great deal from being cared for by different people if the circumstances are suitable for their age and development and they feel safe and loved. Nevertheless, it is better for us, and for our children, to manage the change to a new carer as sensitively as possible.

FINDING SUITABLE CARE

Most childcare experts now agree that it is best for children under one year to be cared for by a limited number of familiar carers. Some more socially conscious governments have responded to this research by allowing mothers and fathers to take several months' leave to be with their babies in the first year. Where that is not possible, it is important to ensure that your baby has one main carer apart from you. She can be based in your home, in her home or in a nursery (see page 150); the important thing is not the setting, but the relationship of carer and child.

SETTLING IN

Somewhere between six and eight months, babies start to learn that their principal carers are not actually attached to them, they can go away. The knowledge of separateness is frightening and many children at this stage become clingy and anxious. This "separation anxiety" is likely to persist to some extent until the child is at least three years old and may go on for longer. You can help your child to manage this anxiety. Visit the new carer together before you are due to start work and stay for a while to show your child that this is someone you trust to care for her. It will also give you an opportunity to observe their relationship and the care environment at first hand. Your child may hate you to leave. This is quite natural, but try not to add to her anxiety with your own. Be cheerful (even if you don't feel it), tell her you will be back (even if she does not understand), and leave. You can always phone later to make sure she has calmed down.

FOLLOWING YOUR INSTINCTS

Your child may take a while to settle down, and may be very tired in the evening, but if there is a significant change in behaviour – perhaps she seems withdrawn or unruly – do not ignore it. Good childcare is good for children. You can expect your child to be happy and developing well in your absence. If he or she is not, you are the only person who can intervene to change things. Try to find out just what the problem is. Your child may be reacting to tensions at home, but if you suspect the problem lies with the carer, make an unannounced daytime visit to check. If a change is necessary, try to avoid temporary solutions. Frequent changes of carer are distressing.

> 66 He cried a lot at the beginning. I was dying to have time without him and I felt guilty because I was so relieved to get back to work. 99

Thinking about Childcare

Your choice of childcare is probably one of the most important decisions you will make in your child's life. It is worth thinking hard and doing as much research as you can. Every society has its own norms for the care of young children and something one group considers normal, another may consider intolerable, but some basic ground rules are given in the chart below.

When choosing carers, always meet them in the place where they will be looking after your child. Spend time there and follow your heart as well as your head. Ask yourself some of the following questions:

- Are the other children happy?
- Is there plenty for them to do?
- Is there space for them to run around?
- Will they be able to make a mess with water and paint?

In a nursery, find out about staff working conditions if you can. If the turnover is high, staff may be underpaid and overworked and, in the end, it is the people who matter. You want your child to be cared for by people who will not change every month, who will be loving and calm and provide a safe place for your child to explore and grow.

TYPE OF CARE

Childcare costs vary according to the type and quality of care (for details of the options see pages 150–51). Experienced, qualified carers cost more than inexperienced, unqualified staff, and if you want one-to-one care, it will be more expensive than group care of a similar quality. Start by doing some research. Your local council will be able to provide most of the information you need to

ASSESSING YOUR CHILD'S NEEDS

Though most experts agree that children under a year need one-to-one care, there is much controversy about staffing ratios for 2–5-year-olds. This chart provides guidelines that are broadly acceptable in Northern Europe, Australia and America.

Requirements	Under 9 months	9 months–2 years
Ideal staffing ratio	1:1–2	1:2–3
Ability to cope in a group	Must be with a known carer	Can cope in a small group with known carers
Continuity of care	Can cope with more than one regular, known carer	Very sensitive to changes of carer; needs continuity for language acquisition
Need for play	Short bursts only	During most of waking time
Need for education	Learns through play	Learns through play
Minimum desirable one-to-one care	Full time: mainly from parents via maternity and parental leave	A substantial part of the day, either with parent or carer

NAME: Gail Butler

OCCUPATION: Hospital administrator

AGE: 30

"As I am working flexitime and my husband, Rob, works rotating shifts for the railways, we work out the childcare arrangements a week in advance. If he is on an early shift, I go into work late and drop the baby off at the childminder on my way in. Then Rob has her in the afternoons. If he is on evenings, I go to work early and Rob drops off the baby at lunch-time. Then I collect her at 4 o'clock in the afternoon. Our arrangement means that on average we only need to pay for childcare for 20 hours a week, although we both work 35 hours a week."

know, but you could also chat to other local parents, look on noticeboards or phone childcare facilities.

THE QUANTITY OF CARE

The hours of childcare need to cover both your working and commuting times comfortably. But you may be able to cut the overall amount by working out a co-operative arrangement with your partner (or with a friend), so that one delivers and one collects. If you can use flexitime to your advantage (see page 139), you may find that you will only need to cover six hours a day. Or perhaps each person can take off half a day per week, cutting paid childcare time down to four days a week. If you work erratic hours, try to create some certainty for children. Never make promises to be back that you cannot fulfil.

2–3 YEARS	3–5 YEARS	5–11 YEARS	11 PLUS
1:4–5	1:15	1:25	1:25
Happy in a small group, with known carer, for whole day	Up to 30, but needs quiet periods, especially at the end of a day	Up to 30 or more, but may prefer quieter period after school	May resent after-school groups organized by adults
Learning to cope with changes of carer; may enjoy visits to friends or playgroups; wants familiar carer for quiet times	Relates more to peer group, but still looks to a familiar adult to help with disputes and provide comfort	Relates primarily to peer group, but wants someone familiar to come home to	Needs clear framework and monitoring by parents, with access to parents when needed
During most of waking time	During most of waking time	At least half of waking time	Needs daily work-free time
Needs some directed play	Play-based nursery education	Not more than half waking hours	Should include self-motivated learning
Every evening and weekend, preferably with a parent or familiar carer	After nursery; needs a quiet wind-down time before bed	Quiet after-school care; time to talk to parents in the evening	Time when asked for; may not be often, but should not be missed

66 By lunch-time the first day I was crying and dripping milk. I rushed over to the nursery to find my baby, who had refused ever to suck from anything but me. She was sleeping happily, having just polished off a whole bottle of milk. 99

CHILDCARE OPTIONS

Choosing childcare means coming to some sort of compromise between your child's developmental and emotional needs, your own need for flexibility and time, and your ability to pay. You will probably opt for different kinds of care, or different combinations, at various times as your children grow. Consider also the developmental needs of children shown in the chart on pages 148–49, bearing in mind that they are as different as we are. Some may opt for football every day after school; others may just want to curl up with a book.

AT HOME

This includes private care in your home by a nanny, mother's help or au pair.

ADVANTAGES You do not have to worry about dropping off or collecting and it does not matter too much if you have a last-minute meeting or get called away. A live-in nanny, a mother's help, or an au pair once children start school, provides continuity of care to cover all the wrinkles in your life and the changing needs of your children. Many people with demanding jobs opt for this kind of care. Make sure you do not exploit your carer – she may abandon you.

DISADVANTAGES It is difficult to monitor your carer's performance. You may have problems of high turnover. As your child gets older, he or she may feel isolated. You might want to consider sharing a nanny or sending your child to a part-time playgroup as well.

COST You have to cover the whole carer's salary yourself.

CHILDMINDERS

Minders look after children in their own homes and should be registered, which means they are regulated by the local authority and usually have access to resources such as toy libraries.

ADVANTAGES No mess! Childminders are often older mothers with children of their own and you can benefit from their experience. They care for children in "family groups" so, as your child gets older, there will be others to play with and talk to. Childminders often take and drop off at local schools or playgroups.

DISADVANTAGES You have to drop off and collect and minders tend to be less flexible about time (though you may strike lucky). It can be hard to ask for special treatment for your child, though most minders are quite used to parents with different lifestyles.

COST Relatively low because you share the minder's wage with other parents.

GROUP CARE

DAY NURSERIES Usually private or, more rarely, a local authority facility. Local nurseries may have waiting lists.

ADVANTAGES Unlike a nanny, nurseries do not leave you. Your child can stay in a day nursery until she starts school; all her changing needs are catered for.

DISADVANTAGES Few nurseries can really give the one-to-one care that babies need. They are inflexible about time.

COST An expensive form of care for children under 2 years old.

VOLUNTARY PLAYGROUPS These may be organized under the auspices of a national playgroup organization or established by a local group, possibly of childminders.

ADVANTAGES A voluntary playgroup has all the advantages of a day nursery. Additional advantages include direct involvement by the users and ease of regular monitoring.

DISADVANTAGES You may be asked to take on a bigger role than you have time for. Playgroups rarely tolerate late parents, though informal evening arrangements may be easy to negotiate.

COST Usually very reasonable.

SCHOOL NURSERIES These vary widely from country to country. In France, for example, most children start nursery school before they are 3 years old. In Sweden, nurseries are available for all 6-year-olds. In Britain, some areas have no nurseries at all, while some have provision for most 3-year-olds, but only for three hours a day.

ADVANTAGES Good nursery education is an excellent start to education and should be available to all children as a statutory right.

DISADVANTAGES Hours may fit in badly with your working day, making additional childcare arrangements necessary.

COST Usually free.

AFTER-SCHOOL GROUPS Your child's school or a local community centre may run these groups. Sometimes known as latchkey schemes, they are for children of school age.

ADVANTAGES Children who enjoy being surrounded by other kids enjoy the range of activities on offer.

DISADVANTAGES These schemes are not often geared to the youngest children and some children prefer a quieter end to the day. They are rarely flexible about time.

COST The cost is usually modest, and may be subsidized for those who qualify.

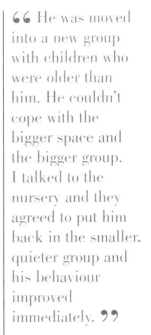

66 He was moved into a new group with children who were older than him. He couldn't cope with the bigger space and the bigger group. I talked to the nursery and they agreed to put him back in the smaller, quieter group and his behaviour improved immediately. 99

GROUP CARE
Nurseries offer an excellent start to education.

66 I rush home.
When I open the
door, there are
crumbs trodden
into the carpet,
the children are
quarrelling about
the TV and instead
of being pleased to
see them, I start
yelling at them. 99

MANAGING YOUR TIME

• SURVIVAL STRATEGIES • CLOTHES STRATEGIES

WOMEN TODAY HAVE SO MANY OVERLAPPING TASKS and roles, so many things that all seem to need doing at the same time, that it seems impossible to find time for ourselves, and often equally impossible to do anything as well as we would like to. In the effort to balance our own needs with the needs of employers, partners, friends, children and other family members, we often squeeze ourselves right out of the picture.

Time management techniques are more often used in the workplace than in the home, but the principles are the same. If you have too many things to do, and no baseline from which to allocate your time, you are likely to panic, try to do everything at once, and achieve nothing. Time management will allow you to set goals, establish priorities and make sure that, even on the days when you are forced to skimp, you do what you can do as well as you can.

PLANNING FOR SURVIVAL

If you are overburdened, it is hard to stand back and work out your priorities. Using the chart opposite as an example, fill in the time columns on the blank chart on page 182 to show how you and the other members of your household spend time in an average day. If you have children, help them to fill in charts too. Then use the ideas below to help analyse your daily routine.

ANALYSE YOUR TIME CHART Look at how much time you have for: yourself, your partner or your children (if you have them), friends, work, housework, entertainment, sleep. How does this compare with your partner's chart?

DECIDE WHAT NEEDS CHANGING Are your needs getting swamped? Do you spend enough time alone with your partner? Do you feel you have adequate time for yourself alone and uninterrupted? Write a list of all the changes you would like to see in an ideal world.

CONSIDER CONFLICTING NEEDS You may find that your partner wants more time to himself and that your children (if you have them) want more time with you, but that you want more time with your partner and feel too guilty to ask for time to yourself. These may seem to be conflicting needs, but sometimes conflict is a result of lack of clarity, which can lead to guilt and resentment. If you agree with your partner clearly to set aside regular time to be alone as well as to be together, there should be less conflict over, for example, the times when work spills over, making you feel anxious and harassed.

If you have children, establish clear times when you give them your undivided

---

TIME-SAVING TIPS

■ **Time for yourself** Give yourself an extra half hour once or twice a week to have a drink with a friend, soak in a hot bath or do some exercise (see page 42).

■ **Housework** Share it with everyone in the house. Explain that you will be a more pleasant person to live with if everyone helps. Make a rota and stick it on the wall. If something is not done, everyone will know who did not do it.

■ **Working hours** Negotiate an early finish once a week in return for an early start. Pick your children up from school once a week to keep in touch with their work, friends and other parents. Your employer will benefit from your reduced anxiety.

■ **Fathers** Children and fathers need time alone. Plan for it, insist on it, even if you do not live together: they will thank you.

■ **Children** Make some time to be together each day without the distraction of a newspaper, radio or television.

attention. With less conflict over your roles you will work more efficiently and release more time to be with your friends and family or just alone with a book. If you live alone, make a special time when you put on the answerphone and concentrate on your own needs.

SET TARGETS You should now feel more able to write down the changes you would like to make in your life immediately and in the future. Here is an example of changes that could make life easier:

NOW: Sharing housework or childcare to release uncluttered time.

SOON: Writing regular "time out" sessions into your *work* diary to enable you to plan around them.

IN THE LONG TERM: Negotiating a change in working hours may be something to aim for in the future.

> 66 I drop them off at school and go home to clear the breakfast, but what I really want is to lie down and go back to sleep. I never stop feeling tired and I never achieve anything either. 99

TIME-PLANNING CHART

These charts were filled in by Julia and her husband, who have two children. Each bar represents the time they spent on key activities. Their charts showed how little time they were spending doing things they enjoyed.

They agreed to clarify their childcare responsibilities, to keep one evening a week to themselves, and to write school events (which neither managed to attend) into their work diaries. There is a blank chart to fill in on page 182.

JULIA'S CHART

Time alone												
Time with children												
Time with partner												
Time with friends												
Work												
Housework												
Entertainment												
Sleep												
Hours	1	2	3	4	5	6	7	8	9	10	11	12

JULIA'S PARTNER'S CHART

Time alone												
Time with children												
Time with partner												
Time with friends												
Work												
Housework												
Entertainment												
Sleep												
Hours	1	2	3	4	5	6	7	8	9	10	11	12

SURVIVAL STRATEGIES

Our working lives are crowded, and we too often live on the edge of what we can manage to do. In time to come, perhaps we will arrive at a more harmonious way of living, but until then we can all use some basic survival strategies to help us cope.

CREATE A VILLAGE

Atomized individuals in one-to-one communion with computers may look good in the workplace, but self-reliance is never enough. Everyone needs a wider framework to life, and building connections in your community may literally prove to be a lifeline in a real emergency. At the most basic level, the time you spend getting to know your neighbour may save you a missed appointment or a garage bill when your car won't start in the morning. More seriously, for women living alone, the sense of belonging to a community can make a busy city feel safe, and there is absolutely no substitute for a friendly neighbour when you are stuck in a traffic jam and a friend is about to arrive at the front door.

For working mothers, time spent getting to know other parents is never wasted. The bigger your children's social network, the more people you have to call on in emergencies who will know you and your children. Mutual assistance is a far better back-up than any childcare agency. You may be frantically ringing around everyone you know when your nanny gets flu, but as far as your children are concerned, Auntie Valerie is picking them up from school today. It may be a crisis for you, but for them it is merely an interesting variation on normal arrangements.

CREATING COMMUNITIES
*Building a sense
of belonging is fun.*

CLOTHES STRATEGIES

Fashions change but there are a few basics that will always look smart.

"I regularly travel by air to meetings. How can I avoid looking as though I've slept in my clothes?"
- Loose-woven or knitted fabrics show fewer creases and cope better with splashes than smooth suits.

"Why is it that other women can arrive for a weekend with a small bag and then turn up in a completely different outfit twice a day?"
- Interchangeable separates provide variety as well as simplicity.
- Choose plain, not patterned, fabrics and flattering colours that work together (see pages 22–23) to create many looks from a few items.
- Take something glamorous to liven up clothes for evenings, such as a couple of silky tops, sparkly earrings, a string of beads or bright lipstick.

"I am about to return to work, but how can I ever manage to look like an efficient executive with baby puke on my shoulder and milk rings on my blouse?"
- Buy a loose-weave jacket in beige or cream. It will cover a multitude of sins.
- Choose items that are machine-washable.
- Keep a spare outfit in case the baby throws up on you as you are leaving.

"How does anyone with children ever get anywhere on time?"
- Assume that the time taken to get ready and leave the house can be multiplied by the number of people leaving. With a child under five, double it.
- Keep a bag ready-prepared by the door with nappies, bottom cleaner and a complete spare set of clothes for each child. Refill the bag when you get home and don't raid it when you run out of clean clothes: it must always be ready and suitable for the season.
- If travelling, keep this bag with you constantly. Even quite competent children spill drinks, wet themselves or throw up when moving at speed.

"I am going on a research expedition this summer and will be visiting a family friend. I know she will organize a party, but how can I carry suitable clothes in a backpack?"
- Buy a sarong or two metres of non-crush fabric. You can roll it up in the bottom of your backpack and wear it tied around your waist like a long skirt with a matching vest top.

"I've been unemployed for a year, so I have very little money, nothing smart to wear and I've just been offered a job interview. What can I do?"
- Start with your shoes. If you have a decent pair, polish them until they gleam. If not, buy or borrow plain beige or black pumps or white canvas shoes in summer.
- For a classic look, stick to neutral colours. Keep the skirt at knee length.
- Tie straggly hair back with a scarf to match your outfit, or wear it up.
- Wear either earrings, a brooch or a necklace – not all three.

A SURVIVAL LARDER

For a surprise visitor, or a treat at the end of the day, you need a well-stocked larder. Go for high-quality trimmings, such as: extra-virgin olive oil or walnut oil; sun-dried tomatoes, olives and anchovies; Thai green or red curry paste and a can of coconut milk; parsley, basil, mint and chives grown from seed on your window sill; garlic and fresh ginger.

Use them to liven up low-cost basics to complete a sumptuous meal, including pasta, rice, potatoes or frozen chicken breasts. Then all you need to buy on the day is good bread, fruit and salad in season.

Electrical safety and repairs

The basic tool kit

Unblocking a sink

Repairing a puncture

PRACTICAL LIVING

We have all heard the story of the nuclear physicist who had to ring his wife because he couldn't programme the washing machine, but how many of us have shamefully to admit that we wait for a man to come by when there are repairs to be done? Too often we avoid learning how to do things, not because they are difficult, but because they don't fit in with ingrained ideas about our role in life. But as more and more of us choose to live alone, we cannot expect to leave half of life's skills to our other halves; we have to learn to be whole people ourselves. From basic plumbing repairs to changing a car tyre, the pages that follow reveal exactly what to do.

HOME SAFETY

• FIRES • IN-HOUSE DISASTERS • CRIME PREVENTION

I S YOUR HOME A SAFE HAVEN, a retreat from the hurly-burly, or a death-trap full of disasters waiting to happen? If there is water dripping from a light socket and your towel rail is hanging off the wall; or your washing machine is flooding the flat below and your bicycle has a puncture, here is how to sort it out yourself.

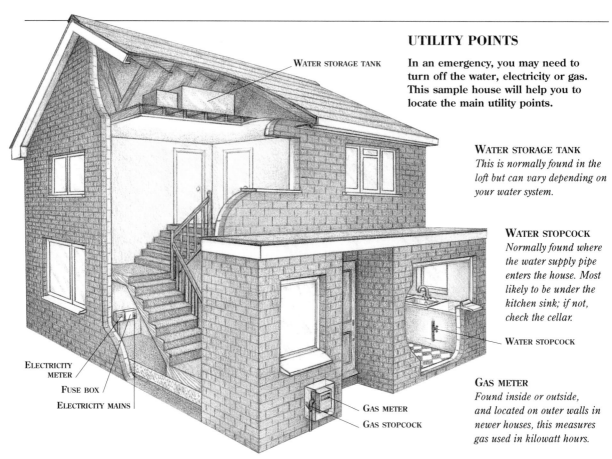

WATER STORAGE TANK

ELECTRICITY METER

FUSE BOX

ELECTRICITY MAINS

GAS METER

GAS STOPCOCK

WATER STOPCOCK

UTILITY POINTS

In an emergency, you may need to turn off the water, electricity or gas. This sample house will help you to locate the main utility points.

WATER STORAGE TANK
This is normally found in the loft but can vary depending on your water system.

WATER STOPCOCK
Normally found where the water supply pipe enters the house. Most likely to be under the kitchen sink; if not, check the cellar.

GAS METER
Found inside or outside, and located on outer walls in newer houses, this measures gas used in kilowatt hours.

ELECTRICITY MAINS
Find the switch on or beside the fuse box. Before you start any electrical repairs, turn off the electricity at the mains.

FUSE BOX
Located by the front door in some countries. Always replace a blown fuse with one of the same amperage.

ELECTRICITY METER
Usually found next to the fuse box, this monitors electricity consumption per hour, measuring it in units called kilowatt hours.

GAS STOPCOCK
Normally located next to the gas meter. To stop the supply in the event of a gas leak, pull the handle down so it is at a right angle to the main pipe.

SAFETY AWARENESS IN THE HOME

POSSIBLE DANGER	PRECAUTIONARY MEASURE	POSSIBLE DANGER	PRECAUTIONARY MEASURE
Sockets	Do not overload sockets with too many plugs and adaptors as this is a fire hazard. Have extra sockets fitted if necessary.	**Loose flexes**	Do not allow them to trail where people can trip over them. Do not run under carpets or staple down.
Open fires	Always use a fireguard, especially to protect small children and to ensure nothing trails into an open fire.	**Corrosives & combustibles**	Lock safely away or store in high cupboards out of the reach of children.
Ashtrays	Make sure that matches and cigarette ends are properly extinguished, especially before going out or going to bed.	**Stair banisters**	Make sure they are not wobbly or insecure.
Electric blankets	Do not allow electric blankets to come into contact with water or get creased: they can cause electrocution.	**Loose rugs**	Buy anti-slip products to keep them in place and prevent danger of tripping.
Gas heaters	May leak toxic carbon monoxide fumes which can kill, so service regularly. Fuel-burning appliances need good ventilation.	**Fabrics & furnishings**	Should be fire-resistant or treated with a fire-resistant spray. Check the labels.
Fan heaters & electric fires 	Do not position near curtains or furniture. Never dry clothes on them.	**Frayed flexes**	Repair immediately. May lead to electrocution or start a fire.
Floor surfaces	Ensure they are non-slip in the bathroom and kitchen.	**Saucepans**	Keep pan handles turned away from the front of the hob – they could be knocked or pulled off.
Stair carpet	Ensure it is properly fitted and not loose or frayed – you could trip up.	**Washing machines**	As with any electrical appliance, do not operate in the bathroom.
Electric appliances	Switch off at the mains or unplug appliances that are not in use, especially when the house is empty.	**Kettles**	Cordless are best, but a coiled flex gives flexibility which may prevent spillage of boiling water.

FIRES

Fires can be started by faulty electrical wiring, unguarded open fires, a smouldering cigarette, a candle left to burn down unattended, even a light bulb left on and in contact with paper or fabric. Fires often happen at night and you may have very little time to escape, so it is worth planning escape routes in advance. Most fires can be prevented with care, but if the worst should happen, you need to know how to put out a small fire and how to escape if it begins to spread.

FIRE PROCEDURE

TYPE OF FIRE		ACTION
Fat fire		Immediately turn off the heat under the pan. Smother the flames by putting a large lid or plate on the pan or throwing a damp towel or fire blanket over it. Never try to move the pan – this will fan the flames. Never throw water on it – the flames will spread.
Electrical fire		Immediately unplug the appliance or turn off the electricity at the mains. Smother the flames with a rug or fire blanket. Never touch the burning appliance. Never use water or fire extinguishers in an attempt to put the fire out.
Open fire		Keep a safe distance and throw water on the fire. Pull any rugs or carpet out of the way.
Burning foam furniture		Do not attempt to tackle this fire. Leave the room immediately, shut the door and phone the fire brigade. The thick, black smoke given off by fires caused by foam furniture is lethal if inhaled and can kill in under 2 minutes.

SMOKE ALARMS

Install smoke alarms between bedrooms and rooms where there is a fire hazard, such as the kitchen and basement.

■ The best place to fit a smoke alarm is on the ceiling, in the centre of a room or hallway. If a room has a sloping ceiling, locate the alarm on the wall, 1 metre (3 feet) from the top.

■ Do not fit smoke alarms near windows, doors or fans, or in very dusty areas: wind and dirt can hinder their sensitivity.

■ Test your smoke alarm weekly.

MAJOR FIRE STRATEGIES

In a major fire, you haven't got much time, so make sure you know what to do:

- If it is confined to one room, shut the door so draughts cannot fan the flames.
- Get everyone out of the house quickly (do not stop to collect possessions).
- Call the fire brigade from a neighbour's house.
- Alert all neighbours – they may also be at risk if the fire spreads.
- If you are trapped upstairs, close the door and block the gap beneath it with (preferably wet) bedding or rugs. Open a window and shout for help.
- If the room fills with smoke, lean out of a window or lie down below the level of the smoke.
- As a last resort, make a rope of sheets, clothes, towels, belts, or anything that comes to hand, and climb down it to safety.

In-house Disasters

Knowing how to detect an impending disaster is the best way of preventing it, but even in the best organized of homes, the occasional crisis will occur. Some disasters only destroy property, others are capable of destroying lives. The faster you react to minimize a problem, the less damage will be done. You can save time in an emergency if you know where to locate your gas stopcock and water and electricity mains (see page 158).

DISASTER PROCEDURE

TYPE OF DISASTER	ACTION
A strong smell of gas	Put out cigarettes, extinguish naked flames and turn off electric fires. Do not touch light switches. Turn the gas off at the mains and open all windows. Phone the gas board from a neighbour's house if possible – a single spark could cause an explosion.
A slight smell of gas	Take the same precautions as above. Try to trace the source of the leak – check pilot lights and the burners on your cooker. If you cannot locate the source and switch it off, open all the windows and call the gas board.
Carbon monoxide poisoning	If you experience unexplained headaches, sickness, lethargy or muscular weakness while in the same room as a gas appliance, turn it off and have it checked by the gas board. Carbon monoxide is odourless and difficult to detect, but it can be fatal (see right).
Burst pipes	Turn the water off at the mains. Mop up water quickly – it can do serious damage. If water collects in a bulge in the ceiling, place a bucket underneath and pierce the bulge with a sharp instrument. If water seeps into light fittings, remove the fuse from the mains fuse box and do not replace it or switch on lights until the area is dry.
Overflowing washing machine	Mop up as much water as quickly as you can and follow the procedure for when pipes burst (above) to minimize damage. A dehumidifier is useful for drying out a room. Check that you did not use the wrong washing powder or too much.
Leaking roof	Most often caused by slipped, cracked or missing roof tiles. Minimize water damage by collecting drips in a bucket and laying down plastic sheeting. If water seeps into the ceiling and starts to bulge, follow the procedure for when pipes burst (above). Check light fittings.
Flooding	Turn off gas, electricity and water at the mains. Fill plastic bags with rolled-up blankets or soil and lay them along the outside of exterior doors. If the flood level rises, do the same at the windowsills. Move valuables, especially rugs and carpets, to upper floors. Be prepared to evacuate.

WARNING

Carbon monoxide is given off by faulty or badly installed gas (or other fossil fuel) heaters. In an unventilated room, it can kill. In a ventilated room, it can cause headaches and flu-like symptoms. You cannot smell or see carbon monoxide, although you can buy special detectors. You should turn an appliance off and have it checked if you notice:
- Yellow or brown staining around the appliance.
- A yellow or orange gas flame (it should burn blue).

CRIME PREVENTION

Burglars will always go for the easiest targets. They look for homes that are obviously unoccupied, easy to enter and, if possible, reasonably secluded. They would also prefer a house where they can see a number of easily located, portable consumer goods. They are looking for money or items that are easy to sell, such as jewellery. As a precaution, do not lock internal doors and drawers; they create a target and you may end up with damage to add to the cost of loss. If you have valuable items that are not in use, keep them in a bank. Make friends with neighbours, particularly those who are at home during the day, so you can keep an eye on each others' homes.

GENERAL PRECAUTIONS

There are some basic precautions that every householder needs to take to keep the home safe:

- Change the locks when you move into a new house. Someone could have taken the key from the previous occupants or real estate agent and copied it.
- Do not label your keys and, if you have your handbag stolen with your keys inside, have your locks changed.
- Ensure valuable consumer goods cannot be seen from the street.
- Install locks on windows and doors (see opposite) and remember to use them.
- Keep front hedges low so they don't provide cover.
- In a high crime area, consider installing a burglar alarm.

WHILE YOU ARE AWAY

If you go away, the best precaution is to find someone to house-sit. Failing that, make sure the house is properly secured and don't provide obvious signs of your absence. The following ideas may be useful:

- Cancel all deliveries so they don't pile up on the doorstep.
- Ask a trusted neighbour to open and close curtains in the evening.
- Don't leave keys under the mat, in a plant pot or on a string.
- Don't leave a message on your answer machine giving details of your absence.
- If you are regularly away for long periods, install automatic timers on lights and radios so the house appears occupied.

IF YOU ARE BURGLED

A burglary is always upsetting, but it may help to know that burglars are no keener on confrontation than you are. They want to get out as fast as they can.

- If you are alone in the house and you think you hear burglars, turn on lights, call out, and make it sound as though you are calling to someone. Ring the police from the room you are in if you can.
- If you arrive home and discover a burglary, do not enter the house. Leave and go to a neighbour's, or to a phone box, and call the police. Wait until they arrive before entering.
- If you do confront a burglar, try to keep calm. If you can get out, do so; if not, make sure you are not blocking the way to the exit.

LOWERING YOUR INSURANCE PREMIUMS

A no-claims bonus will lower your premiums, which vary according to the area you live in. Most insurance companies offer a discount of at least 5 per cent if you comply with the following safety regulations:

- Install 5-lever mortice deadlocks on exterior doors.
- Fit appropriate window locks.
- Have a burglar alarm professionally installed on an annual maintenance contract.
- Install a safe for valuables.
- Join a neighbourhood or home watch scheme.
- Mark valuable items, either by etching or with indelible ink.

CHOOSING THE RIGHT LOCKS

LOCKS FOR DOORS

Invest in good locks; cheap ones are flimsy and, from a security point of view, useless. A good lock is only as secure as the door and frame it is fitted to – make sure both are heavy and solid. Fit rack bolts or barrel bolts at the top and bottom of a door to prevent it being kicked in.

LOCKS FOR FRONT DOORS

A cylinder nightlatch (a snib that is clicked up to bolt the lock, or locked with a key) is not secure because it can be tripped with a credit card. If the door has a glass panel, a burglar can break the panel and reach in to trip the lock. Fit additional locks or bolts.

A mortice deadlock is the most secure lock (a 5 or 7-lever is best); it can only be unbolted by turning the key. These locks are difficult to pick and cannot be levered open with a credit card.

A latchbolt will suffice as a single lock on a front door. It has a handle on the inside but can only be opened with a key from the outside.

LOCKS FOR BACK AND SIDE DOORS

Often hidden from view, back and side doors are the most common points of entry for burglars – make sure they are secure.

A mortice deadlock, with or without handles, is a good choice (see above), as is a **sashlock**, which has a bolt and handles on both sides.

For extra security, fit another mortice deadlock at either the top or the bottom of the door. Alternatively, fit two or three **mortice rack bolts** at the top, middle and bottom to ensure the door is securely reinforced. They are operated with a cylindrical key. Traditional **barrel bolts** or **tower bolts** are also very effective if fitted at the top and bottom of the door.

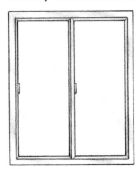

LOCKS FOR PATIO DOORS

Two proprietary locks should be fitted to the inside door to secure the frames to each other. They are most effective when positioned at the top and bottom of the door. Fit them to a wooden door with wooden screws and to a metal one with self-tapping screws.

LOCKS FOR WINDOWS

Fit additional locks to any easily accessible windows. Never leave keys for the lock in the window; keep them out of view but nearby in case of an emergency, when you may need to use the window as an escape route.

LOCKS FOR FRENCH WINDOWS

Mortice rack bolts should be fitted to the top and bottom of the window that opens first and screwed securely into the frame.

Hinge bolts can be fitted to both windows to reinforce weak hinges.

LOCKS FOR SASH WINDOWS

Dual screws will lock the inner and outer frames together. Fit one at each side of the window if it is large.

A surface-fitted bolt will restrict how far the window can be opened, but should open wide enough to allow for ventilation.

LOCKS FOR METAL WINDOWS

A surface-fitted lock should be fixed at the centre of the window, close to the opening edge.

A cockspur bolt secures a cockspur handle, a long-handled levered catch.

LOCKS FOR CASEMENT WINDOWS

Mortice bolts, two at each end of the opening edge, are suitable for wooden windows and are secure because they are fitted into the frame.

Surface-fitted locks will secure windows with narrow wooden frames.

A cockspur bolt must be fitted to the frame to jam the handle if cockspur handles do not secure with a key.

BASIC TOOL KIT

FOR A STRIPPED-DOWN KIT, invest in an electric screwdriver with interchangeable heads, a selection of screws and some rawl plugs, together with a good hammer and some nails. These basics will allow you to stick up most things that fall down. Add an adjustable spanner, a pair of scissors and some insulating tape and you will be able to cope with most minor emergencies. The tool kit shown on these pages will arm you for most essential repairs around the home.

HAMMER
Hammer down on a nail at a right angle to ensure the nail does not bend. Use the claw end of the hammer for levering out toughly entrenched nails.

TACKS AND NAILS
Tacks secure lightweight materials. Flat-head nails lodge firmly and won't pull through. Lost-head nails are easily concealed and cannot be levered out.

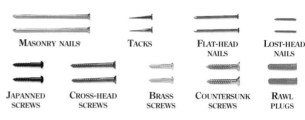

MASONRY NAILS   TACKS   FLAT-HEAD NAILS   LOST-HEAD NAILS

JAPANNED SCREWS   CROSS-HEAD SCREWS   BRASS SCREWS   COUNTERSUNK SCREWS   RAWL PLUGS

SCREWS AND RAWL PLUGS
Screws create a stronger join than a nail because of their spiral threading. A screw should not be more than $\frac{1}{10}$ the width of a piece of wood, or it may split it. Japanned screws are anti-rust. Countersunk screws lie flush with the surface. Inserting a rawl plug before a screw will ensure that the screw fits tightly.

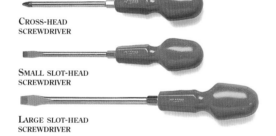

CROSS-HEAD SCREWDRIVER

SMALL SLOT-HEAD SCREWDRIVER

LARGE SLOT-HEAD SCREWDRIVER

ADJUSTABLE SPANNER
A good investment because it is very versatile and fits most nuts and bolts.

SCREWDRIVERS
Different sizes and heads fit different-shaped screws. The cross-head variety generally provide a better grip when screwing than the slot-head.

WOOD DRILL BITS   MASONRY DRILL BITS

ELECTRICIAN'S SCREWDRIVER
Essential for any minor electrical repairs. The built-in bulb illuminates on contact with an electric current.

BRADAWL
Good for boring a hole to guide a drill or a screw.

ELECTRIC DRILL AND BITS
The best option for boring holes through metal, plastic, wood and concrete. Some drills have reverse options that make them useful for unscrewing stubborn screws.

ELECTRIC SCREWDRIVER
These have a variety of screwheads and are a must for anyone without wrestler's arm muscles.

ENGINEER'S PLIERS
Good for general purpose tasks where you need to get a firm grip on something.

SPIRIT LEVEL
Essential to ensure surfaces are really level; also allows you to measure a 45-degree angle.

STEEL RULER
Durable and a good choice for marking out precise measurements.

CHISELS
Use when cutting into wood and when prizing up tiles or floorboards.

CRAFT KNIFE
For trimming and cutting items that are difficult to tackle with scissors, such as wallpaper, carpet and floor tiles.

INSULATING TAPE
Useful for many temporary repairs and for holding lagging together.

STRING
Every tool kit should have some – it will always come in handy.

RADIATOR KEY
You need this to bleed a radiator (see page 167).

MEASURING TAPE
Handy when measuring long stretches or around corners.

PLUNGER
Should unblock any sink or toilet – good for saving money on plumber's bills.

SCISSORS
A good pair of general purpose scissors is invaluable.

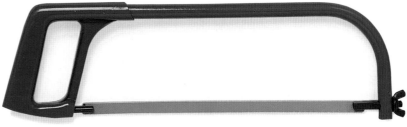

HACK SAW
Best for cutting through metal or plastic – pipes in particular.

PANEL SAW
Use for cutting through wood. Saw with an even, rhythmic action.

ESSENTIAL REPAIRS

- ELECTRICAL • PLUMBING • CAR MAINTENANCE
- CAR TROUBLE • BICYCLE MAINTENANCE

BASIC HOUSE REPAIRS can seem daunting if you don't know one end of a screwdriver from the other and have no idea what a rawl plug is used for. The following pages will put simple repairs easily within your grasp.

ELECTRICAL

Many electrical repairs are simple if you observe basic safety rules: never touch wiring that is attached to the mains without first unplugging or turning off the supply; make sure you attach live to live and earth to earth; and never allow bare wires to touch each other or to touch any other metal surface.

WIRING A PLUG

Make sure that the plug has the correct fuse (3, 5 or 13-amp) for the appliance you are attaching it to – check the manufacturer's handbook if you are at all uncertain.

The electrical wires in the flex are colour coded:
- **In a modern plug, brown is live, blue neutral, and green and yellow is earth.**
- **In an older plug, red is live, blue neutral, and green earth.**

1 Using a craft knife, strip 6–12mm (½in) of casing off each of the wires in the flex, exposing wires long enough to reach each of the terminals in the plug. Twist the wires in each separate casing together if they begin to fray.

2 Undo the screw that holds the plug together. Undo one of the screws in the small arm at the base of the plug that holds the flex in place and push the arm to one side.

3 Undo the screws at each of the terminals and feed each of the three wires in. Place the live wire into the terminal marked L, the neutral into the terminal marked N, and the earth into the terminal marked E. Secure each wire in its terminal by tightening the screw that holds it in place.

4 Screw down the arm at the base of the plug to hold the flex in place. Screw the cover back on to the plug.

CHANGING A MAINS FUSE

In a household electrical system, the different appliances, switches and lighting are powered by circuits. If a circuit is overloaded or there is a fault on it, the fuse will blow.

Your fuse box will contain one of three types of mains fuse (right). Always switch off at the mains before touching the fuses. Once you have located the blown fuse, switch all appliances and sockets on that circuit off. Depending on the type of fuse, replace it or switch it back on (see right). Switch on each appliance and power point until the fuse blows again. If the fuse blows when everything is on, the circuit is overloaded and you should use fewer appliances.

A cartridge fuse
Look for evidence of burning to help identify the blown fuse. Remove the fuse carrier and replace the blown fuse with one of the same amperage.

A miniature circuit breaker (MCB) system
You can locate the circuit that has fused because the switch will have moved to the off position. Turn the switch back on.

A rewirable fuse
The wire will have broken in the blown fuse. Unscrew the terminals at each end, remove the broken wire and insert fuse wire of the same amperage or thickness. Reassemble.

PLUMBING

Plumbing is mostly a matter of logic plus, in many cases, muscle power to shift stuck or rusted metal. With a bit of effort and common sense you can repair small blockages and leaks yourself, but do not touch your gas supply – call in a plumber with a recognized qualification.

CLEARING A BLOCKED TOILET

A toilet can block in the bend running from the bowl to the outside, or in the drains that remove the effluent. Try unblocking the toilet with a mop and plastic bag (right). This is normally effective, but if it does not work, you may need to call a specialist drain-clearing company or borrow some drain-clearing rods. These bend and extend some distance. With enough wiggling you should be able to dislodge any obstruction.

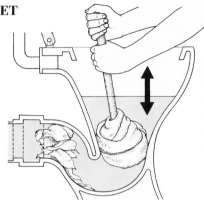

1 Use an old mop; it will not be useful in its previous role again. Tie a plastic bag or an old towel over the mop head and secure it with string. If the floor is carpeted, cover it with plastic sheets.

2 Insert the mop into the bowl to fill the drainage hole. Move the mop up and down to create suction. This should dislodge the blockage.

REPAIRING A CISTERN

If the cistern overflows, it could mean that the ball float is not working properly, since the ball float controls the inlet valve by closing it automatically.

If the toilet cistern requires repeated efforts to make it flush, there could be a problem with the flap valve, which is situated at the base of the siphon assembly. You may need to call a qualified plumber to deal with this.

Use the same technique to stop a cold water cistern or water tank from overflowing as you would for a toilet cistern (right).

1 Before working on the cistern, empty the water out. Place a piece of wood across the top of the cistern and tie the arm of the float to the wood. This will prevent the cistern filling up with water. Flush the toilet.

2 If the ball float is damaged, unscrew and replace with a new one of the same size.

3 If the ball float is in good condition, check the float arm. It may be at the wrong angle so that the ball float is too high. This will keep the inlet valve open, allowing water to continue flowing

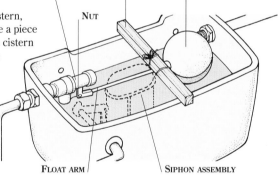

INLET VALVE   WOOD   BALL FLOAT
NUT
FLOAT ARM   SIPHON ASSEMBLY

into the cistern. If the arm is plastic, loosen the nut to lower the ball. If it is metal, use a spanner to bend the arm down. Untie the wood to let the cistern refill.

BLEEDING A RADIATOR

If a radiator feels hot at the bottom and cool toward the top, it has air in it, preventing efficient heating. At the beginning of winter, it is sensible to bleed radiators to release any trapped air. Buy a special key that fits the vent valve at the top end of the radiator.

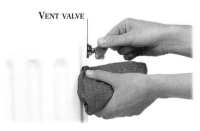

VENT VALVE

Releasing trapped air
Hold a rag underneath the valve to catch any water. Using the special key, open the valve until air starts to hiss out. Do not open the valve too far or it may come out. Be ready to close the valve as soon as drops of water start to leak from it.

TYPES OF TAP

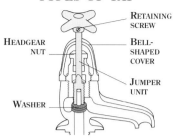

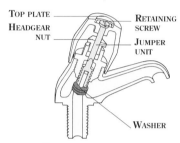

CAPSTAN-HEAD TAP
*Undo the retaining screw
and the handle and then take
off the bell-shaped cover.*

SHROUDED-HEAD TAP
*Either pull off the shroud head
or prize off the top plate to get
to the retaining screw.*

FIXING A LEAKING TAP

**A dripping tap wastes
water and can be fixed by
replacing the washer. In a
modern tap with ceramic
discs, dripping can be
caused by grit lodged
between the discs and
you should call a plumber.
Before starting plumbing
repairs, turn off the water
supply to the tap either at
the main indoor stopcock,
the gate valve located by
the water tank, or the gate
valve near the tap you are
working on. Then turn the
tap on and run it until no
more water comes out.
Put the plug in the sink
to prevent any small parts
falling down the drain. As
you dismantle the tap, lay
the parts out in the order
you remove them. When
you have reassembled the
tap, turn the stopcock or
valve back on and wait for
water to run out of the
tap before turning it off.**

1 Remove the top plate or
bell cover (see left) and
undo the retaining screw and
knob to expose the headgear.

JUMPER UNIT

3 Hold the edge of the
jumper unit with pliers
and unscrew the nut that
holds the washer in position.

2 Unscrew the headgear
nut with an adjustable
spanner and remove it from
the body of the tap.

4 Replace the old washer
with a new one and
reassemble the tap following
the steps in reverse.

CLEARING A BLOCKED SINK

You will find either a U-bend or a trap under your sink.

1 Block the overflow hole
with a rag and bail out the
water. Place a rubber plunger
over the plughole to cover
it completely. Work the
plunger up and down to
create suction, dislodge the
blockage and drain the sink.

2 If you are unsuccessful
with the plunger, put a
bucket under the sink and
unscrew the U-bend. Undo
the top joint first, then the
lower one.

3 If the blockage is stubborn,
unscrew the whole U-bend
and clean it thoroughly. If
the sink still will not drain,
use a straightened wire
clothes hanger to probe
into the pipes and poke out
the blockage.

CLEARING A TRAP

If you have a plastic trap,
place a bucket under the
pipe and unscrew the bottom
section. The blockage and
waste should dislodge. You
may have to poke a piece of
wire into the pipe to loosen
the blockage.

PIPE LEAKS AND BURSTS

At the first sign of a leak, make sure that the water supply to the leak is turned off. If in doubt, turn off the water at the mains and turn off any central heating.

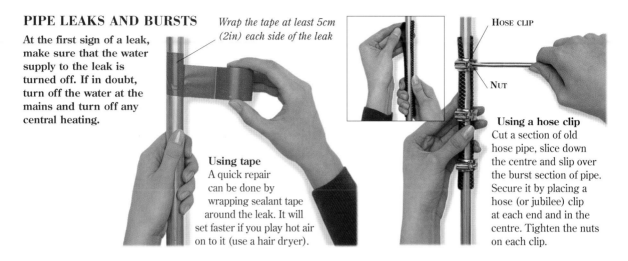

Wrap the tape at least 5cm (2in) each side of the leak

HOSE CLIP

NUT

Using tape
A quick repair can be done by wrapping sealant tape around the leak. It will set faster if you play hot air on to it (use a hair dryer).

Using a hose clip
Cut a section of old hose pipe, slice down the centre and slip over the burst section of pipe. Secure it by placing a hose (or jubilee) clip at each end and in the centre. Tighten the nuts on each clip.

FROZEN PIPES

In cold weather, water that does not flow may freeze in a pipe. Any thawing should be done gently, or the pipe might crack.

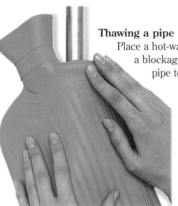

Thawing a pipe
Place a hot-water bottle over a blockage in an accessible pipe to thaw it gently.

Heating with an appliance
Play an electric heater or hair dryer over a frozen section of pipe to thaw it.

PREVENTATIVE MEASURES

Sensible preventative measures can be taken to prevent pipes bursting in the first place. Lag hot and cold water pipes situated in parts of the house that are subjected to extreme cold, such as the attic and under ground-floor floorboards. When insulating an attic, do not insulate the area under water tanks. Heat rising from the house keeps them warm and less likely to freeze.

Foam tubing
The easiest way to lag pipes is to cover them with commercial foam tubing. This can be bought ready-moulded in standard sizes. Slip it over the pipes and secure with adhesive tape.

Strip lagging
For difficult short sections of pipe, use any suitable insulating material – an old tea towel, for example. Wrap it around the pipe and then hold in place with adhesive tape.

CAR MAINTENANCE

Surveys have shown that 80 per cent of women are overcharged by garages and that women are routinely charged up to two thirds more than men for minor repairs and servicing. They think they can see you coming, so when you get your car serviced, it will help if you at least sound as if you know what you want the mechanic to do. Keep copies of all your old bills (which should always be itemized). When you take the car in, remind the garage of what was fixed last time and provide a list of what you want them to check. Ask them to phone with an estimate *before* starting work and to keep parts they replace for you to see.

REGULAR CHECKS

Basic maintenance will not only prolong the life of your car, it will make it safer as well.

PETROL
Keep the petrol level about a quarter full and always fill up before a long journey. Dirty residue in petrol dregs can clog the engine.

FUSES
Normally located under the dashboard, but check your handbook. Carry spares and learn how to change them.

WINDSCREEN
Ensure screen washer is not too low. Buy a special additive to prevent the windscreen icing (not anti-freeze, which can harm the paintwork). Make sure the wipers are not worn – an indicator of this is "juddering". Dirty windows distort your view, especially dangerous at night.

OIL LEVEL
Check weekly when the engine is cool. Consult the handbook if you have trouble locating the dipstick or are unsure of the grade of oil to use. Running out of oil while driving can damage the engine irreparably.

BATTERY
Batteries that are "sealed for life" require no maintenance, but older ones need the fluid level checked monthly. Top up with distilled water to the marked maximum level (or until the plates are covered).

SPARE TYRE
Usually in the boot

FUSES
May be under the dashboard or bonnet

EXHAUST
Watch out for harmful emission levels. Ask your mechanic to check.

TYRES
Check the condition and air pressure weekly. Tread depth should comply with the latest regulations. Uneven wearing can indicate a serious problem, such as faulty wheel alignment.

SPARE TYRE
Check that this is in sound condition. In many countries it is illegal to drive without one.

WATER LEVELS
Check weekly, but never unscrew the radiator cap (or expansion chamber) while hot. Cars with sealed systems do not need topping up.

HOW A CAR WORKS

If you don't want to be ripped off, you need to know at least a little about what happens under the bonnet of your car. Here is a basic grounding.

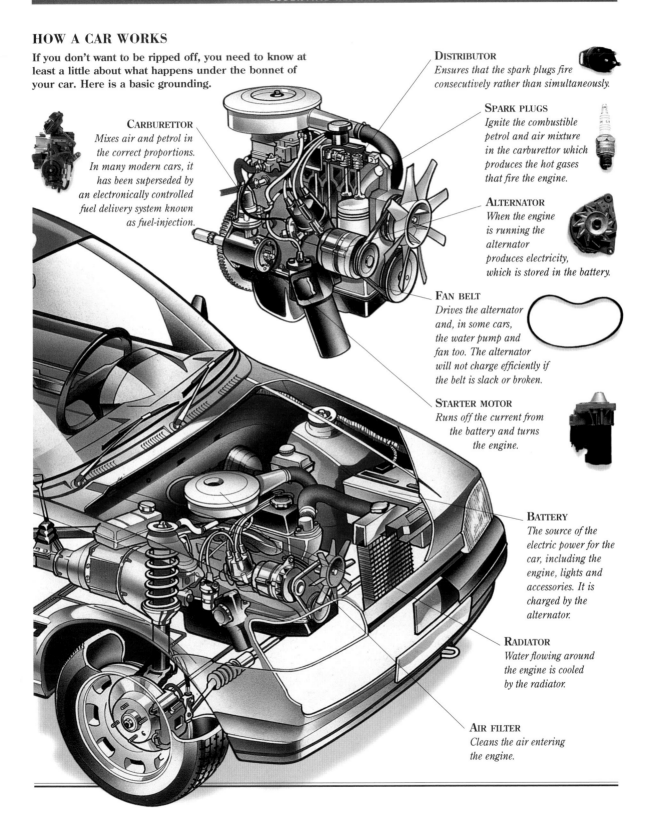

DISTRIBUTOR
Ensures that the spark plugs fire consecutively rather than simultaneously.

SPARK PLUGS
Ignite the combustible petrol and air mixture in the carburettor which produces the hot gases that fire the engine.

CARBURETTOR
Mixes air and petrol in the correct proportions. In many modern cars, it has been superseded by an electronically controlled fuel delivery system known as fuel-injection.

ALTERNATOR
When the engine is running the alternator produces electricity, which is stored in the battery.

FAN BELT
Drives the alternator and, in some cars, the water pump and fan too. The alternator will not charge efficiently if the belt is slack or broken.

STARTER MOTOR
Runs off the current from the battery and turns the engine.

BATTERY
The source of the electric power for the car, including the engine, lights and accessories. It is charged by the alternator.

RADIATOR
Water flowing around the engine is cooled by the radiator.

AIR FILTER
Cleans the air entering the engine.

WHAT TO DO IF YOU BREAK DOWN

■ On an arterial road, park on the hard shoulder, turn on your hazard-warning lights and follow the arrows on marker posts to the nearest emergency phone. After phoning, return to your car and remain outside it but away from the road.
■ On other roads, drive or push your car into a safe position. Turn on the hazard-warning lights and put the bonnet up. If you cannot get to a public phone, sit in the car, lock the doors and windows and wait. When someone stops, ask them to phone your motoring organization, or a garage, to come to your rescue.

CAR TROUBLE

Running out of petrol is the most common reason for breaking down, but if anything else should go wrong, the chart on the right will help you to diagnose the problem, even if you cannot fix it yourself.

JUMP STARTING A CAR

A car will start, even with a flat battery.

1 Park another car close enough for the jump leads to reach, but make sure that the two cars do not touch.

2 Clip the black lead to the negative (–) terminal on each battery. Attach the red, positive (+) lead to the positive terminals. Do not let the clips touch.

3 Start the car with the healthy battery. When it is idling smoothly, start the car with the dead battery. Ensure the lights are off.

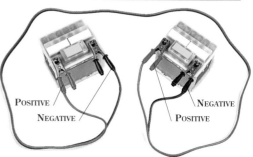

POSITIVE

NEGATIVE

NEGATIVE

POSITIVE

4 Disconnect first the positive, then the negative leads. Keep the engine running for at least 10 minutes to recharge the battery.

HOW TO CHANGE A TYRE

Make sure treads are not worn, that tyres are properly inflated and that wheel alignment is checked at each service. Good tyres rarely let you down, but be sure to carry a jack (most cars come with one) and learn how to use it. Ensure your spare tyre is in good condition.

1 With some models of car, you have to remove the hubcap to get to the bolts – it is normally easy to prize off. Loosen the bolts (turning anti-clockwise) with a spanner while the weight of the car stops the wheel turning.

BOLTS

2 Position the jack securely under the car and at a suitable jacking point (this varies with different cars, see your handbook). Do not attempt to change a tyre on anything but firm, unsloping ground.

JACKING POINT

3 Either wind or pump the jack up so the car is lifted well off the ground. Then fully unscrew the bolts (put them somewhere safe) and lift away the wheel.

4 Fit the spare tyre and, using moderate force, tighten the bolts diagonally opposite each other to ensure the wheel is centred. Wind down the jack to lower the car. Fully tighten the bolts using the car's weight to hold the wheel in place. Refit the hubcap.

CAR TROUBLE-SHOOTING CHART

SYMPTOM	POSSIBLE CAUSE	ACTION
1 Engine fails to turn or is dead when ignition key is turned.	• The battery is flat. • Battery connections are loose or corroded. • Starter motor wiring loose or broken.	• Start the car using jump leads or by push-starting. Do not push-start cars with catalytic converters or automatic gears. • Tighten connections; if terminals are corroded, clean and remake connection. • Consult a mechanic.
2 Engine turns normally but fails to start.	• No fuel in tank. • Fuel not reaching engine. • Excessive choke – engine "flooded". • Insufficient choke – engine is too cold. • Faulty or dirty spark plugs. • Ignition failure.	• Check petrol gauge – in an old car they cannot always be trusted. If you suspect a faulty gauge, take the fuel cap off, rock the car and listen for the sound of sloshing petrol. • Check for leaks on the fuel lines running from the fuel tank to the carburettor. Ask your mechanic to investigate blockages. • With a manual choke, leave the car for 15 minutes. Try starting without choke, but use full accelerator. No DIY attention is possible for cars with fuel injection. • Pull choke out fully when trying to start car, but beware of flooding the engine. • Remove and clean. Could indicate more serious problem. • Consult breakdown service or mechanic.
3 Engine cuts out and will not restart.	• Damp distributor cap or spark-plug leads. • Fuel not reaching engine. • Ignition fault.	• Check distributor cap and spark-plug leads for dampness – wipe or leave to dry. Use a proprietary water repellent spray. • See 2 above. • Consult a mechanic.
4 Engine misfires and then cuts out and will not restart.	• Wiring fault. • Dirt in fuel system. • Possible ignition fault.	• Check for loose wiring. • This can be caused by driving on petrol dregs. Refer to mechanic. See also 3 above. • Consult a mechanic.
5 Engine overheats.	• Low coolant level. • Cooling fan not working. • Leaking joints or hoses.	• Check and top up. Check hoses and radiator for leaks. • Check fuses if fan is electric. • Tighten if possible. N.B. Never add cold water to a hot engine – major engine damage is likely to result. Do not remove radiator or expansion pressure caps while hot – risk of injury from escaping steam.
6 "Pinking" noise in the engine.	• Incorrect grade of fuel. • Incorrect ignition timing.	• Check car handbook for correct type of fuel. • Consult a mechanic.
7 Screeching noise in the engine.	• Worn out or loose fan belt.	• Check the condition and tension of the fan belt; it should be taut and unfrayed.
8 Horn, wipers, indicators, both headlights or both rearlights do not work.	• Dirty or blown fuse.	• Pull the relevant fuse (it should be marked) from its terminals. Fuses are colour-coded according to rating. Always replace an old fuse with a new fuse of the same rating. If the fuse blows again, there may be a short circuit. Consult a mechanic.

BICYCLE MAINTENANCE

As urban roads clog up with traffic and rural public transport disappears, the humble bicycle really starts to come into its own. The bicycle keeps you fit, is economical, causes no pollution and is faster than walking. In fact, in big cities, where rush-hour traffic can be reduced to a crawl, cycling is faster even than the car. The growing popularity of the bicycle as a viable form of transport has meant that manufacturers are making bikes lighter yet more durable, and more high-tech. Maintaining your bike will lessen the likelihood of a mishap on the road, but carry a pump, tyre levers and a puncture repair kit or a spare inner tube at all times, and familiarize yourself with the basics of bicycle repair, just in case.

REGULAR CHECKS

Look after your bicycle; journeys will be safer.

WHEEL REFLECTORS
An essential safety precaution, especially if you ride at dusk or night. Attach them to the front and back wheels.

SADDLE
It is the correct height if, when you sit on the saddle with your foot on one of the pedals in the down position, your leg bends only slightly.

BRAKE CABLES
Check for worn cable housing and any fraying.

BRAKE BLOCKS
Make sure they are correctly aligned with the rim of the wheel. Remove any grit which may make brakes less effective.

WHEEL REFLECTOR

BRAKE CABLES

BRAKE BLOCKS

CHAINSET

CHAINSET
Keep chainrings clean and check they are not bent and that no teeth are broken. Use oil or a synthetic lubricant.

CHAIN
Check that it does not become worn or stretched and that the links have not jammed. Keep well lubricated.

PEDALS
Check for cracking and tighten if they become loose. Toe straps can fray and may need replacing.

WHEELS
Check tyre pressure regularly and replace tyres when the treads wear down. Remove embedded gravel and grit.

CHANGING AN INNER TUBE

With some models of bicycle, you may need to release and detach the brake cables first.

1 Unscrew the valve cap and locknut. If there is no locknut, use your finger or a pen to push the valve in and deflate the tube. Push the valve through the hole in the rim.

2 To separate the tyre from the rim, work your way around the tyre pressing back and forth and pinching the sides of the tyre together.

3 Place the tyre levers between the rim and the tyre about 2cm (1in) apart. To hook the tyre over the rim, hold one tyre lever in place and slide the other around.

4 You should now be able to remove the tube and repair the puncture (see below), or replace it with a spare inner tube.

5 To refit an inner tube, partially inflate it to avoid creasing. Tuck the tube inside the tyre and push the valve through the valve hole in the rim.

6 Working back and forth, and away from the valve, use your thumbs to press the side of the tyre over the rim. Fit the locknut, reinflate the tyre and replace the valve cap.

REPAIRING A PUNCTURE

Carry a puncture repair kit consisting of sandpaper, adhesive, a patch and some chalk.

1 Take out the inner tube (see above) and inflate it; hold it to your ear and listen for a hiss. If you over-inflate the tube, you should be able to feel, or even see, the nick.

2 Use sandpaper or a cement surface to roughen the area around the hole. Smear the adhesive over an area slightly larger than the patch you are going to apply.

3 Allow the adhesive to become tacky before peeling the foil off the patch and applying it. Press the patch firmly in place, making sure not to trap air bubbles.

4 Let the patch set, pull off the cellophane back and dust with chalk to prevent any glue sticking to the tyre. Refit the inner tube (see steps 5 and 6 above).

First Aid

SHOULD THERE BE AN EMERGENCY, this chart will advise you on temporary measures in the short term, until professional medical advice can be sought. You should not carry out first-aid procedures without training, but there may be situations where there is no one else to help.

SYMPTOM	ACTION
Anaphylactic shock Symptoms can include anxiety, tightness in the chest and difficulty breathing, blotchy red skin, puffiness around the eyes, swelling of the face and neck, a quickened pulse rate.	THIS IS A SEVERE ALLERGIC reaction that normally occurs as a result of the injection of a particular drug, the sting of a particular insect or marine animal, or from having eaten a particular food. The condition can be fatal. Reassure the person in shock and keep them sitting up to ease any breathing problems. Call an ambulance and get them to hospital immediately.
Bleeding	PULL ANY CLOTHING AWAY from the wound and apply firm pressure with a clean pad or dressing. To control the bleeding, raise the injury above the level of the heart. If blood seeps through the dressing, do not remove it, apply a new dressing on top. Secure the dressing by bandaging the wound, using a scarf or handkerchief if there is nothing better to hand. Tie the bandage firmly, but not so tight as to cut off the circulation. Seek medical advice.
Burn	COOL THE BURN by running it under cold water for at least 10 minutes; this should alleviate some of the pain. A burn will swell; remove any clothing or jewellery that may constrict this. Cover the burn with a clean, non-fluffy dressing that will not stick to it. Never apply sticky plasters; never rub fat, ointment or any greasy lotion on the burn; never burst a blister. You can use a plastic bag or cling film as a temporary dressing. A very painful burn is usually an indicator of only superficial damage to the skin. A burn that has charred the skin or turned it grey or black and caused peeling but is not too painful, may be very serious. Seek medical advice immediately.
Choking	FOR A CHOKING ADULT OR CHILD, lean them forward and, using the heel of your hand, give up to five sharp blows between the shoulder blades. Try to hit hard enough to dislodge the item. If this does not work, for an adult, stand behind the person, reach around and put one fist below the breastbone, thumbside in, and grasp with the other hand. Pull in sharply. The aim is to pull the top of the abdomen up against the bottom of the lungs. The force of the remaining air in the lungs being pushed out should dislodge the blockage from the air passage. For a child, perform a chest thrust: place the heel of your hand on the lower breastbone and push downward five times. If this fails, place the heel of your hand midway between navel and breastbone; push upward five times.
Drug overdose Symptoms can include vomiting, hallucinations, extreme dilation or contraction of the pupils, sweating, breathing difficulties, unconsciousness.	CALL AN AMBULANCE IMMEDIATELY. Check and clear the person's airway; resuscitation may be necessary (see unconsciousness). Do not try to make the person vomit; this can cause more damage. Try to ascertain which and how much of the drug was taken. Take any pill bottles, a sample of vomit, if possible, and any suicide note to the hospital with you.

SYMPTOM	ACTION	
Grit or harmful chemical in the eye	TILT THE PERSON'S HEAD to one side, hold the eye open and gently pour cool, clean water over the eye to rinse it. If the eye is cut or wounded, or has an object embedded in it, lay the person down, making sure the head is supported.	Cover the eye with an eye pad and secure with a bandage that covers both eyes – this minimizes eye movement. Reassure the person and seek medical advice.
Head injury	KEEP YOUR FINGERS out of any wound, place a clean dressing over it and apply firm pressure to control any bleeding. Secure the dressing with a bandage. If the person is sick or drowsy or has been	unconscious, even for a few seconds, seek medical advice. If you have to transport them, keep them in a lying-down position; make sure the head and shoulders are constantly supported.
Insect and marine stings	REMOVE AN INSECT STING still in the skin with tweezers: grasp it close to the skin and pull firmly. A plastic bag half-filled with ice (or even a bag of frozen peas) and wrapped in cloth will reduce swelling and alleviate pain. If the person has been stung in the mouth, swelling could restrict breathing; get them to hospital	immediately. Sucking ice cubes will help to reduce swelling. For marine stings, inactivate the venom by pouring household vinegar or seawater over the wound, then dust with talcum powder or meat tenderizer (used for barbecues). In both cases look for signs of anaphylactic shock (see left).
Nosebleed	SIT THE PERSON DOWN, making sure the head is tilted forward, and gently pinch the nose just below the bridge. Do not allow the head to tip back as blood can run down the back of the throat and cause vomiting. Gently mop up the blood	and clean around the nose. Advise the person to breathe through the mouth. Seek medical advice if the bleeding persists for longer than 10 minutes or clear fluid is mixed with the blood – it may indicate a more serious condition.
Swallowed chemicals	TRY TO FIND OUT WHICH CHEMICAL has been swallowed. Household cleaners such as bleach and disinfectant are dangerous if swallowed. If the chemical is corrosive and has burnt the person's mouth or	throat, give cool water or milk to sip slowly. Do not induce vomiting. Call an ambulance and get them to hospital immediately.
Knocked-out tooth	IT IS POSSIBLE TO REIMPLANT an adult tooth, so if it has been lost, it is worth looking for it. When you find the tooth, do not wash it as this may damage the delicate tissues that will help it to reroot. Put the tooth back in its socket and keep it in	place by gently holding a clean dressing or pad over it. If you cannot place the tooth back in its socket, store in the person's cheek or in a glass of milk. Get the person to a dentist or hospital as soon as possible.
Unconsciousness	IF THE PERSON IS NOT BREATHING, roll them on to their back, tilt the head back, open the mouth and clear any *obvious* blockage with a finger. Pinch the nose with your thumb and forefinger and breathe gently into the mouth, removing your mouth from theirs to allow the lungs to empty of	air between breaths. Once breathing is regular, turn the person carefully on to their side, folding the lower arm so their hand is under their cheek. Pull the upper arm and upper leg out at right angles to the body to support it. Do not move unless absolutely necessary.

PERSONAL RECORDS

KEEP A RECORD of essential information and you will always have it easily to hand without having to rummage through piles of paper to find things in a hurry. It also acts as a safeguard should an important document be destroyed, lost or stolen. If you photocopy this page, you will always have a clean copy to update.

HEALTH RECORDS

Doctor

Address

Telephone

Dentist

Address

Telephone

Well woman clinic

Address

Telephone

Health number

Blood group

Height

Weight

Allergies

Regular prescriptions

Emergency contact in case of accident

Address

Telephone

Vaccination records

It is wise to have the necessary vaccinations if you travel to countries with conditions that may pose health risks. Make sure you keep a record of the type and date of any vaccinations. The inoculations you will need do change, so check with your doctor or a health clinic before travelling.

Tetanus

Polio

Typhoid

Yellow fever

Hepatitis A (a booster may be advisable if travelling to a high-risk area)

Diphtheria

Meningitis

Tuberculosis

Others

PERSONAL/FINANCIAL

National Insurance number

Tax number

Bank

Address

Telephone

Sorting code

Current account number

Deposit account number

Card number(s)

24-hour emergency number

Building Society

Address

Telephone

Code number

Current account number

Deposit account number

Card number(s)

24-hour emergency number

Credit card number(s)

24-hour emergency number

Pension number

Company

Address

Telephone

Life assurance number

Company

Address

Telephone

Mortgage number

Company

Address

Telephone

Landlord or estate agent

Company

Address

Telephone

Building insurance number

Company

Address

Telephone

Contents insurance number

Company

Address

Telephone

MENSTRUAL RECORDS

THE SYMPTOMS OF THE CYCLE are different for every woman. Use the charts and calendars on these pages to introduce some degree of order and predictability into what can be a very volatile time of the month. If you photocopy these charts, you can re-use them and keep a more long-term record.

CHARTING THE CHANGES IN YOUR CYCLE

Often you are only able to identify the symptoms of your period after it has arrived. You may feel inexplicably touchy, overemotional or suffer debilitating backache for a few days before your period. Similarly, at other times in the month you may feel sensual, glowing and sociable. Charting the occurrence of symptoms, both physical and mental, will enable you to detect any patterns and explain changes in mood.

There will probably be many other symptoms that you can add to the lists on the right. Record any changes over four consecutive months in the charts below.

PHYSICAL CHANGES

W	Weight fluctuations
B	Breast changes
S	Spots
H	Headaches
N	Nausea
D	Diarrhoea
R	Water retention/ bloating
P	Heavy bleeding
p	Light bleeding
C	Cramps
A	Backache

MENTAL CHANGES

D	Depression
S	Snappiness
C	Clumsiness
T	Tearfulness
F	Cravings
H	Heightened libido
L	Diminished libido
A	Appetite
Z	Disturbed sleep/ dreams
Y	Creativity
P	Paranoia

MONTH

Physical																	
Mental																	
Day	1	2	3	4	5	6	7	8	9	10	11	12	13	14	15	16	17

MONTH

Physical																	
Mental																	
Day	1	2	3	4	5	6	7	8	9	10	11	12	13	14	15	16	17

MONTH

Physical																	
Mental																	
Day	1	2	3	4	5	6	7	8	9	10	11	12	13	14	15	16	17

MONTH

Physical																	
Mental																	
Day	1	2	3	4	5	6	7	8	9	10	11	12	13	14	15	16	17

TYPE OF CYCLE

If you ring the date of the first day of your period over consecutive months, you will soon see a pattern emerge. If the circled dates are in a straight line, your cycle is a predictable 28-day cycle. If the line slopes down from left to right, you have a longer cycle, between 28 and 35 days, which is constant. If the line slopes upward, your cycle is shorter than 28 days. If there is no straight line in any direction, you have a variable cycle.

Jan 1	29	26	26	23	21	18	16	13	10	8	5	3	31
2	30	27	27	24	22	19	17	14	11	9	6	4	Jan 1
3	31	28	28	25	23	20	18	15	12	10	7	5	2
4	Feb 1	Mar 1	29	26	24	21	19	16	13	11	8	6	3
5	2	2	30	27	25	22	20	17	14	12	9	7	4
6	3	3	31	28	26	23	21	18	15	13	10	8	5
7	4	4	Apr 1	29	27	24	22	19	16	14	11	9	6
8	5	5	2	30	28	25	23	20	17	15	12	10	7
9	6	6	3	May 1	29	26	24	21	18	16	13	11	8
10	7	7	4	2	30	27	25	22	19	17	14	12	9
11	8	8	5	3	31	28	26	23	20	18	15	13	10
12	9	9	6	4	Jun 1	29	27	24	21	19	16	14	11
13	10	10	7	5	2	30	28	25	22	20	17	15	12
14	11	11	8	6	3	Jul 1	29	26	23	21	18	16	13
15	12	12	9	7	4	2	30	27	24	22	19	17	14
16	13	13	10	8	5	3	31	28	25	23	20	18	15
17	14	14	11	9	6	4	Aug 1	29	26	24	21	19	16
18	15	15	12	10	7	5	2	30	27	25	22	20	17
19	16	16	13	11	8	6	3	31	28	26	23	21	18
20	17	17	14	12	9	7	4	Sep 1	29	27	24	22	19
21	18	18	15	13	10	8	5	2	30	28	25	23	20
22	19	19	16	14	11	9	6	3	Oct 1	29	26	24	21
23	20	20	17	15	12	10	7	4	2	30	27	25	22
24	21	21	18	16	13	11	8	5	3	31	28	26	23
25	22	22	19	17	14	12	9	6	4	Nov 1	29	27	24
26	23	23	20	18	15	13	10	7	5	2	30	28	25
27	24	24	21	19	16	14	11	8	6	3	Dec 1	29	26
28	25	25	22	20	17	15	12	9	7	4	2	30	27

18	19	20	21	22	23	24	25	26	27	28	29	30	31	32	33	34	35

18	19	20	21	22	23	24	25	26	27	28	29	30	31	32	33	34	35

18	19	20	21	22	23	24	25	26	27	28	29	30	31	32	33	34	35

18	19	20	21	22	23	24	25	26	27	28	29	30	31	32	33	34	35

TIME MANAGEMENT

EFFECTIVE TIME MANAGEMENT is only really possible if you can identify exactly what you currently do with your time and exactly what you would like to do with your time. The charts on these pages may offer some useful time-planning suggestions. Photocopy them so you can re-use them.

ASSESSING YOUR TIME

Think about what you spend your time doing and who you spend it with. Break a typical day down and colour in the appropriate number of hours on each bar of the chart below to give a visual representation. If you can learn to organize your day and prioritize tasks (pleasant as well as unpleasant), you will find you can use your time more beneficially. See page 153 for a sample chart that has already been filled in.

YOUR CHART

	1	2	3	4	5	6	7	8	9	10	11	12
Time alone												
Time with partner												
Time with friends												
Time with children												
Work												
Housework												
Entertainment												
Sleep												
Hours	1	2	3	4	5	6	7	8	9	10	11	12

TARGETS FOR CHANGE

Now use the information from the chart above to plan changes in your routine that would allow you to spend more time doing the things you want to. Plan changes you could make immediately, over the next few weeks or months, and in the long term.

NOW	SOON	LONG TERM

TO DO PLANNER

Take the time to plan your week. Set aside realistic blocks of time to get things done. Don't forget to allow yourself time to do the things that you really want to do – and to relax.

PLANNER	MORNING	AFTERNOON	EVENING
MONDAY			
TUESDAY			
WEDNESDAY			
THURSDAY			
FRIDAY			
SATURDAY			
SUNDAY			

FINANCIAL RECORDS

WHETHER YOU ARE STRUGGLING to make ends meet or living comfortably within your means, keeping track of exactly what you spend your money on will give you greater control over it and enable you to plan for the future.

LEARNING HOW TO BUDGET

A simple budget sheet provides you with a good general financial overview. If you are constantly in the red, it is time to take control of your spending; money that is frittered away could be saved for a luxury that now seems financially out of reach. Record even the smallest amounts of outgoings and subtract the sum from your total income.

OUTGOINGS	
Rent or mortgage	
Food	
Eating out	
Clothes and shoes	
House contents insurance	
Building insurance	
Life insurance/endowments	
Pension payments	
Electricity	
Gas	
Water	
Telephone	
Council tax or local rates	
TV licence	
Travel costs – public transport	
Car insurance	
Car maintenance and MOT	
Petrol	
Car breakdown insurance	
Credit card payments	
Dry cleaning	
Club memberships	
SUBTOTAL	

CARRIED OVER	
Subscriptions	
Newspapers, magazines, books, etc.	
Window cleaner, cleaner, gardener	
Hairdressing	
Toiletries	
Medical costs, including optical & dental	
Bank charges	
Childminder/nanny	
Children's pocket money	
Educational costs	
Holidays	
Entertainment	
Cigarettes, alcohol, snacks	
Incidentals	
TOTAL	

INCOME	
Take-home pay	
Interest from savings and investments	
Other incomes, such as rent, gifts, etc.	
TOTAL	

CURRICULUM VITAE

Y OUR CURRICULUM VITAE (CV) is your chance to get yourself noticed and to make it to an interview. Aim to sound accomplished and interesting, and include all relevant achievements, but beware of embellishments that stretch the truth.

A SAMPLE CV

Try to keep your CV to one page and make it as clear, concise and neat as possible.

Start with your most recent job and work backward

Use concise bullet points, not lengthy sentences; only mention what is relevant

If you have just left education, put this section first

Examination grades are less important if you have a degree; there is no need to include your grades; omit any exam failures

Curriculum Vitae
EMILY DEWHURST

Flat 6, 10 Grove Road, Belling NW6 3NA

Work telephone: 0273 625 1875   *Date of birth: 17.08.74*
Home telephone: 0273 222 4578   *Nationality: British*

Career
1995 – 1996 (October – May) Hillmore Press
   • *Editorial Assistant*
   • *Acquired proofreading and copy-editing skills*
1995 (January – August) Office Temps
   • *Temporary Secretary*
1994 (July – December) Lycée de Saint Etienne
   • *Teacher*
   • *Taught English as a foreign language*

Work experience
June 1994 – Assisted the features editor on 'Working Woman Magazine'; gained experience in sub-editing and proofreading
Regularly contributed book reviews to the university magazine, 'Refresher'

Education
1987-1989 The Downs School, Blackford
1989-1991 St Agatha's School, Newtown
1991-1994 Greenhill University

Exams passed
7 GCSEs in Maths, English Language, English Literature, Geography, French, History, Biology
3 A LEVELS in French, History, English
BA HONOURS in English
CERTIFICATE IN TEACHING ENGLISH AS A FOREIGN LANGUAGE

Skills and Achievements
Quark XPress
Typing – 45 w.p.m.
Fluent French
Full driving licence

Interests
Contemporary fiction, swimming, photography, scuba diving, making jewellery

Your name should be in capitals and bold type

Include your date of birth, not your age; mention marital status or children only if it is relevant to the job

Make sure every year is accounted for – don't leave any gaps

Anything out of the ordinary will make you stand out

YOUR RIGHTS

These are your statutory rights in Britain in 1996;
the law does change, so keep yourself up-to-date.

MATERNITY RIGHTS

YOUR LEGAL RIGHTS

You have the following legal rights:
- You cannot be sacked for becoming pregnant.
- You can take 14 weeks maternity leave or up to 40 weeks if you have been with the same organization for more than two years and three months.
- You can claim a small amount of Maternity Pay for up to 18 weeks and, if you have worked for nine months with the same employer before the baby is born, you can claim ninety per cent of your pay for six weeks and a small weekly allowance for up to twelve weeks.

MATERNITY BENEFITS

The Social Security Contributions and Benefits Act 1992 forms the legal basis for Britain's maternity benefits. There are two types of maternity benefit available, but you are only eligible to collect one at a time.
- **Statutory Maternity Pay** This is paid by your employer.
- **Maternity Allowance** This is paid by the Department of Social Security (DSS).

If you discover that you are not eligible for either of these, you may still be able to claim Sickness Benefit.

STATUTORY MATERNITY PAY (SMP)

This is a weekly payment that you receive from your employer. It can be paid to you for a maximum of 18 weeks. The amount you receive is calculated as a percentage of your earnings. You must have worked for your employer for at least 26 weeks at the time of giving up work to have your baby. You can claim this benefit even if you are not intending to return to work.

HOW TO CLAIM SMP:

You cannot claim SMP until the 11th week before your baby is due, but this period may be negotiable with your employer. SMP is conditional providing that you:
- Give your employer at least 21 days' notice (preferably in writing) of the day you intend to leave work to have your baby.
- Supply your employer with written medical evidence of your pregnancy, either as a maternity certificate or as a letter from your doctor or midwife.

MATERNITY ALLOWANCE (MA)

If you are not eligible for SMP, you may be able to claim Maternity Allowance. You must have been employed or self-employed and have paid the standard rate of National Insurance contributions for at least 26 weeks. (These 26 weeks must fall within the 66 weeks that lead up to and include the week before the week in which your baby is due.)

HOW TO CLAIM MA:

The earliest MA can be paid is the 11th week before the baby is due, but the DSS may be flexible on this point. You must also do the following:
- Fill in the relevant form, available from your DSS office or from your maternity or child health clinic. This information will be used to calculate how much benefit you are entitled to.
- Provide evidence of when your baby is expected; ask your doctor or midwife for a maternity certificate. (This can only be given 14 weeks before the week in which the baby is due.)

ABORTION RIGHTS

According to the 1967 Abortion Act, a woman may only have an abortion if two doctors believe that her pregnancy poses a risk to her life or will have an adverse effect on her mental or physical health or her existing children. The law also permits an abortion if the child will be seriously handicapped.

Although a doctor is fully within his or her right to refuse you an abortion if it conflicts with his or her conscience, the law is open to liberal interpretation in that it permits a doctor to consider "the actual or reasonably forseeable environment" of the woman. This means that if a doctor believes you would suffer severe depression if forced to have the child, you will be allowed an abortion for the sake of your mental health. Similarly, if a doctor considers that your living conditions render it too stressful for you to go through a pregnancy, if you live in adverse poverty or poor housing, you may be advised to have an abortion.

In 1990 an amendment to this law put a 24-week time limit on abortion. Exceptions that allow a doctor to waive this law are:
- A pregnancy that will result in serious injury or pose a threat to the mother's life.
- A discovery that the foetus is severely handicapped.

COMPUTERS AND EYESIGHT

Health and Safety (Display Screen Equipment) Regulations that came into force on 1 January, 1993 state that an employer must comply with the following requirements:
- You should be able to adjust the screen to a comfortable viewing angle.
- You should be able to control the brightness and contrast of the screen.
- The screen should not be attached to the keyboard; you should be able to adjust it to a comfortable height.
- The screen should not flicker or glare; images and words should be legible.
- The working day should be structured so there is time to take frequent short breaks from the screen.
- Employees should be offered an eyesight test upon request.

RESOURCES

BIBLIOGRAPHY

Taking Control, Lyndsey de Paul,
Boxtree Books, 1995 (page 28)
The Art of Starvation, Sheila McLeod,
Virago, 1980 (page 38)
*Blood Relations: Menstruation and the
Origins of Culture*, Chris Knight, Yale
University Press, 1991 (page 55)
The Trick Is To Keep Breathing, Janice
Galloway, Polygon, 1989 (page 83)
*Primary Love and Psychoanalytical
Technique,* Michael Balint, Karnac Books
Ltd, 1935 (page 100)
The Hite Report, Shere Hite, Hamlyn,
1977 (page 104)
*This We Can Say: Talking Honestly About
Sex,* Nine Friends Press, 1995 (page 106)
Preferences for Work and Leisure, F. Juster,
The Time Squeeze, Demos 5/1995, UK
Henley Centre for Forecasting, 1994
(page 130)
Beyond Certainty, Charles Handy
Hutchinson, 1995 (page 131)
British Social Attitudes Survey, The Time
Squeeze, Demos, 1993 (page 131)
The Empty Raincoat, Charles Handy,
Arrow, 1994 (page 140)
A Good Enough Parent, Bruno
Bettelheim, Thames and Hudson, 1987
(page 145)
The Care of Young Children, Barbara
Tizard, Thomas Coram Research Unit,
1986 (page 147)
Our Bodies, Ourselves, ed. Angela
Phillips, Jill Rakusen, Penguin, 1989
Talking from 9 to 5, Deborah Tannen,
Virago, 1994

USEFUL ADDRESSES

PREGNANCY AND CONTRACEPTION
**British Pregnancy Advisory Service
(BPAS)**
Austy Manor, Wootton Wawenn, Solihull,
West Midlands B95 6BX
Tel: 0121 643 1461

Brook Advisory Centres
233 Tottenham Court Road,
London W1P 9AE
Tel: 0171 580 2991

Family Planning Association (FPA)
27–35 Mortimer Street,
London W1N 7RJ
Tel: 0171 636 7866

Health Education Council (HEA)
Information Service
c/o Health Promotion Information
Centre, Hamilton House,
Mabledon Place,
London WC1H 9TX
Tel: 0171 383 3833

**National Association of Ovulation
Method Instructors**
47 Heathhurst Road,
Sanderstead, South Croydon,
Surrey CR2 0BB

**Natural Family Planning Centre
Birmingham Maternity Unit**
Queen Elizabeth Medical Centre,
Edgbaston, Birmingham B15 2TG
Tel: 0121 472 1377 ext 4219
0181 399 4789

Pregnancy Advisory Service (PAS)
11–13 Charlotte Street,
London W1P 1HD
Tel: 0171 637 8962

PARENTING
Gingerbread National Group
35 Wellington Street,
London WC2E 7BN
Tel: 0171 240 0953

Maternity Alliance
15 Britannia Street, London WC1X 9JP
Tel: 0171 837 1265

National Childminding Association
8 Masons Hill, Bromley,
Kent NBR2 9EY
Tel: 0181 464 6164

**National Council for One Parent
Families**
255 Kentish Town Road,
London NW5 2LX
Tel: 0171 267 1361

Pre-school Playgroups Association
61 Kings Cross Road, London WC1
Tel: 0171 833 0991
Helpline: 0171 837 5517

Parents at Work Helpline
Tel: 0171 628 3578

MEDICAL MATTERS
Action on Smoking and Health (ASH)
109 Gloucester Place, London W1H 4EJ
Tel: 0171 935 3519

Alcoholics Anonymous
General Office, P.O. Box 1,
Stonebow House, Stonebow,
York YO1 2NJ
Tel: 0171 352 3001/01904 644 026

Body Positive
51b Philbeach Gardens,
London SW5 9EB
Tel: 0171 835 1045
HIV Helpline: 0171 373 9124

**British Association for Mental
Health (MIND)**
Granta House, 15–19 Broadway,
Stratford, London E15 4BQ
Tel: 0181 519 2122

British Homeopathic Association
27a Devonshire Street,
London W1N 1RJ
Tel: 0171 935 2163

Cruse Bereavement Care
Cruse House, 126 Sheen Road,
Richmond, Surrey TW9 1UR
Tel: 0181 940 4818
Helpline: 0181 332 7227

Eating Disorders Association
Sackville Place, 44–48 Magdalen Street,
Norwich, Norfolk NR3 1JE
Send SAE for information.

Herpes Association Helpline
Tel: 0171 609 9061

National AIDS Helpline
Tel: 0800 567 123

**National Association for
Pre-menstrual Syndrome**
P.O. Box 72, Sevenoaks,
Kent TN13 3PS
Tel: 01732 741 709

National Tranquillizer Advice Centre
25a Masons Avenue, Wealdstone,
Harrow, Middlesex HA3 5AH

Positively Women
5 Sebastian Street,
London EC1V 0HE
Tel: 0171 713 0222
Counselling for HIV positive women.

Repetitive Strain Injury Association
Tel: 01895 238663

Standing Conference on Drug Abuse
Waterbridge House, 32–36 Loman Street,
London SE1 0EE
Tel: 0171 928 9500

Terence Higgins Trust
52–54 Grays Inn Road,
London WC1X 8JU
Tel: 0171 242 1010
HIV and AIDS helpline.

ASSAULT
National Harassment Network
University of Lancashire,
Harrington Building,
Preston PR1 2HE
Tel: 01772 892512

Rape Crisis Centre
P.O. Box 69, London WC1X 9NJ
Tel: 0171 837 1600

The Suzy Lamplugh Trust
14 East Sheen Avenue,
East Sheen, London SW14 8AS
Tel: 0181 392 1839
Personal safety courses and information.

Victim Support (Head Office)
39 Brixton Road,
London SW9 6DZ
Tel: 0171 735 9166

Women Against Sexual Harassment
242 Pentonville Road,
London N1 9UN
Tel: 0171 837 7509

COUNSELLING
Association of Sexual and Marital Therapists
Student Health Centre,
University of Manchester,
Manchester M13 9QS
Send SAE and details of nearest sex therapist or clinic will be forwarded.

British Association of Counselling
1 Regent Place,
Rugby, Warwickshire CV21 2PJ
Tel: 01788 578 328

Child
Tel: 0142 473 2361
Infertility self-help support group and counselling information line.

Gay and Lesbian Switchboard
Tel: 0171 837 7324 (24-hour)

Issues (National Fertility Association)
509 Aldridge Road, Great Barr,
Birmingham B44 8NA
Tel: 0121 344 4414

Lifeline
Main Road, Holland Ward, Ashbourne,
Derby DE6 3EA
Tel: 01262 674505
Counselling for violent and abusive men.

London Lesbian Line
Tel: 0171 251 6911

Relate
Herbert Gray College,
Little Church Street,
Rugby CV21 3AP
Tel: 01788 573241
Counselling for couples.

Samaritans (Look up in your local telephone book under Samaritans.)

Women's Therapy Centre
6–9 Manor Gardens,
London N7 6LA
Tel: 0171 263 6200

WORKING LIFE AND
MONEY MANAGEMENT
Citizens' Advice Bureau (CAB)
Middleton House,
115–123 Pentonville Road,
London N1 9LZ
Tel: 0171 833 2181

Consumers' Association
2 Marylebone Road,
London NW1 4DX
Tel: 0171 486 5544

Equal Opportunities Commission
Overseas House, Quay Street,
Manchester M3 3HN
Tel: 0161 833 9244

Financial Intermediaries, Managers and Brokers Regulatory Association
22 Great Tower Street,
London EC3R 5AQ
Tel: 0171 929 2711

National Association of Volunteer Bureaux
St Peter's College, College Road, Saltley,
Birmingham B8 3TE
Tel: 0121 633 4555

Redundancy Payments Service
Tel: 0188 848489

The Women Returners Network
8 John Adam Street,
London WC2H 6EL
Tel: 0171 839 8188

Women and Training Limited
Hewmar House, 120 London Road,
Gloucester GL1 3PL
Tel: 01452 309330

PRACTICAL LIVING
Automobile Association (AA)
Fanum House, Basingstoke,
Hants RG2 1EA
Tel: 01256 20123

British Security Industry Association
Security House, Barbourne Road,
Worcester WR1 1RS
Tel: 01905 21464

Crime Prevention Officers
Contact your local police station.
Offer advice to ensure your home is safe.

Driving Instructors' Association
Safety House, Beddington Farm Road,
Croydon, Surrey CR0 4XZ
Tel: 0181 665 5151

Fire Protection Association
140 Aldersgate Street,
London EC1A 4HX
Tel: 0181 207 2345

Royal Automobile Club (RAC)
RAC House, M1 Cross,
Brent Terrace,
London NW2 1LT
Tel: 0171 930 9142/3/4

Royal Society for the Prevention of Accidents (ROSPA)
Canon House,
The Priory, Queensway,
Birmingham B4 6BS
Tel: 0121 200 2461
Information on safety legislation.

INDEX

ACKNOWLEDGMENTS

DK would like to thank:
Kwik Fit, Cricklewood; LV Engineering, West Hampstead; Renault London; Freewheel Bike Shops, West Hampstead and Covent Garden; Dr Ruth Curzon, Vicky Padbury and Jane Winfield at the FPA; Brett Lees, holistic self-defence instructor; Rachael Leach for picture research; Lyn Greenwood for the index; Linda Sonntag for proofreading; Ellen Kramer for make-up; Gary Ombler at the DK studio; Andrew Macdonald, David Burnie and Coral Mula for illustrations; Anna McMurray and Annabel Martin for editorial assistance.
Models: Lara Maiklem, Zoe Sanders, Joshua Jones, Ann-Marie Campbell, Laura Hill, Jo Smith, Carine Daribo, Prashila Dayal, Kirsty Drury, Amanda Waddington, Sooz Bellerby, Jacqueline Phillips, Sultana Qureshi, Sarah King, Thomas Keenes, Valerie Horn, John Dinsdale, Nasim Mawji and Jane Heyes.

The author would like to thank:
Dr Janet Millar, for reading and commenting on the health section; Annie Bracx of MIND for comments on mental health; Sheila Ernst for commenting on relationships and eating disorders; Sara Dove, of Amazon Women's Gym, for initial comments on the exercise section; Ruth Evans for comments on work; Alex Sturrock for trying some of the questionnaires and commenting on them; Ben, Josh, Jake and Grace Jones for reading and commenting on questionnaires; Sara Peraton and Sarah Hemstedt for research; editors Charyn Jones and Nasim Mawji for their comments throughout the book and their patience; friends and women I have interviewed over the years, for their contribution (witting and unwitting) to the stories and examples I have used.

The publisher would like to thank the following for their kind permission to reproduce their photographs.
t= top, b= bottom, a= above, c= centre, l= left, r= right.
Cosmopolitan: Jenny Aitchingson front cover br, Tim Hill back cover bl, Syriol Jones 154 b, Mauricio Nahas front cover cr, Oliver Pearce back cover cra, Eliot Siegal front cover bl, spine t, Peter Woolf 130 tl. **Robert Harding Picture Library:** 127 br. **Image Bank:** Gio Barto back cover tl. **Sandra Lousada:** 3, 105. **Panos:** Micheal Pickstock 21 b. **Tony Stone Images:** Peter Carrez 114 bl, Margaret Gowan 20 bl, David Madison 51 b, Andre Perlstein 43 b, Rick Rusing 95 bl, 101 c. **Zefa:** Sander back cover crb. **Additional photography:** Dave King, Jane Burton, Maureen Barrymore, Steve Gorton, Liz McAulay, Clive Streeter, David Murray, A. Heywood, Debi Treloar, Jules Selmes, Tim Ridley, Jane Stockman, Steve Shott, Ranald Mackechnie and John Garret.